Momfluenced

Momfluenced

INSIDE THE MADDENING, PICTURE-PERFECT WORLD OF

Mommy Influencer Culture

SARA PETERSEN

BEACON PRESS ■ BOSTON

BEACON PRESS
Boston, Massachusetts
www.beacon.org

Beacon Press books
are published under the auspices of
the Unitarian Universalist Association of Congregations.

26 25 24 23   8 7 6 5 4 3 2 1

This book is printed on acid-free paper that meets the uncoated paper
ANSI/NISO specifications for permanence as revised in 1992.

Text design and composition by Kim Arney

Library of Congress Cataloging-in-Publication Data
is available for this title.
ISBN: 978-0-8070-0663-4
e-book: 978-0-8070-0664-1; audiobook: 978-0-8070-0837-9

For my mother

CONTENTS

1

"Performing Motherhood with a Hashtag"

I'm not a momfluencer. I suck at taking selfies, I don't have the patience to corral my children into pinafores and corduroys for an Insta-friendly photo shoot in a pumpkin patch, and I'm too jaded to caption said photo with musings about wanting my littles to stay little. That said, I possess many qualities that could set me up for momfluencing success.

First of all, I have kids. Three of them. None of them have hit the awkward stages of adolescence, but only one of them is young enough to be truly innocent as far as legit candid photography goes. My house (when not trashed, which is rarely if I'm the parent in charge) features things like retro floral wallpaper, letterpress nursery prints of red and white toadstools, a blond-wood butcher block kitchen island, and at least one macrame wall hanging. I found some incredible animal decals for one of my kids' walls from a French artist thanks to a vintage Cup of Jo post about kids' rooms. Most of my other walls are painted in Benjamin Moore Simply White (included in nearly every momfluencer's "best white paint colors" roundup), and my bathroom counter is strewn with products I was able to get at 20 percent off, thanks to whichever momfluencer convinced me I needed whichever facial oil or brightening serum I ended up buying. Swipe up!

I've always favored ochre as one of the chicest neutrals. And when I apply makeup (which is almost never these days but doesn't stop me from clicking on links that promise a natural "flush" to cheer up my winter-wan cheeks), I present as reasonably attractive. I'm thin, white, and have enough of a disposable income to get sun-kissed highlights for my naturally drab dishwater-blonde hair. I know how to style a Babaa sweater with faded fake-vintage Levi's. I have Superga sneakers. I have Blundstone boots. I've yet to master a bold red lip—the red is always too pink—but maybe someday.

The only real drawback to my pursuing a career in momflu-encing is the fact that the bulk of what I have to say about mother-hood in America is laced with expletives. First, there are the huge systemic inequities: workplace exclusion of mothers, unequal pay, laughable prenatal and postnatal care networks, even more laugh-able paid-parental-leave legislation, Black maternal mortality rates, family separation at the border, a persistent failure to recognize women's reproductive rights as rights, a capitalist system that uses mothers and other care workers to uphold the primary concerns of buying and selling while denying those same mothers and care workers adequate compensation or even cultural respect for their indispensable work.

Then there are the personal reasons. I love my kids, but I often don't love being a mother. The other day, in a text thread with friends also sick of nonstop pandemic parenting, I wrote, "I just want to listen to podcasts and keep them alive." It's so boring, so hard, and so thankless. I'm often bad at it. Which is why I'm fascinated by the thousands of mothers on Instagram who make it look magical, like the only thing anyone would ever want to be.

Naomi Davis (@taza) was my gateway drug. I remember dis-covering Naomi when my two older kids were tiny and exhausting, and I was drawn to her bright colors, big grin, and the unabashed joy she seemed to derive from motherhood. In 2019, her Instagram bio read: "Always surrounded by a handful of littles," followed by both the sunglasses and party hat emojis. As of May 2022, it reads simply: "Mama of 5," followed by the yellow heart emoji.[1] She hasn't posted in a few months; the momfluencer world is abuzz with speculation.

Hooked up to a breast pump in 2014 in the dark of 5:30 a.m. while my Velcro-swaddled newborn "napped" in the hideous but effective Fisher-Price Sweet SnugapuppyDreams Cradle 'N Swing (the groaning back-and-forth hums of which are now almost as PTSD-inducing as the whishy-whishy sounds of breast pumps), I stared at my phone. Taza stared back at me from a kayak, smiling big, seated between two cherubic toddlers, both of whom were also smiling, a fact that might not be particularly jarring unless you've ever tried coercing a child under the age of four into a lifejacket. "Have you seen this woman?" I texted my friend Steph. "What's her deal?" Steph texted back immediately (she also had a newborn, which is to say she was also enjoying a very intimate relationship with her phone). "She has super cute bangs. She seems so happy—what's up with that?"

Taza did have cute bangs. She always has a cute *something*. But it was the happiness, really, that sucked me into momfluencer culture, because I, too, couldn't quite figure out "what was up with that." It seemed suspicious, like a mystery to get to the bottom of. For me, and for every mom I knew, motherhood was like the title of Jennifer Senior's book about modern parenthood: *All Joy and No Fun*. I wasn't a miserable hag of a mother, but I was more likely to be caught in an open-mouthed smile when talking shit about motherhood with my friends than when kayaking with my toddlers. The very idea of kayaking with a toddler makes my jaw tighten. The onset of motherhood injected my soul with a love too big to ever really comprehend, but the day-to-day experience of mothering is mostly the mundanity of *doing*. Not really *being*.

Taza made me want things. Bangs, Anthropologie mirrors, eyelash extensions, a husband who regularly wore bow ties, an

Upper West Side apartment. Freckles. Sometimes she even made me want to get pregnant. Again.

A few years ago, for the *New York Times*, I wrote about my fraught decision to have a third kid. I was six months pregnant with that kid, which was slightly weird. But upon rereading the piece—which notes my desire to keep myself tightly wedged into the box of young, sexually desirable womanhood implied by pregnancy and childbearing—I think I missed the fact that maybe my longing for a third baby was also impacted, at least a little bit, by momfluencers like Taza who made pregnancy and motherhood look good. I forgot to credit them for being one of the many fucked-up reasons I craved another baby. To clarify: my baby is delicious, and I'm unhealthily obsessed with him. The murkiness surrounding my reasons for wanting him, though, remain.

When I first discovered Taza, I was unfamiliar with the concept of professional influencing; I think most people were at the time. Maybe influencing's lack of transparency made influencers and momfluencers more powerful in those bygone years of innocence between 2014-ish and now. It wouldn't be until 2018 or so that "influencer" became a common term to describe someone who commodifies a lifestyle or an identity for the purposes of selling something, whether that something is a product or an idea or a belief or a way of being.

Back then, to me, Taza was just a person on Instagram, someone who made motherhood look way better and more rewarding than my own experience, and I wanted more. Whether that *more* was tricks or tips for figuring out how to wear my motherhood so it fit more comfortably and was more flattering, or whether that more was just a citron-yellow maxi dress or suggestions for entertaining children on an airplane, I didn't know. I just knew that the more I consumed Taza, the more I wanted.

To understand what a momfluencer is, we must understand their predecessors: mommy bloggers. Taza started out as a mommy blogger, personal-essaying about her life as a mom and wife alongside women like Heather Armstrong of *Dooce* and Natalie Lovin of *Hey Natalie Jean*. Some of these early blogs were truly revolutionary in terms of expanding conversations about motherhood. In their heyday, mommy bloggers bitched, they snarked, they talked about postpartum depression. They made a huge impact on normalizing the harder, bloodier, more taboo sides of motherhood. And some of their blogs served as sites of aspiration—something we've come to expect from contemporary momfluencers. In 2011, Nona Willis Aronowitz wrote this about Natalie Lovin for *Good Magazine*, which I think quite accurately describes both the central appeal of that first wave of mommy bloggers and the current appeal of momfluencers: "Natalie is a character you want to be. Her life is one you want to have."[2]

Mommy bloggers monetized their work primarily through banner ads, which initially generated enough income for some women to make good money from their blogs. But eventually banner ads died out as a viable revenue source, and this is when mommy bloggers turned to sponcon. Sponsored content (and, of course, the rising power of Instagram as a more lucrative, effective platform than a personal blog) brought about a huge sea change. Mommy bloggers, who initially drew audiences in with their voicey, intimate writing, morphed into momfluencers, with a focus on curated images and products. Natalie Lovin, who partnered with brands like Tiffany, told *Elle* in 2019 that she became so invested in utilizing each and every lifestyle choice for content that, in the end, her apartment became "her showroom."[3]

In an article for *Wired* about the history and rise of influencer culture, Paris Martineau notes that mommy bloggers were some of the first influencers to successfully monetize their identities by turning to sponcon, something that was initially met with outrage by industry insiders and consumers alike, inspiring articles with inflammatory headlines like "PayPerPost.com Offers to Sell Your Soul," and "Polluting the Blogosphere."[4] It's worth noting both the outrage as well as the efficacy with which mothers were able to simultaneously create communities centered around the common experience of motherhood while selling community members something in the process.

The simplest definition of a momfluencer is someone who monetizes her identity as a mother on a social media platform. In a 2019 essay for *Topic* magazine, Lyz Lenz writes that a momfluencer is someone who masters the monetization of maternal identity "through Instagramming, blogging, podcasting, Facebooking, working with advertisers, knowing [her] angles." A momfluencer is someone who can "perform motherhood with a hashtag."[5]

But for the purposes of this book, I'm interested in expanding the definition to consider other ways in which momfluencers— even those who haven't monetized their accounts—can impact us. Shanicia Boswell, who has certainly monetized her work as a momfluencer, agrees that the definition of a momfluencer is bigger than someone who simply hawks strollers and bamboo diapers. Shanicia, a speaker, author, and founder of the Black Moms Blog, is a self-described momfluencer with thirty thousand followers on her personal Instagram account and nearly five hundred thousand followers on her blog's account. When we spoke about momfluencing, Shanicia referenced the astrological origins of the term *influencer*, which dates back to the early 1600s, in her attempts to define what a momfluencer does: "I give that background to first identify how we, as humans have shapeshifted the word into 'influencer' and how it still references the movement of ideologies, lifestyles, and political and social movements."[6]

This definition seems prescient in the 2020s, when influencers in general, and momfluencers in particular, are being held to increasingly complicated, mercurial standards in terms of aesthetic, moral, and political trends. Shanicia reported that the key to her success as a momfluencer has to do with a focus on authenticity, which to her means engaging in real time, and speaking up when motherhood isn't particularly photogenic. Yes, she hires a professional photographer to take a slew of photos two or three times a year, but she captions those beautiful photos with candid thoughts about motherhood, some of which are pretty, some of which are not. She's leveraged her platform to write three books, start a self-care retreat, raise funds for a charity that donates menstrual care products to unhoused women, and has started the Period Party, which fosters conversations between mothers and daughters about "menstrual health, wellness, and acceptance."[7]

Shanicia is one of many momfluencers who create vibrant, inclusive, engaged online communities that speak to vital issues impacting mothers, but many momfluencer followers don't seem to know that creators like her even exist. To a lot of people, momfluencers are a homogeneous group of perfectly pretty mama princesses, and many understandably find this off-putting. But many also find it fascinating. In chapter 3 I'll dig much deeper into the various, multifaceted reasons we consume momfluencer culture, but here it's worth understanding, even on a surface level, that, just as momfluencers are far from a monolith, the same can be said of their followers. And the symbiotic relationship between what motivates momfluencers to create content and what motivates their audiences to consume that content is necessary to understanding the culture as a whole.

Many momfluencer followers get their first taste of the larger culture sort of like I did: by finding a mother whose performance of motherhood shocks you, inspires you, enrages you, or helps you better understand something about yourself—good or bad. Actress Alice Greczyn doesn't have children, but she recently responded to one of my momfluencer-centric tweets by saying that momfluencers "color my impression of modern motherhood, even tho I know it's a total illusion. The contrast of shitshow selfies and my-kids-drive-me-crazy memes between perfectly staged, hair-blown-out dinner spreads is horrifying and envy-inducing all at once. Like a cautionary dream."[8]

Maya Kosoff, another momfluencer follower who seems to view momfluencer culture mostly through the lens of voyeuristic, car-crash entertainment, is particularly interested with trad wives. Trad wives (or trad moms) are notoriously tricky to define. Some of them make all of their own clothes, grow and raise all of their own food, and live totally off the grid in the middle of the woods. Some of them reside in the suburbs and prioritize keeping their houses clean, ensuring that their kids don't make too much noise around their husbands once those husbands "get home from work" and, for some reason, making their husbands lots of sandwiches. The single feature that unites most of them is a celebration of the nuclear family and traditional gender roles. In an essay entitled "Help! I'm Obsessed with Trad Wife Influencers" for *Medium*, Maya refers to a momfluencer as someone with whom she has "nothing in common."

> They homeschooled their kids before it became medically necessary to do so because of COVID. They would take one look at my boring life in Brooklyn and call me a baby-killer communist hedonist whose eggs are dying, or something. And yet here I am, scrolling through my feed, undeterred, unbothered, with an air of parasocial familiarity that I'd absolutely loathe to have applied to me and my boring Instagram, or worse, my Twitter.[9]

Maya's essay is funny and a little snarky, but, to be fair, momfluencer culture sort of invites snark (which is why there are hundreds of threads on Reddit devoted to the sport, called Blogsnark). Maya's momfluencer catnip of choice is Kelly Havens Stickle, who can best be described as Anne Shirley without the sense of humor. Please understand, she is not a modern version of Anne Shirley; she is a 1917 version of Anne Shirley. She wears homespun floor-length dresses and pins her red braids to her head in a coronet. (I have much more to say about her in chapter 3.) Stickle's central mission seems to be celebrating maternal self-sacrifice as a beautiful and worthy pursuit. In a verbose post about devoting every bit of oneself (or "abandoning yourself") to the work of homemaking and mothering, she concludes with a quote from Mark Twain that is meant, I think, to be inspirational: "My mother had a slender, small body, but a large heart—a heart so large that everybody's grief and everybody's joy found welcome in it, and hospitable accommodation."[10] Perhaps the "slender, small" mother in this scenario is so sated by everyone else's feelings she has no room for her own?

After reading Maya's article, I emailed her to get more dirt, or at least to ask her what a momfluencer is to her, and why she keeps scrolling, despite very obviously viewing that culture with some skepticism and a little disdain. She was a "bit ashamed to admit" that her consumption of momfluencers has to do with feeling a little bit better than them.

> The feeling of righteousness you get when you see people proudly posting stuff you would never do or post. Imagine yet another picture of baby Thaddy [Kelly Havens Stickle's son] taken with him lying flat on his back in a pile of frost-tinged leaves, for some reason, or Kelly Havens Stickle's husband proudly not wearing a mask at Home Depot. A "momfluencer," to me, is any person who self-describes as a "mama," meaning she has children, and posts about her life, their lives, and her family's life on social media. The momfluencer does this in pursuit of clout for being a mother, and projects a specific image of motherhood—whether that's being a Girl Boss and living with your family in Manhattan or homesteading on the farm in Montana with your husband and your seven sons.[11]

Maya makes a really important point here: that not all momfluencers monetize their influence, and that a projection of imagery of motherhood is central to being identified as (or self-identifying as) a momfluencer. Her observation that momfluencers might engage in their work to achieve "clout for being mothers" also makes sense, given that motherhood is a job where clout is hard to come by. Instagram allows mothers to curate their own versions of motherhood, to pick and choose scenes they want to represent themselves, to edit the content according to their personal aesthetics or belief systems. And why not? The actual labor of motherhood is private and rarely celebrated in any meaningful ways. There's something empowering about mothers controlling their own narratives and imagery, when, for much of history, the story of motherhood was largely told (or wholly ignored) by men.

I can also deeply relate to the sense of righteousness Maya mentions, the smug coziness of feeling better about myself because I think someone else is doing ____ wrong. My most current momfluencer obsession is Hannah Neeleman, who had 157,000 followers when I started writing this book, but in 2022, has 1.7 million followers as @ballerinafarm. She is married to the son of JetBlue founder David Neeleman, but does little to advertise this fact, since her whole schtick revolves around being a scrappy homesteader on the prairies of Utah with her stalwart husband, Daniel; their seven kids; their farm dog, Hoss; their beloved milk cows (RIP Dandy); Hannah's sourdough starter, Willa (I am not making this up); and countless other unnamed animals.[12]

Hannah's followers may not know she was crowned Miss New York City as Hannah Wright in 2011 and studied ballet at Juilliard before scrapping a dance career in favor of marriage, motherhood, and ranching. I know a lot about Hannah Neeleman. I've seen her wedding pictures. I've read about her Mormon modesty in an article I found in the *Deseret News*, which points out that she was the only beauty queen who wore a one-piece bathing suit during the Miss New York City pageant.[13] I've found old Instagram photos that show Hannah on a beach drinking margaritas instead of sipping steaming mugs of raw milk sourced straight from Dandy's teat. I've seen her grow out her peroxide-blonde bob to better suit her new role as homesteading's golden girl. Now her presumably natural maple-sugar-blonde hair floats in waves down her back. It makes more sense this way.

Anyway, I will scroll through @ballerinafarm's feed and huff to myself, "An indoor wedding without masks. What the fuck," and then go about the rest of my day, feeling plenty of insecurity, doubt, and confusion about my own motherhood, but at least assured that I'm following sane pandemic protocol. Hannah's sourdough might be home-baked in her twenty-thousand-dollar hunter-green Aga oven (named Agnes), and Hannah might seem like a happy, relaxed, fun mother who has the patience to actually involve her children in cooking by allowing them to crack eggs, but I'm a smart feminist mom who reads (and writes!) about important things like mothers being completely fucked during a global pandemic. I'm not running around to flower-arranging workshops packed with forty mask-less attendees pre-vaccine and blithely posting photos of pink peonies. I'm not posting time-lapse videos of myself doing dishes, nor am I giving a thumbs-up to the camera upon finishing those dishes. Doing dishes is a drag, and I will not pretend otherwise. Thumbs way, way down. My following of Hannah Neeleman exists as a perpetual teetering between self-loathing and self-righteousness.

In the *Deseret News* article mentioned above, I found the following quote from Hannah, which feels almost like a premonition, a foreshadowing of her future as one of the top-tier trad-wife momfluencers. It communicates so much about the confusing space between reality and performance squarely occupied by momfluencer culture. In the article, Hannah responds to a question about her choice to preserve her modesty and sense of self by wearing a one-piece suit instead of a bikini during her several years as a beauty pageant contestant: "When you stick to who you are, they (the judges and the other contestants) notice you more. I was representing myself, not playing a role, so modesty, for instance, was really important to me always."[14]

Hannah asserts that she was not playing a role (in a beauty pageant!) despite the fact that a "representation" of oneself rather than an embodiment of self is the very definition of role-playing. Just as sharing a video of dishwashing in which she magically does the dishes of a family of nine in thirty seconds and (if the smile and thumbs-up are to be believed) is made giddy by such labor, is a representation of motherhood designed to be "noticed."

Hannah recently entered the Mrs. Utah beauty pageant and won.

Alexandra Tanner wrote an essay for *Jewish Current*, called "My Mommies and Me," in which she recounts spending her year of quar (a cutesy abbreviation of the decidedly uncute experience of being quarantined at home during a global pandemic!) scrolling through the lives of her various "mommies," some of whom wrote about purchasing black market chicken pox viruses to deliberately expose their children so they could join the "great awakening." The essay is a lyrical musing on the darker underbelly of momfluencer culture, where pretty "mamas" wax poetic about protecting their "littles" from the New World Order; or from Hillary Clinton and Rihanna, who seek to eat the souls of white children; or satanic Halloween; or satanic yoga; or the satanic Super Bowl. Many of Alexandra's mommies, though, are simply conventionally attractive Mormon women wearing tie-dyed leggings. "Some of the outfits were cute," she writes in the essay. "And I thought: This is why Instagram is showing me these women! It wants me to buy things. I did not buy the mommies' special clothes and I felt superior, smarter than the algorithm."[15]

Via email, I asked Alexandra to try and quantify what exactly kept her hooked on momfluencer content for an entire year, and how her consumption of it impacted her ambivalence about becoming a mother herself. She said she believes momfluencers absolutely impact women without children, if not directly through algorithm crossover (a woman searching for tie-dyed leggings, for example, might easily find herself in momfluencer territory), then through the way their influence bleeds into how we think of "momming" as a full-contact sport, an endeavor to be mastered, an identity that is less an identity and more an indicator of whether or not you are "successful"—at breastfeeding, homeschooling, crafting, nursery designing, buying the right toys, feeding kids the right foods, being sexually desirable despite of and in spite of your motherhood. The list is inexhaustible.

Whether or not to have kids is a question I've wrestled with a lot in the last year or so. Spending so much time zeroed in on women who have, you know, 10 children and huge homes and seemingly endless resources and never mention medical bills or dealing with learning disabilities or family troubles . . . ever . . . does make a certain vision of motherhood seem daunting and unattainable. But also, I think on my particular mommy-blogging journey last year, I saw a lot of women doing things to their children that seemed like . . . highly reportable offenses! Posing their children with literal stacks of cash or tons of products, posting videos of their children angrily crossing out Barack Obama's face in their history textbooks or carrying signs at anti-mask rallies or any of the other wild things I saw made me feel more protective of children, more confident in my potential ability to care for a child, etc. So there's that constant pull of insecurity/superiority, which is how, of course, every social media platform keeps its hooks in us, deflating and inflating us like 15 times a minute.[16]

Alexandra points out that this push and pull between disdain and aspiration is not so very different from how we've always viewed ourselves in comparison to others—especially, unfortunately, as women trained to pit ourselves against each other. We've always, after all, judged mothers in parking lots, grocery stores, or even in our own living rooms if the mom in question happens to be a friend or relative. But, in an increasingly isolated world, when the tax on our time is at an all-time high, mothers are perhaps more likely to gauge our parenting success or failures by peering into a tiny screen, by rewriting and revising our own embodiments of motherhood against those of a stranger. A momfluencer.

In Alexandra's article, although she expresses her deep ambivalence toward momfluencer culture, she echoes something I've heard from countless women: that despite it being difficult to assess the benefits she derived from consuming momfluencer content, "still something grabbed [her]."

Momfluencers grabbed something in Jo Piazza, too—so much so that she spent two years researching the momfluencer industrial complex for her podcast *Under the Influence*, determined to figure out why it held such power over her imagination and her purchasing habits. In an interview with *Glamour*, Jo recounted how scrolling and clicking allowed her to envision a different type of motherhood than the one she was experiencing, one that was better, more beautiful:

> I painted my whole house Simply White by Benjamin Moore. I bought a ton of Everyday Oil. I bought a rug from Ruggable. I got Comotomo products. I bought all-natural rubber pacifiers that promise that your kid will never get cancer and metal feeding bowls that look like dog bowls because, again, the mom influencers were telling me that plastic was bad for my kid. I got, like, three different kinds of baby slings. I bought the Solly baby wrap. These things make motherhood look beautiful, right? And I'm like, "I just want to look beautiful again." I wouldn't remember a lot of it either. A package would arrive and I'd be like, "I didn't order this. Someone is sending things." Most moms will understand this: Being awake in the middle of the night with a screaming baby is kind of like being blackout drunk.[17]

Simply White. I'm telling you.

I called Jo to ask her all the things, and, first of all, she does *not* recommend the Ruggable rug, which I was sad to hear because I've been coveting it for my kids' basement playroom disaster for several months. We spent the first five minutes talking about our joint love of Smeg fridges despite the fact we're 100 percent certain that actually owning one would be wholly impractical. Jo says that while her podcast began as an effort to flesh out her own fascination with momfluencers, she quickly came to appreciate the monetized momfluencer industry as a hugely powerful financial player. To all the haters who dismiss momfluencers as vapid attention seekers, Jo says this: "We should care about momfluencer culture and we have to care about it because it is driving billions of dollars in commerce. Moms control the majority of family spending decisions and they are now being influenced in those decisions by this continually growing army of women. Influencing is quickly displacing traditional advertising as the way that consumers choose how to spend their disposable income."[18]

It's easy to hate momfluencers, and it's clear that people love to hate them, but Jo is quick to point out the inherent misogyny in denigrating a multibillion-dollar industry dominated by women. She told me that momfluencers are "EICs of their own little media companies, and my research has given me a ton more respect for the work they do. These women are working hard and also benefiting off the unpaid labor of motherhood, which does feel like a coup." We spent the last few minutes of our call sharing pandemic parenting sob stories before Jo ended the chat abruptly by saying, "Shit. I gotta go. My baby is trying to eat matches."[19] Which I absolutely get.

Momfluencers are not the only ones making money in the Wild West of momfluencer culture. Entire professions have been forged in service to the industry. Lissette Calveiro (@lissettecalv) spent the majority of her career in public relations and marketing and was director of influencer marketing at Ogilvy before starting her own business coaching influencers and helping them get paid for their work. She has eighty thousand followers on Instagram and is passionate about garnering respect for the work of influencing, about highlighting the fact that it is indeed *work*. HBO Max released a documentary about influencer culture called *Fake Famous*, which was widely panned by influencer insiders and people who actually study the culture. *BuzzFeed* writer Stephanie McNeal called the film "so condescending," writing that "the documentary mocks influencers for a grueling hour and a half, casting an entire ecosystem primarily built and run by women as, one male talking head put it, people who are 'not employed' and 'without a sense of purpose.'"[20] Shortly after the film's release, Lissette Calveiro posted about the widespread disdain for influencers on her Instagram:

> I'm tired of influencers having to say "I don't like using that word" because the word has been made so stigmatized and dirty. I'm tired of the endless hours spent building community, mastering a rapidly changing social media space, and many times wearing 277,382 hats running a business, to not be given the congratulations they deserve. So, next time you think about calling the industry a "joke," think about the multi-Billions of dollars involved and let me know if you still have reason to say it is.[21]

Tiffany Mitchell is one of those women who wears 277,382 hats. She has 180,000 followers as @tifforelie and was a style/travel influencer before she was a momfluencer. Prior to her son Noah's birth, her feed was dominated by fashion, home decor, and pictures of camping trips seeped in '70s rock and roll nostalgia. Tiffany has long wavy hair that she recently dyed rose-gold, and her vibe is warm and boho. She came under fire in 2018 for posting photos immediately following a motorcycle accident, which critics claimed were posed for the purpose of selling ads for Smartwater. The photos, which Tiffany has removed, featured her lying on the road, bruised and looking distraught, next to her motorcycle. In the foreground of many of them, there's a bottle of Smartwater. In an article about the incident for *BuzzFeed*, Tanya Chen wrote that the comments under Tiffany's post about the accident "became mixed with more critical and cynical observations. For one, people were taken aback by the optics of taking, and then sharing, professional-grade photos of her actual accident."[22]

Tiffany has spoken at length about the controversy in a high-lights reel on her Instagram page, denying that the accident was staged or contrived. In a podcast interview, she explained that her friend Lindsey (a fellow creative and a photographer) had her camera with her at the time, which wasn't at all unusual. "She just loves capturing all the time," Tiffany said. "She's got her camera with her all the time."[23] Following the accident, Tiffany was in "shock," in part because she had lost someone very close to her only a few years prior in a motorcycle accident. As for the Smartwater, Tiffany explains in the interview that a witness to the accident (also riding a motorcycle) had pulled over and placed the bottle by her head, "in case I wanted it so I could reach it, it was right there."[24]

Tiffany opened up on Instagram about her decision to switch from breastfeeding to formula, and, as is typical when a mother has the audacity to make her own decisions for her own child, she dealt with a fair share of intrusive, misogynistic comments. Via email, Tiffany told me she fielded one comment from a man who diagnosed her (over DM) with postpartum depression and chastised her for "giving up" on nursing.[25]

Demystifying the work of momfluencing is critical to a thoughtful, holistic critique of the culture itself. So I asked Tiffany to walk me through a typical day in her Nashville life, balancing family and work with her husband, Steve, and son, Noah. Unsurprisingly to any mother with a baby, she says that her time is dominated by Noah's sleep schedule, and that being able to work around his needs is one of the main reasons she's grateful for the flexibility her career affords. The following quote is long, but I think cutting it down would also unfairly reduce an honest reckoning of Tiffany's work juggling time, energy, daylight, and childcare.

> I really only have 2 windows of possibility to get my shooting done (the first 2 naps) because I need natural light. Once I have all the raw content, I'll take Noah's evening nap (or wait til he's down for the night) to sift through everything, choose selects, write captions and send everything off to the client. I have to try to book my shoots with a lot of wiggle room before deadlines because if Noah's naps are off, or he's up all night, I have to push back which gets super stressful if I

didn't plan right. The scheduling also has to include product testing (as I can't move forward with a partnership if I haven't tried and liked the product) and a block of time to work out creative. I can typically get all that done during a single nap. Once the client receives all my content, they send approval and I make sure to post whatever I need to on the designated date. This takes probably an hour or 2 total, as I try to stay available to respond to comments and DMs throughout the day. The last step is sending off post/story analytics a few days after posting. Sometimes I do have to work while Noah's awake and Steve's recording, so I try to wear him since he really likes that, or keep him in the sit-me-up with some toys next to my computer. In this phase, he's very clingy though so I have to work fast in those situations haha![26]

To any parent who works from home, this schedule will likely feel familiar: a little chaotic, a little uncertain, a little messy. But freelancing or running one's own business can often feel like a more humane and achievable career option for mothers who don't want—or can't afford—full-time childcare. And it's clear that Tiffany's many hats showcase her many bankable skills: marketing, content creation, photography, styling, interpersonal communication, copywriting, personal writing, accounting, data analysis, time management, baby-wearing! Momfluencing is her chosen profession (although hopefully, she says, a launchpad for different creative projects in the future), and she is good at it. It's hard to imagine anyone reading about Tiffany's typical workday and having qualms about the fact that she is paid for her work. And yet.

Erin Boyle started her blog, *Reading My Tea Leaves*, in 2009 as a creative side project. On it, and now also on her Instagram page, she writes about minimalism, environmentalism, and mindful consumption, and posts tutorials for making potholders out of hardware-store twine alongside essays about practicing anti-racist allyship as a white woman, and how patriarchy is to blame for her landlord requiring her father's signature on her most recent Brooklyn lease. Her aesthetic is spare and soft without feeling unattainable, and my purchasing of a vintage milk-glass lamp shade is directly due to her influence.

To prepare for our phone call, which took place during Our Year of Virtual Learning, I plunked my three kids in front of the TV show *CoComelon* (which I won't tell you much about save to recommend it as a certifiable toddler gateway drug toward a healthy TV addiction), loaded them up with Goldfish and graham crackers, and told them in a Very Serious Voice to keep the baby safe. Then I locked myself in the bathroom, where the glare of daylight forced me to confront the growing forest of white hairs sprouting from the center of my scalp. Erin, for her part, spent our call scraping paint from an old bookshelf while her husband taught a college biology class via Zoom, her oldest daughter attended a first-grade class via Zoom, and her two younger children lived their best lives at daycare.

In 2013, Erin was newly pregnant with her first child as an associate editor at a lifestyle site, when she was asked by her boss to participate in an ad campaign for a big paper towel company, posing as a mom, with child models. She recalls the ad copy being "incredibly sexist and obnoxious," and she was less than thrilled that her employer would reap all the benefits of her performance as the "happy cleaning mommy" while her paycheck would remain absurdly low, especially given the cost of living in New York City.[27] She thinks refusing to participate was the beginning of the end of her career at the lifestyle company.

However, it was this incident that made her take a hard look at the future of the women's media landscape and her place within it. As an associate editor at a big media company, Erin was barely making enough to live on, and her husband had an equally untenable salary. She knew the job would not contribute enough income once her baby was born, and she recognized that a company had wanted to use her identity to sell something—but only to profit the company, not her, the actual person with the actual identity.

Both from a financial point of view and an ethical point of view, this struck her as fundamentally wrong.

> Rather than being used by big media companies who want to commodify my identity without paying me for that commodification, I thought, *I should go do this by myself.* So that's what I did. And for me, this is very much a job. I get to write about things that interest me, and the funding model means that sometimes I have to do annoying advertised advertisements for companies. For me, it's very straightforward. But of course, I think the trickiness comes in with, like, it's not straightforward for everyone.[28]

Bekah Martinez (@bekah) has more than seven hundred thousand followers on Instagram, and creates funny, unexpected, refreshing content in a genre often dominated by conformity. Think sponcon pranks on April Fools' Day and photos of herself with her kids with captions that read: "When you're the only one that looks good in the photo but you post it anyway."[29] When we spoke on the phone, Bekah told me she constantly fields intrusive questions about her work that would not be asked of a man. "It's so interesting to me how many mom bloggers and influencers constantly get told to, like, *Get a real job*, or deal with comments like *Wait, you get paid what?* And I think it's super misogynistic. Let's look at male-dominated jobs, like a hedge fund manager, for example. Look at what these guys are making, and what the fuck are they doing at their offices all day? Why are people so appalled at how much momfluencers make?"[30]

In addition to misogyny, Bekah thinks that critiques of monetized momfluencers can also be understood in the context of women's collective longing for the ever-elusive work/life balance.

> I think it still makes some people uncomfortable to see women succeeding outside of the home. And other people want a mom to be spread so thin she can barely function.

Like, working nine to five outside the home, keeping the house, picking up the kids from daycare, making dinner, whatever. And I think when other moms critique momfluencers for making as much money as they do, it's coming from a place of wishing they could find work they were passionate about while still supporting their families, you know? And I completely understand that.[31]

When I think about Erin taking control of her own commodification; or Bekah pointing out that America still makes it nearly impossible for most women to even dream of "having it all" (if having it all means simply being able to function); or when I consider Tiffany's summation of her daily work responsibilities; it *does* seem, as Erin said, "straightforward." In our current capitalistic system, we're always being sold to, so why not happily give ad money to people like Erin, Bekah, and Tiffany—mothers running their own small businesses—to support their families? And if identities can be (or must be) monetized, shouldn't those identities be profiting the people they actually belong to? Why shouldn't a momfluencer control her own narrative, as well as her own financial destiny? Erin thinks it has to do with the "cult of personality," and the fact that most consumers are accustomed to giving their money to faceless corporations—which feels like an impersonal transaction—whereas, to some, following someone on Instagram, being privy to little snapshots of their lives, and then being served up an ad for Dove deodorant, feels like cognitive dissonance. They want their momfluencers to be better than money-grubbing corporations. They want their momfluencers to be human. To be real. To be authentic. Authenticity, as we'll learn in later chapters, has become the gold standard of effective momfluencing.

The veneer of authenticity—and the effort such authenticity requires—might be one reason Myleik Teele (@myleik) referred to herself as an "accidental influencer" during our Zoom. Myleik was kind enough to explain that she looked as phenomenal as she did (in full makeup, wearing non-sweatshirt-clothing, against very cool green-velvet wallpaper), because she had a work thing immediately afterward. "Otherwise," she said, "I'd look like you!"[32] I can't remember what I was wearing at the time, but an elastic waist was probably involved, and I know my background lacked green velvet (and sadly, still does).

Myleik is the founder of CURLBOX, a subscription service specializing in products made for curly hair, and the mom of two. Most of Myleik's content has to do with her business, but she also shares what she's learned from motherhood with other moms that might be like her, who haven't chosen the "traditional approach or route to motherhood." Because of her large platform (213,000 followers), brands often approach her for mom-centric partnerships; however, Myleik has never pursued momfluencer work full time, partially, she says, because even taking photos of her kids on Halloween can be a struggle. "I tried," she said. "And I literally was like, *How do you do it. How do you do it?* Because the squirming, the crying, I couldn't get the costume on. How the hell do momfluencers get a costume on? I have not been able to get a costume on my kid for three years."[33] I mean, yes.

In addition to the inherent challenges of working with one's own children, Myleik explained what is entailed in a momfluencer gig coming out well. "It's a lot of work," she said. "It's hair, it's makeup. It's video. It's acting! And then it's edits. A lot of these brands don't give you a concept; they come to you for the concept, which is the reason I'm like, *I can't do it for less than twenty thousand dollars, you know, because you'd like me to dream up the thing.*" Even if Myleik was paid twenty thousand dollars for a momfluencer job, she figures she typically pays three to four thousand dollars for a videographer if she wants "something that looks good," and another one to two thousand dollars for hair and makeup.[34]

She told me about a recent job she did for Bounty, which was, she says, "a complete disaster. [My son] sees the videographer setting up all the lights, you know? And he's like, *What's happening in in my house?*" When they finally shot the first take, something had blocked the roll of Bounty on-screen, so they had to set up to do it all over again, and Myleik's son "lost it."[35] She ended up not including him in the ad because, screaming kid.

Myleik also thinks the industry itself can be disorganized and unpredictable, and a little "predatory." She reported, "I have rarely gotten a job that wasn't last minute. I have rarely had somebody reach out to me and say, *Hey, we're working on a Bounty ad in six months or three months or one month.* It's like, *Hey, we need you to turn this around in a week.*" Myleik is grateful that she doesn't "need" her momfluencing jobs, and feels empathy for moms whose entire livelihoods are dependent on creating mom content, who don't have a choice about "having to drop everything and turn this stuff around." Myleik finds the industry "so annoying . . . It's aggressive and it's like, *do this, do that.* It definitely has an air of game playing to it. It feels like gambling a little bit."[36]

Influencers of color are notoriously paid less than white influencers, and Myleik "hates" how brands will reach out to see how much she charges without first explaining what is expected and when. She always starts negotiations by asking for the brand's budget first. Because there are so many moms trying to monetize their accounts, though, most brands have no problem saying "no" to a momfluencer demanding to be paid fairly for her time and skill. Myleik thinks Black momfluencers in particular, even when they have more followers, or more influence than white momfluencers, are often rendered powerless in these negotiations because a brand can simply "throw one dollar" at the next mom on the list. There are no meaningful industry standards. No "minimum wages."[37] There's no HR department.

In addition to lack of oversight, Myleik also explains how short-sighted most companies are in failing to recognize the market power of Black creators, often because there are no Black people on the other side of the negotiating table. "If you don't employ Black people, you legitimately don't even know how well they're doing, you know?" She told me when she first started CURLBOX, she would pitch companies by referring to a specific "holy grail" Herbal Essences product Black women had used for years to illustrate the gap in the market. And the people she was pitching had no clue—either about the product she was referring to, or the market gap. "So I think that you've got people at these companies that don't know the culture, they don't know that these [Black influencers] can sell, sell, sell, and instead they just kind of tokenize them or overlook them. Which is a bummer."[38]

Perhaps the most existential problem of momfluencing work (at least for Myleik) is how it makes her vulnerable to unsolicited comments and interactions having to do with her motherhood. Once she started posting publicly about motherhood on Instagram, she was "shocked by the harassment. . . All of a sudden you've got strangers who are now the police of my kid, you know? Once I talked about how I don't have mom guilt, you know? Like, I just don't have it. And I got bashed via email that I didn't have it!"[39] First of all, WHAT. Second of all, fuck yes to divesting ourselves of bullshit mom guilt that has been foisted on so many of us without our consent! I told Myleik that I've never felt a *ton* of mom guilt either (and am grateful!). I don't particularly "miss" my kids when I'm away from them for a weekend. I savor being away from them for a weekend.

Myleik totally gets this, and we laughed in solidarity over our shared disdain for treacly mom platitudes, some of which "irritate the shit" out of us. "When people say things like *My kids are my whole world*, and it's like, no, they're not! Or, *I can't remember my life before kids*. On a weekend when my three-year-old's whining, my one-year-old is, like, on my leg, and I'm trying to make lunch, and it's not the right thing, and I'm now on my third type of cheese, my husband will say, *Can you imagine what you'd be doing without kids?* And it's like, *Yeah! I'd be poolside in Mexico having drinks!*"[40]

Cheers.

Hitha Palepu's toddler did not want to watch *Adventure Bay*. Or *CoComelon*. Or the *Paw Patrol* movie. As I drove myself and my daughter to a sleepover with friends (hers and mine) through a sheet of rain on the stretch of Route 95 connecting New Hampshire to Massachusetts, Hitha tried to quell her toddler's demands for attention with TV. Because, obviously. As he gently squawked, my daughter smirked in the backseat. She's experienced her share of TV negotiations with her own toddler brother.

"What about *Octonauts*?" I suggested to Hitha. "My toddler just discovered *Octonauts* and was absolutely entranced."

"Wanna try *Octonauts*?" Hitha said enticingly in a tone I recognized.

They tried *Octonauts*, and Hitha and I continued our conversations about how furious she is with the misogynistic misconceptions about the creator economy in general, and mom influencers in particular. She "hates" the term "momfluencer," by the way and doesn't want to be "qualified by [her] gender."[41]

"Do not take away my accomplishments by putting these cute little adages on it," Hitha fumed. "I also hate 'girl boss.' I'm just a boss. I think these terms, while probably shared with good intentions, or for great SEO, deprive us of the power we have worked so hard to earn. I think it is disrespectful. Yeah, I think it is frustrating beyond all belief. I want to ditch the sort of qualifiers and embrace the ampersands."[42] For the record, I totally agree, despite the name of this book! Hitha's frustration with the term "momfluencer" mirrors my own irritation when people talk about "mommy writers," as if my choice to write about motherhood— one of the most dramatic, life-shaking, archetypal journeys of the human experience—is somehow less worthy or important than a [male] writer choosing to write a bildungsroman about a guy going through some shit in his twenties. Do we call him an "artsy sensitive man writer"? I've chosen to use the term "momfluencer" for the title and throughout the book at least in part because of what it connotes in terms of demeaning gender assumptions. I've also chosen it for simple convenience: to distinguish a mom influencer from a style influencer or a fitness influencer or a wellness influencer.

Hitha (@hithapalepu) is the creator of #fivesmartreads and the author of *We're Speaking: The Life Lessons of Kamala Harris: How to Use Your Voice, Be Assertive, and Own Your Story*. She has nearly sixty thousand followers on Instagram and made a name for herself due to her thriving professional partnerships with businesses like Taco Bell, Athletic Greens, and the Girlfriend Collective. After *Octonauts* had worked its magic, Hitha told me she feels like momfluencers are "still fighting for our place in terms of respect."

> And the influencer economy keeps growing because think about what's happening for women and moms in traditional workplaces. You're not getting paid leave, you're not getting flexibility, you're facing the very real motherhood tax. And if you continue to work, you have to work even harder than you did before you had kids. And you're killing yourself for scraps, instead of being able to take what you've learned in a myriad of industries, and create your own business and work on your terms. And be able to give yourself the dignity really in most workplaces.[43]

To explain how her creator work grants her dignity, Hitha told me about a "dream" partnership with Taco Bell. She spent four weeks moderating a series of culture summits all over the world for Taco Bell's internal purposes. At the final summit, the chief people officer of Taco Bell gave a speech acknowledging Hitha's work and thanking her for it, highlighting how Hitha had "paused her life" despite having young kids at home and a variety of other work commitments.[44]

"And that was the first time I actually felt like a brand saw and valued my whole self," Hitha explained. "Not just a sliver of myself. And I was paid well for it, my travel was covered. And it was one of the most fulfilling projects I've ever done professionally. It gave me a lot of hope for the future." During our phone interview, Hitha also drew attention to our respective work/life contexts, to indicate how we were both showing up as mothers (me with a kid on a way to a sleepover, her dealing with a kid's mercurial TV preferences) *and* as people engaged in serious work. She pointed out that our back-and-forth about which shows might be most effective at keeping a toddler at bay needs to be normalized as a standard part of working while being a parent. "I'm so excited for the future because, you know, if we can show up as our full selves, and have it be celebrated, and have these types of interruptions be normalized the way any other work challenge would be normalized, we'd all be in a better spot."[45]

Agreed.

On a cold, gray afternoon in snow-covered New Hampshire, I Zoomed with Shanicia Boswell. Clad in a citrus-colored sweatshirt and surrounded by houseplants, Shanicia was like a little virtual beam of warmth despite the fact that it was thundering and downpouring on her side of the screen in Atlanta. Five minutes into the call, I heard my toddler start to cry and my daughter screaming "Mom!" despite the fact that I had instructed her to "get Dad" if anything went awry. I dug my fingernails into my thighs until Brett hustled them away from the door. Shanicia commiserated, saying she was deep in homeschooling "fun" with her second grader. Recalling my conversation with Erin Boyle about people getting pissed about moms posting sponcon (and daring to lay bare their desire to be paid for their work), I asked Shanicia why she thought momfluencer consumers often felt scammed by sponsored content popping up in their favorite feeds.

> People go online to escape reality. Say I'm following the world's greatest momfluencer. Her life is perfect. I love the way she cooks for dinner. Her children are beautiful, her husband is so loving, and then—BOOM—buy some deodorant—and I'm like, *Oh, my god, this is all a lie.* It's almost like it shakes you out of your dream. Okay, this is fake, she's making money off of this, it can't be authentic anymore. I think it kind of challenges reality for people. When people fall in love with an influencer, they're like, *This is my person.* They feel ownership over your life because you're influencing *their* life. What you do matters. Our job as influencers is to make people think they know us.[46]

Shanicia went on to describe strangers approaching her on the street for hugs to illustrate her point that momfluencer work is deeply personal to many content consumers in a way that traditional women's media simply isn't. Toward the end of our Zoom, Shanicia's eyes grew a little pensive. "I think for both the momfluencer and the person following," she said, "everything is very subconscious. [Both the content creation and consumption of the content become] as simple as breathing. Maybe people don't realize how much they actually do need it."[47]

Matt Klein is a cultural theorist and cyberpsychologist studying our relationships with technology. He says that momfluencers occupy a unique place in the influencer landscape, that they're "different" from other influencers because they've largely remained immune to the greater shift toward less glossy imagery and more gritty, raw content that other genres of influencers are currently grappling with.

> While all influencers are tasked with pushing products, Momfluencers also sell something more profound: idealistic fantasy. It's escapism. It's performance. It's aspirational. Unattainable, we still really don't care. It's what we signed up for. Knowing how impossible this is, is part of the fun and appeal. It's pleasurable. It's voyeuristic. It's unrealistic. We know it's not good for us, but it feels so good.[48]

Matt astutely points out something that's always puzzled me: that mothers, a demographic group most likely to consume momfluencer content, know without a shadow of doubt that motherhood is anything but glamorous, peaceful, or easy, but we seek those very things in representations of motherhood on Instagram. The strange kismet between momfluencers and their audiences full of fellow mothers has to do with the fact that we moms are in on the scam. We know it's a ruse. Or, as Matt says, "there's an unspoken suspension of disbelief. There's a fake-ness, or at least complete concealing of the seams."[49] As mothers, our everyday lives are full of gritty motherhood rawness, of children refusing to wear snow pants in blizzards, or the strain of holding back tears and curses upon stepping on another fucking Lego. Of fish sticks. Of dishes. Of middle-of-the-night sheet changes. Why would we want to spend our spare time consuming someone else's rawness when we're sick and tired of our own?

Matt confirms something I've long suspected, that "momfluencers can act as a mirror. Moms see bits and pieces of themselves in others. Here there's relatability . . . the part that helps sell. But this mirror is in fact a fun-house mirror, accentuating and exaggerating the parts we like, shrinking and ignoring the parts we don't. Many can see their best selves in momfluencers."[50]

Their best selves. Yes. And their worst selves. When Hannah Neeleman drives her tractor or milks her cow or hikes through the scrubby Utah range with her kids in tow, I recall my past weekend spent shoving chunks of granite into place to repair an old, crumbling stone wall in the woods behind my house. I feel good in knowing that I rattled off some cursory historical information about New England's stone walls and that I gave my older kids helper jobs to do, directing them to toss smaller rocks into appropriate nooks and crannies. My daughter helped the toddler make a stone wall for the fairies. This small aspect of my own motherhood, of my own self, the outdoorsy, history- and fairy-loving bit, is reflected back to me by Hannah chattering about early pioneer wives as she directs her kids to help her patch a wooden fence, and I feel a little more solid in myself, in my mothering. But then I see Naomi Davis playing some sort of make-believe robot game with her troop of children—and seemingly loving it—and that solidity wobbles a bit. I hate make-believe. Playing with my kids is often boring, and not something I always cherish. Of course, this makes me feel bad. Not like a bad mom, but like a mom that could be (maybe should be) better. Both the bursts of feeling good and of feeling bad are nearly imperceptible—I might not even consciously be aware of them in the moment—but they pile up somewhere inside of me. I can't even really be sure how big the pile is or where I keep it.

Many people have asked me why this book is focused on momfluencer culture and not influencer culture in general, and, while my reasons are plentiful, the primary answer is that motherhood renders all mothers powerless to an extent, and momfluencer culture offers us power and control. We cannot control our bodies during pregnancy. We cannot control who our children will be. We cannot control who we will turn out to be as mothers. I harbored grand fantasies of being a serene earth goddess mother before having kids, the type who would think about traveling across time zones with her baby as an adventure rather than a logistical, sleep-deprived nightmare. We cannot control how motherhood will make us feel. I am continuously shaken by the nuance of feeling that motherhood ushers in. How I feel when my six-year-old daughter tells me she doesn't want me to put her hair in a bun because it isn't "pretty enough"; how I feel when I don't get an invite to a mom-hang; how I feel when my first baby tells me how big a whale's brain is. Motherhood can hurt us just as deeply as it can bring us joy; it is a role defined by vulnerability. And momfluencer culture is defined by trusting ourselves and others to respect that vulnerability. As we'll see throughout this book, this trust can be beautiful. And, as we'll explore in chapter 6, this trust can also be dangerous. Power and trust can always be used for good and evil.

Ultimately, momfluencer culture allows us to control—at least to an extent—the mythology of our own motherhood. I don't have a ton of followers on Instagram, but every mom-centric photograph or caption I post is chosen to communicate something specific about my motherhood, about the type of mom I want others to see when they look at me.

I want people to know I have a sense of humor and am not precious, so I post a photo of some dumb kid selfies with quippy, dry captions, or maybe of a Snickers wrapper found nestled between cushions. I want people to know I'm thoughtful, that I value the beautiful, liminal moments of motherhood, so I post a photo of sea-sprayed baby curls. I want people to appreciate my personal style, so I post a photo of the baby in a onesie dappled with indigo-colored block prints of seaweed made (obviously) by a little-known Brooklyn-based company; the photo is well lit, the composition is good. I want people to know I'm smart and care about things bigger than myself, so I post about motherhood literature and maternal advocacy. I want people to know I'm a cool mom, sometimes even a hot mom, so I post a photo of myself in a hand-knit ochre sweater (my love for ochre will never die) and jeans that make my ass look perky. In the photo I'm wearing makeup, but it's meant to look like I'm too cool to care about makeup or how I look. I want people to know I am loved and therefore I must, to some extent, be a decent mom, so I post a photo of smiling kids snuggled in my lap. A couple thousand people digest my mythology, and who's to say it doesn't impact how they think of their own motherhood mythologies? I am a mother on Instagram. And what I choose to show influences those who watch. I am a momfluencer. If you are a mother on Instagram, so are you.

2

In Pursuit of Clean Countertops and a Shoppable Life

M y Care/of vitamin packets live in a drawer littered with spare rubber bands, ChapSticks, paper clips, Eric Carle–themed name labels for kids' water bottles and backpacks, and receipts that will never be needed. I haven't taken the vitamins all week, and although I'm telling myself that I'll remember to take them today because I'm writing about them, I don't have particularly high hopes that'll actually happen.

Instagram has been trying to sell me Care/of vitamins for a while now, mostly through targeted ads, but it wasn't until Julie D. O'Rourke served me an ad in one of her Instagram stories that I finally took the plunge. There was a discount code (of course), and O'Rourke, whom you can find as @rudyjude on Instagram, is exactly the type of momfluencer most likely to make me buy something. She lives on an island in Maine with her obscenely hot partner and two kids, who both know how to whittle and weave. When not working on her clothing line (also named Rudy Jude), which features simple, timeless pieces like billowy white sailor blouses and her trademark high-waisted non-stretch jeans, O'Rourke makes her own butter and seems to love hand-embroidering tiny baby dresses with spotted toadstools. Lest you think she's at all precious, she is *not.* She projects an extremely appealing air of not giving many fucks and she seems more chill as a mother than I could ever pretend to be. Anyway, she sold me the Care/of vitamins.

Momfluencers sell me a lot of things. They sell a lot of us a lot of things! In selling motherhood and a particular version of womanhood, momfluencer content has largely taken the place of celebrity endorsements, glossy women's magazines, and traditional advertising. And because we can voluntarily access them all the time anytime, momfluencers exercise an outsized impact on the consumer habits of the women who scroll. Even discerning, anti-consumerist, feminist mothers (like me!) follow momfluencers and are liable to become avid customers.

By creating distinct, recognizable brands, momfluencers can more effectively reach their target audiences to sell baby slings, Vitamin C serums, workshops, life-coaching sessions, parenting manuals, anti-vaccine propaganda, white supremacy, or social justice. Many also sell their own photo filters, called "presets," which allow consumers to color their own lives so that they look just like those of their favorite momfluencers. These presets are literal rose-tinted lenses.

But before momfluencers can sell us anything, they must first sell us on motherhood itself, and often, on Instagram and within the culture at large, motherhood is made beautiful and aspirational through a domestic lens. Of course, motherhood and domesticity have long been entangled in the consumer market, and advertisers have always sold mothers the idea that their ultimate panacea is domestic bliss. In an *Aeon* article about mid-century advertising powerhouse Jean Wade Rindlaub, Ellen Wayland-Smith writes, "Rindlaub's Betty Crocker ads hammered home this message of sentimental domesticity, promising that if women felt 'troubled' by the world outside their front doors, relief was just a cake away."[1] It only takes a few minutes of Instagram scrolling to determine that this message from 1954 is alive and well.

Even liberal Instagram moms tend to tout devotion to children and home as a type of resistance, when in fact this aligns them with advertising that has historically deliberately portrayed the labor of caregiving and housework as a combination of joy and feminine moral duty. By convincing a mom that she can cure her hopelessness by cooking and tidying up (consider the title of Marie Kondo's book *The Life-Changing Magic of Tidying Up*), momfluencers are able to gain new customers for a powder-pink Always pan or artisanal laundry basket. In other words, momfluencers promoting a domestic-goddess version of motherhood online help to create a particular class of new mamas to whom they can then continue to sell products.

Momfluencers have made the domestic fantasy more visible and more "shoppable" than ever before. Meanwhile, the effect of momfluencing on the way we spend our money (and time) remains mostly unexamined and not very well understood. Emily Hund, a postdoctoral research fellow at the Center on Digital Culture and Society at the University of Pennsylvania's Annenberg School for Communication, has been studying influencer marketing, particularly on Instagram. Along with her colleague, Lee McGuigan, assistant professor at the UNC Hussman School of Journalism and Media, she coined the term "shoppability" to define how the "integration of commerce and personal technologies has become a central pivot of lived experience in the early 21st century."[2] When we scroll through momfluencers' feeds, we are consuming their performances of motherhood, sure, but we're also just as likely to be shopping, and Instagram is no longer a platform solely devoted to sharing doctored-up photos with family and friends, but a platform from which billions of dollars are spent and made. And most of these dollars are being spent by women, many of them mothers.

In their paper "A Shoppable Life: Performance, Selfhood, and Influence in the Social Media Storefront," Hund and McGuigan explain that shoppability has its roots in catalogs and infomercials. Whereas I could project very little onto a nameless model in a J.Crew catalog wearing a rollneck sweater—I don't know her name, I don't know how many kids she has, I can't commiserate with her about teary preschool drop-offs—I can do all that and more when shopping from my favorite momfluencers' pages. When they give me an ad or affiliate link, I feel like my shopping choices have been vetted by someone I kind of (feel like I) know, and it is parasociality that makes this possible. "Parasociality" refers to the psychological phenomenon of forming bonds with celebrities, public figures, or, in this case, momfluencers, that fulfill similar roles to IRL friendships.[3] These parasocial relationships make shoppability so much more powerful, because they enforce the idea that we're buying something via someone we trust or feel like we know. Parasociality helps distinguish the modern era of shoppability from traditional magazine or TV ads targeted toward women and mothers.

What hasn't changed, however, is the clear understanding among advertisers and marketers that, to effectively sell a product to mothers, one first must define the parameters of what makes a "good mother." These, of course, depend on cultural mores and expectations, which have changed quite a bit throughout modern consumer history but, in many critical ways, have remained stubbornly the same.

For the purposes of understanding momfluencer culture and shoppability, with its overarching emphasis on domesticity and all that it entails (nurturing, homemaking, cooking, aesthetics), I think it's helpful to hitch up our petticoats for a little jaunt down memory lane to visit everyone's favorite cult, the Cult of Domesticity, which had its heyday in the late nineteenth century. The central goddess worshipped by members of this cult was the Angel in the House. Beautiful, selfless, attentive to her husband's and children's every whim, and devoted to everything domestic, she was made famous by Coventry Patmore's 1854 poem "The Angel in the House":

> *Man must be pleased; but him to please*
> *Is woman's pleasure; down the gulf*

Of his condoled necessities
She casts her best, she flings herself.[4]

Patmore's Angel did not live for herself. Rather, she gave all of herself (or, at least, the best of herself) to her husband. And, according to Patmore, it was her pleasure to do so. It's worth nothing that yesterday's housewife is today's stay-at-home mother, and that the fetishization of the model wife has given way to the fetishization of the model mother. We might all scoff at Patmore's rendition of the selfless Angel wholly devoted to her husband's needs, but the notion of the selfless Angel wholly devoted to her children's needs is not only still celebrated but also expected as natural and necessary.

To make things a bit more ideologically thorny, assuming the mantel of stay-at-home-mother often carries with it the assumption of choice—or the illusion thereof. In their book *The Mommy Myth: The Idealization of Motherhood and How It Has Undermined All Women*, Susan J. Douglas and Meredith W. Michaels argue that today's era of intensive mothering, or "the new momism," has created a generation of women determined to define themselves by their perceived "success" as mothers. Douglas and Michaels define "the new momism" as the media-led "insistence that no woman is truly complete or fulfilled unless she has kids, that women remain the best primary caretakers of children, and that to be a remotely decent mother, a woman has to devote her entire physical, psychological, emotional, and intellectual being, 24/7, to her children."[5]

This sounds remarkably like what was expected of nineteenth-century mothers, but Douglas and Michaels point out that, today, thanks to second-wave feminism, some women are free to make the *choice* to become wholesale domestic goddesses, and in that choice lies both a celebration and rejection of feminism: "[As compared to pursuing fulfillment in a toxic workplace culture], the June Cleaver model, if taken as a *choice*, as opposed to a re-quirement, is the truly modern, fulfilling, forward thinking version of motherhood."[6] Consider Alexa (on Instagram as @wearethe browns) regarding her embrace of motherhood as the ultimate expression of identity. On Mother's Day 2021, she posted a photo of herself clad in a long white cotton dress sprinkled with blue flowers. She's holding her baby, whose chubby hand is reaching out to touch a lilac bush, and looking down adoringly at her other small child, who is pointing a vintage-looking toy camera at us, the voyeurs on the other side of the screen: "my one-word answer to the question hanging from the gate key to any worlds beyond this one: what it is i did with my one (holy, sweet, all too brief) life. 'them.' 🥀🥀"[7] "Them," of course, being her children. The dead rose emoji, for the uninitiated, is the trademark emoji of a certain subset of mostly white Instagram mamas whose feeds are rich in waxed vintage pine furniture, floor-length dresses, and nostalgic images of babies in bonnets.

Mothers might work outside of the home now, but there's still a tacit expectation that home is where maternity flourishes, that a mother makes a home. There's a reason "dadfluencer" isn't a thing. Dadfluencers exist, yes, but they certainly don't comprise a multibillion-dollar industry, and Instagram is not very densely populated by fathers smiling beatifically while crafting with their rosy-cheeked spawn in whimsically and thoughtfully appointed playrooms.

Most of my background information about the Cult of Domesticity's codification of domesticity as a feminine pursuit and employment outside of the home in the market sphere as a male pursuit come from two excellent books: Lyz Lenz's *Belabored: A Vindication of the Rights of Pregnant Women*, and Sarah Menkedick's *Ordinary Insanity: Fear and the Silent Crisis of Motherhood in America*. I highly recommend both. Prior to the industrial revolution, both women and men labored inside and outside of the home. Both husband and wife would share responsibilities tending crops and livestock and making shoes. Domesticity was not seen as innately feminine, or as on opportunity to showcase one's aesthetic prowess, but simply an integral part of daily life. But once large-scale factory work became the norm, a gender gap—which grew into a chasm—distinguished white, upper-class men as outside earners and white, upper-class women as confined to the doyennes of domestic affairs. The Cult of Domesticity was born from this gender chasm, recasting women as pure, chaste, and precious, and therefore unfit for the dangers of the public sphere, and once domesticity became explicitly linked to femininity, the work of domesticity was simultaneously denigrated as less serious and less worthy of respect than other forms of labor. Domestic work became "women's work."

Given the rapid advance of industrialization and the relocation of production from country to city, home took on new significance as a refuge from the hustle and bustle of economic life. In this way, Angels of the House directly contributed to the economy by rearing the next generation of workers while providing a place of respite in which their husbands could recharge. They were to keep themselves pure from the grime of buying and selling, yet the buying and selling was the entire point. Domestic life was pretty and feminine, a necessary backdrop to the main action of capitalism, and so, too, of course, was the Angel.

Writing about the stubborn survival of the Cult of Domesticity for *Pacific Standard*, Laura Turner notes, "Men had historically been the earners of their families, but this time they were paid not in favors or food but in cash, which was newly tied to the gold standard. This further stratified society into those who made money and those who didn't."[8] Although upper-class white women were really the only women who had the privilege or luxury to devote themselves to flower arranging and general Angel endeavors, all women were judged by the same standards, placing women of color and working-class women in an impossible position.

In *From Slave Cabins to the White House: Homemade Citizenship in African American Culture*, Koritha Mitchell explains how the 1896 Supreme Court decision *Plessy v. Ferguson*, which ruled for "enforced separation of the two races," was an attempt to prohibit Black people from achieving upward mobility while also preventing

Black wives and mothers from attaining the same Angel status as their white upper- and middle-class counterparts.[9] *Plessy v. Ferguson* also contributed to racist depictions of Black women as "whores" and Black men as dangerous defilers of white feminine purity.

To illustrate how firmly racist ideas about Black women were entrenched in white culture, Mitchell quotes an early-twentieth-century newspaper article cited in Ida B. Wells's book *Red* as follows: "It is not the same thing for a white man to assault a colored woman as for a colored man to assault a white woman, because the colored woman had no finer feelings nor virtue to be outraged."[10] It's no coincidence that while the Cult of Domesticity was being upheld as a paragon of (white) feminine virtue, at the same time the "science of racism," or eugenics, was brought forth as a way of upholding white supremacy. Eugenics, which used bogus "science" to create a hierarchy based on race, paired with the ratification of race-based discrimination via *Plessy v. Ferguson*, made it easy for white people to view violence by white men against Black women as nothing to be "outraged" about, whereas threats to white female purity were to be fought at all costs.

In citing Wells again from her 1887 piece "Our Women," Mitchell points out that this type of "know your place" aggression against Black people and the stereotyping of Black women as "immoral amounted to an attempt to obliterate the accomplishments of African American 'mothers, wives and maidens who have attained a true, noble, and refining womanhood.'"[11]

So even if Black mothers had the time and means to devote to achieving some sort of domestic ideal—even if they checked all the Angel boxes—their enactment of "true, noble, and refining womanhood" would never be recognized as worthy of respect or protection by a white supremacist culture. Mitchell writes that the devaluing of Black women's domestic skills and homemaking efforts coincided with the pervading racist belief that a Black woman's "proper place" was not as mistress of her own home, but in service to a white woman and *her* home, a theme that Mitchell says persists today, which she illustrates via a case study of Michelle Obama's stint as First Lady.[12]

Mitchell argues that, since white supremacist ideology still mandates whiteness as part and parcel of "good womanhood," Michelle Obama, more than any other [white] First Lady before her, had to go to extraordinary lengths to prove her worthiness as First Lady. Part of her strategy was emphasizing her maternity. "In claiming the label [mom in chief]," Mitchell writes, "[Michelle Obama] pursued success while acknowledging the violence inherent in how black women are typically understood, as welfare queens but also as servants in, not women of, the nation's house."[13]

Mitchell underscores how stubbornly whiteness remains hinged to America's understanding of a "good woman" and a "good mother," even though we're over a century removed now from the Cult of Domesticity. "In a nation that insists upon linking womanhood to whiteness," Mitchell contends, "a black first lady was disturbing; for many Americans, it therefore became a patriotic imperative to negate her status as a homemaker. In the process, her heteronormative nuclear family somehow faded in importance in national conversations when it would have been cause for endless celebration if she (and it) had been white."[14] If the (Black) First Lady of the United States struggled to be accepted as a modern-day Angel of the House in the early aughts, despite literally referring to herself as "mom in chief," imagine how much more difficult (that is, impossible) it would have been for Black women during the nineteenth-century Cult of Domesticity. And since women could only attain some modicum of agency or power by complying with the rules of femininity laid out by the Cult, Black women, lacking the proximity to whiteness, were also excluded from those—however meager and imperfect—power sources.

To further highlight American racist nostalgia for Black women and mothers raising white women's children in white women's homes, Mitchell argues that the huge success of the movie *The Help* in 2009 was surely due in part to white anxiety over having a Black First Lady.

> The book and movie arrived to offer a reassuring message, that people who believe black women belong in a servant role are correct. It really does make more sense for black women to be housekeepers, not homemakers—and certainly not first ladies. *The Help*'s overwhelming popularity, becoming a franchise with everything from DVDs and T-shirts to packaged tea, cookbooks, and cookware, should be understood as an expression of the unconscious distress caused by seeing a black woman as *woman of the house*.[15]

Mitchell draws an explicit line from Ida B. Wells's National Association of Colored Women—a network of women's clubs founded in 1896 committed to women's suffrage, anti-lynching activism, and advancing civil rights for Black people—to Michelle Obama's failure to be recognized as a "good woman" in the aughts: "Club women literally taught others how to exemplify admirable womanhood with lessons about style, grooming, and comportment, and Michelle Obama's public persona continued that legacy. . . . She exemplified all that U.S. society worked to prevent her from becoming: an impressive lady."[16]

The Black women's clubs of the late nineteenth and early twentieth century pursued not only equality and dignity for *all* people; they also prioritized domestic accomplishment. They followed the rules of the Cult, but they were denied the perks of membership. And, as Mitchell emphasizes, "if, as all Americans are taught to believe, women gain society's respect and protection by creating domestic havens, then Michelle Obama should have been able to trust that she and her family would be revered and safe. Yet, as she embodied Mom-in-Chief, behaving in ways that presumably earned her that assurance, images of her husband in a noose provided the backdrop to her impeccable performance."[17] The Angel of the House is alive and well, and her longevity is intrinsically connected to the persistence of racist ideologies about what constitutes a good woman and mother.

My purpose in outlining the racist underpinnings of the Cult of Domesticity is to point out that present-day idealization of domesticity and motherhood cannot be wholly divorced from its racist roots. I also think it's worth unpacking why certain subsets of momfluencers are celebrated for embracing a maternal ideal and aesthetic that could very easily have existed in the late 1800s. Long, flowing dresses. Mamas in Shaker-style kitchens waxing poetic about domestic duty and maternal sacrifice. It's worth understanding the historical and cultural context of such imagery and belief systems, and interrogating why both remain so popular.

But how does the Angel of the House, so removed from the messiness of the marketplace, figure into our conversation about momfluencers today? How did marketing to moms become the tentpole of modern consumerism and capitalism? In her book *Angel of the Marketplace: Adwoman Jean Wade Rindlaub and the Selling of America*, Ellen Wayland-Smith provides an excellent history of why and how the selling of domesticity became critical to marketing everything from deodorant to Oneida silver specifically to American mothers. Reading her book caused a litany of cartoon lightbulbs to explode for me, and my copy is riddled with expletives and bathed in neon highlighter.

During the Cult of Domesticity, women weren't necessarily supposed to concern themselves with the buying and selling of things, but they were, according to Wayland-Smith, writing and thinking about how to be the best domestic goddesses they possibly could be. As mentioned earlier, Black women's clubs addressed the importance of personal comportment and proper housekeeping skills, and "home experts" instructed women on how to be good mothers and housekeepers in various books and pamphlets devoted to the art and science of domesticity—for example, *The American Woman's Home, or, Principles of Domestic Science* (1869) by Catherine Beecher and Harriet Beecher Stowe (of *Uncle Tom's Cabin* fame). In their book, Wayland-Smith writes, "the Beecher sisters set themselves the task of explaining why the home—and the woman presiding over it—was the moral center of American life."[18] They discussed the science of homemaking (proper kitchen ventilation!) and "argued that female domestic labor deserved to be treated as a profession in its own right alongside male occupations."[19]

By centering femininity within the domestic sphere, and assuring women that homemaking should be taken seriously as a vocation worth studying, the Beecher sisters did their part to keep women out of the market and in the home. Remember Hannah (Mormon rancher goddess who remains one of my primary momfluencer obsessions) from chapter 1? Consider what she writes on Instagram (next to a photo of herself, pregnant, grinning and holding a huge cast-iron pan containing something delicious-looking, flanked by three of her children) about homemaking as a moral imperative, and the home as a powerful symbol of maternal value:

> Many of our best memories are here in the kitchen. Cheering me on are my flower-bedecked wooden tables, freshly churned butter, cast iron pans and creaky floorboards. The children are earnest helpers and often cook their own meals when Daniel needs me out on the ranch. We don't have television, air conditioning nor a microwave. Simple reasons: Lots of good entertainment here on the ranch, high elevation and cool summer nights keep the heat momentary, my always-hot Aga stove replicates the functionality of a microwave. The ranch house is a peaceful place I proudly call my nest.[20]

Where to begin? For Hannah, her kitchen is not the site of ongoing (sometimes thankless) labor, but a "nest," the mention of which highlights the gender essentialism at play—just as it's natural for a bird to feather her nest, so, too, is it "natural" for a good mother to devote herself to care of the home. Her children ("earnest helpers") don't complain about not having a TV, and since the ranch house is a "peaceful place," apparently they don't fight among each other either? Not only is the home a site of nourishment (both physical and otherwise); it's also pretty ("flower-bedecked"), apparently capable of providing "cheer," and devoid of any potentially corrupting modern influences (microwave!). While Hannah doesn't explicitly write, "I'm a good mom and here's why," the message is clear. She is a good mom because she both enjoys and takes seriously her vocation as a maternal domestic goddess. Her butter is freshly churned.

In 1912, Christine Frederick, a "home efficiency expert," brought her own spin to domesticity and the marketplace. As Wayland-Smith writes, "If the Beechers imagined the home as a space apart from the market, Frederick taught homemakers that their purchasing choices fed into a larger economic and social nexus; they would henceforth exercise their moral influence through their pocketbooks."[21] Frederick argued that it was the housewife's duty to be good shoppers, and that if she somehow bought the wrong item or chose the wrong brand, it was "a confession that [her] judgment is defective."[22] This is not so different from how momfluencers sell us the "right" BPA-free pacifier or the "right" way to sleep train babies. The purchasing of goods or services is considered intrinsically linked to one's fitness as a mother. Then, as now, Wayland-Smith writes, mothers and women were "doing [their] gendered part to keep the American ideals of life, liberty, and the pursuit of happiness alive."[23]

Jean Wade Rindlaub came to prominence in the postwar period, a time during which women were systematically pushed back into their homes after making significant contributions to the workforce during both world wars. Looming Cold War anxiety and the still-fresh memory of the Great Depression put added pressure on protecting the home as a symbolic entity of American values, and, of course, this ideal home required an ideal mother safely ensconced within its ideal domestic center. Gender roles became as rigidly circumscribed as they had been during the Cult of Domesticity, and advertisers began referring to men as "Mr. Breadwinner" and women as "Mrs. Housewife."

Rindlaub understood that, to succeed in a man's world of business, she needed to put her feminized domesticity front and center. She was able to position herself as a "good woman" (that is, a woman wholly concerned with wifehood and motherhood who just so happened to also be an incredibly effective and savvy advertising executive) in a way that reminds me of how many contemporary momfluencers refer to themselves as "just regular moms" in their Instagram bios, despite being de facto CEOs of their own businesses. Rindlaub's emphasis on her femininity made her less threatening to male colleagues and translated into huge financial wins for her advertising firm, Batten, Barton, Durstine & Osborn.

As Wayland-Smith notes, Rindlaub was a dogged researcher, constantly polling other women both in her office and elsewhere to better understand their spending habits. In a speech to advertisers, she said, "You probably don't need much more evidence that women are emotional creatures. . . . Not a job worry in a carload. Not a political worry. My man. My home. My mother. My children—these are the things on your customer's mind."[24] And while Rindlaub's research did indicate that women were bored and at least a little depressed in their roles as mid-century domestic goddesses (in one memo, she reports that the American housewife "has a sense of futility because her life is pretty drab and monotonous"), she also recognized that her role was not to "spring women from their trap. It was to make the trap more comfortable."[25] In doing so, she employed what we now recognize as toxic positivity, but was then a direct response to the Christian-centric doctrine of positive thinking, inspired by a group of pseudo-psychological evangelical thinkers, including Norman Vincent Peale, who published *The Power of Positive Thinking* in 1952. Instead of complaining about the monotony of doing the dishes or preparing breakfast, embrace your vocation as homemaker, find the divine in whipping eggs! If home was a "trap," Rindlaub's advertising copy argued, it was only because you thought of it as such. The problem was not stifling gender inequities; the problem was you.

I'm struck by how this head-in-the-sand way of selling to mothers still exists today—if not universally, then at least in certain sectors of momfluencer culture. At the time of writing this, we're barely emerging from a catastrophic global pandemic, the world is literally still burning our children's lives are deemed less important than gun access, and people with uteruses are being denied bodily autonomy and access to healthcare. Things are not great! But, in their emphasis on insularity by way of homeschooling, book recommendations, and macrobiotic diet hacks, certain momfluencers would have you believe otherwise. In an essay about the Nap Dress—a product sold to mothers and women as a soft, flowing, floral reprieve from reality—cultural critic Anne Helen Petersen (no relation but I guarantee her name is misspelled "Peterson" as often as mine is!) writes:

> The Nap Dress, and mommy-and-me dresses more broadly, look inward. The primary connection is the familial one; the kid's dresses effectively create an echo of the self, even when one's understanding of what that self is (Am I mom? An employee? A wife? A respected member of society? Of worth? What do I actually value?) becomes unstable. They don't say fuck it. They say *maybe this will finally make it work*. Millennials, after all, don't give up. They try harder.[26]

The Nap Dress (often worn and sponconned by momfluencers) is one of many antidotes to the thanklessness of motherhood in a culture that systematically devalues our labor. The work of mothering in the 2020s can be just as "drab and monotonous" as it was in 1954, but advertisers would have you believe that relief lies not in structural change but in a Nap Dress, or a better way to mother tied, at least in part, to one's consumer habits.

In another speech, as Wayland-Smith notes, Jean Wade Rindlaub urged women to battle the boredom of their lives by "throwing some 'chopped green pepper or pimento' into Sunday morning's scrambled eggs" or doing some "'daily stretching[s] of the mind' that 'would make your mothering more rewarding.'"[27] Reading this makes me want to smash a jar of pimentos against the wall. The ghosts of this gaslighty argument thrive on Instagram, in images featuring smiling momfluencers wielding handcrafted brooms against attractive slate tiles, or wireless vacuums across cream-colored nursery rugs. While many white middle- and upper-class women stayed home in the 1950s, and theoretically had the time to find "rewards" in homemaking and domestic work, many women of color and working-class women had been working outside of the home before, during, and after the mid-century revival of the Cult of Domesticity. And the women of color who *did* adhere to domestic ideals were precluded from gaining access to the type of respect and protection afforded to their white counterparts. Just as the nineteenth-century Cult of Domesticity excluded many mothers, so, too, does its contemporary iteration. Where do the majority of mothers today (two-thirds of American mothers worked full time outside of the home in 2018) fit into this fantasy of clean rugs and happy hearts?[28]

I was extremely fortunate to be able to pick out tile for my mudroom floor (and extremely fortunate to live in a house with a mudroom). When it came time to choose, I knew exactly what I wanted: large slate tiles. Yes, just like the ones I made fun of a mere paragraph ago. While it's true that I grew up in a house with a mudroom tiled in slate, it's also true that I was consuming a lot of momfluencer content replete in slate when I opted for my own slate tiles. While I'm not expressing shock and awe that my choice of interior aesthetic was influenced by external forces rather than my innate sense of style, I do think there's something seductive about the close interweaving of motherhood with domesticity. Because when I buy things specifically for the home, I do so with my experience as a mother in mind—because how could I not?

When I imagine my future self walking across the slate tile floors, I imagine small muddy boots and dirty backpacks strewn across them. I also imagine the unpleasantness of such inevitable kid-clutter somehow mitigated by the beauty of the cool, soot-colored slate. I imagine myself as happier, more able to register the sweetness of those small boots versus my annoyance at the mud they track in. It's impossible to know if investing time and money in my domestic space is making me happier as a mother, but I'm loath to imagine a world in which my maternal labor is unvalued, unpaid, and disrespected *and* there's no reprieve to be found in buying something to soothe the ache of longing. Apparently, universal preschool is too much to ask, so what's the sense of begrudging ourselves the indulgence in consumeristic hope? Because that's what we're talking about when we talk about shoppability and momfluencers—the insatiable need to believe there's an easier, more comfortable way to inhabit the impossibly fraught role of *Mother* in a culture that demands servitude with a smile. We're all bound by the fetters of capitalism and patriarchy, so shouldn't we at least be able to access small hits of dopamine from buying stuff to make our experiences of motherhood (or to trick us into believing our experiences of motherhood will be) better?

The campaign that most exemplifies the way advertisers in the postwar period sold women the dream of domestic bliss might be Betty Crocker. Jean Wade Rindlaub realized that Betty Crocker, which had been around as a brand since 1921, needed to be refashioned as a relatable every-housewife to best appeal to women. She knew that for Betty Crocker to convince wives and mothers that cake baking might soothe their woes, both quotidian and existential, she first had to sell them on Betty Crocker as a figurehead. Betty Crocker was a momfluencer before her time.

Various versions of Betty Crocker played by various actresses appeared on both radio and TV programs, the goal being to convince housewives that Betty Crocker could be trusted, because she was "just like us." And since Betty Crocker was always played by (or illustrated on the cover of her cookbooks as) a white woman, the "us" in the prior statement is a white "us" with enough money to spend on nonessential cake mix, and enough desire to aspire to be the type of woman Betty Cocker represented: domestic, maternal, devoted to the care of family and home.

Well before the advent of Instagram, Rindlaub astutely understood that there was lots of money to be made from peddling the appearance of authenticity. In a 1956 briefing to General Mills, Jean argued that "one way that has a sound record of sales success is through the use of trusted, believable, recognizable, real personalities."[29] Betty Crocker was by no means a real person, and, of course, momfluencers *are* real people, but the motherhood they share online can never be 100 percent unfiltered. We all perform motherhood, regardless of our platforms, to various audiences, for various reasons, every day. Momfluencers just have bigger stages.

From 1955 to 1958, Betty Crocker regularly appeared on *The George Burns and Gracie Allen Show*, and her appearances were a lot like sponcon on Instagram now. As Ellen Wayland-Smith writes, "Viewers may have suspected that Adelaide Hawley was a paid actress and that Betty Crocker was a fantasy, but it didn't matter in the context of personality-driven television, where entertainment trumped verisimilitude every time."[30] In the next chapter we'll dig into the existential question of *why* we follow momfluencers more deeply, but here it's worth noting that dozens of women have told me that, despite viscerally understanding that motherhood is 90 percent a mess and 10 percent beauty and wonder, they follow momfluencers with uncluttered playrooms and unspattered stovetops not because they believe in such a domestically pure version of motherhood, but because they like looking at pretty images. They are entertained, just as one is entertained by cavernous, impeccably organized closets in a *Real Simple* spread, or stills from a Nancy Meyers kitchen. It's fun to believe, if only for a minute, in a domestic fantasy.

I think this entertainment can often be colored with something else, though, or at least I know it sometimes is for me. It's tantalizing to believe (or choose to believe) that maybe, just maybe, pouring one's whole self into the pursuit of domestic bliss might dull the noisiness of life, that in pursuing an ideal, lived version of domesticity, we might express our inner selves, as mothers and women. I think this ambiguous, unquenchable need to express our inner selves—and to see our inner selves reflected—on social media can be attributed to most women who use social media, mothers or not. Women, after all, are trained to believe in ideals, to believe that a worthy life goal is to chase those ideals, to embody them. No matter the cost.

Cultural critic and author Emily Gould has written quite a bit about her preoccupation with modern domestic goddesses (albeit usually through the lens of food rather than motherhood), so I reached out to see if she had some thoughts about the intersection of reality and fantasy that permeates the way we both sell and consume domesticity through momfluencer culture. Prior to having kids, Gould told me, she devoured books and cookbooks by domestic goddesses like Nigella Lawson and Laurie Colwin, and said the primary hook for her was these women's apparently unfettered enjoyment of domesticity. Citing their effortless embrace of domestic life and motherhood, Gould said, "These women had everything I wanted and really *enjoyed* doing all of those [domestic] things, and that's the important part, like really *enjoyed* being a mother, really *enjoyed* cooking, and really *enjoyed* their creative lives. I literally never thought to question whether it was all true, I guess."[31]

Returning to Julie D. O'Rourke (super chill island Maine mom) for a moment, a large part—maybe the whole part—of the allure of her Instagram account for me similarly lies in the way she seems to so simply *enjoy* felting Montessori birthday crowns for her kids, *enjoy* foraging for pine tips with which to make homemade ice cream, *enjoy* scooping up periwinkles from rocky tidepools with her toddler (which she'll later cook with butter and that the toddler will gobble up with gusto). Her domestic motherhood seems so untainted by doubt, anxiety, and the constant vacillating between despising domestic drudgery and aspiring to domestic bliss. And although I really doubt that Julie is deliberately trying to sell me the idea that domesticity can be salvation as Betty Crocker ads did in 1950 (Julie is not shy about sharing photos of her kitchen sink overflowing with dishes, for example), the effect on the consumer is largely the same. *Do motherhood like this and the rest of your problems won't be as big, will matter less.* Or, as a stated in a Betty Crocker ad, "'I can't change the headlines, but I've got to do something. So I've gone back to baking bread.'"[32]

Gould told me that, prior to having kids, cooking a delicious meal would feel like a "consolation prize" for a bad day, and the creation of that meal, the magical connotation of a domestic fantasy, could fulfill her on a personal, creative level, much in the same way writing a perfect sentence might. But after kids, she said, domestic work no longer "fits in the same box" as it once did. "If you mapped my brain," she told me, "the creative work part has its own code. And then, cooking and entertaining, you know, everything related to maintaining a household, it's filed in the same place as, like, *When am I going to schedule a dentist appointment?*"[33] Despite this, she said, she's not immune to the tantalizing shoppability of momfluencer culture, and most recently bought a fifty-dollar silicon cheese keeper from Food52 because of it.

Domestic-goddess momfluencer content, regardless of individual momfluencers' intent, regularly teases us with the assertion that the pursuit of idealized domesticity might also have the capacity to fulfill us creatively, because it does for them . . . right? This, of course, is far too simplistic, and all the momfluencers I spoke to for this book are real people, not actresses playing modern-day Betty Crockers. They have real lives, with real problems, and real homes (at least sometimes) trashed by real kids. And while some of them spoke about homemaking as a creative act, none of them pretended that the nuts-and-bolts labor of domestic work was anything but that—labor. Joy can be found in a vase of peonies, but first one must haul the kids into the car to buy the peonies at Trader Joe's; then one has to clear some sort of countertop or table for the peonies to rest upon. Grabby toddlers must be distracted with snacks and garish plastic toys lest they decapitate the pretty peonies.

But even though I *know* (we all *know*) that momfluencers are paid by vacuum-cleaner companies to make vacuuming look aspirational, we are all products of a rich history of marketing to moms according to their perceived value as homemakers, and it's hard to shake the subconscious wondering that maybe, just maybe, my Care/of vitamins will give me more energy to enjoy (?) clearing clutter from the kitchen island (or at least more energy to not feel sucked dry from clearing clutter from the kitchen island), or this cleaning spray in a pretty glass bottle will transform the wiping of the kitchen island into something soothing or meditative. It's all bullshit, but we're asked to buy into that bullshit every day, and sometimes it feels better, easier, to allow a little belief in the fantasy to creep in. Which is what makes us buy things. From momfluencers.

Momfluencers' monetization models have changed through the years. While the OG mommy bloggers monetized their work with affiliate links and banner ads, it was only really possible for the biggest of the big bloggers to make a significant income. At her peak in the late aughts, Heather Armstrong, of the popular blog *Dooce*, reportedly made forty thousand dollars a month on banner ads.[34] She was a big fish in a very small pond. Now there is a vast ocean full of fish, some huge but most smallish, and, regardless of the size of their platforms, these hundreds of thousands of successful and aspiring momfluencers all have the ability to sell us something through the multibillion-dollar influencer marketing industry. Influencer marketing, in which participants are paid to create or share sponsored content, really came into its own in the late aughts to early 2010s, and without influencer marketing, momfluencers and the market wouldn't be as inextricably linked as they are now. Whether a momfluencer is selling you a cookbook of her own "kid-approved" recipes, gaining a platform for her burgeoning gift-box subscription service, affiliate-linking to an eyelet Nap Dress, or creating sponsored content for Gain laundry detergent, influencer marketing is what makes it all possible.

In early 2021, I started researching my first big piece about my fraught relationship to momfluencer culture for *Harper's Bazaar*, and, after tweeting about it, got a DM from author and podcaster Jo Piazza, telling me she'd been reporting on momfluencer culture for two years and was now an expert on every single direct-to-consumer bedsheet brand. Since that fortuitous DM, Jo has been like my fairy godmother of momfluencer expertise, and if you haven't yet listened to her momfluencer podcast *Under the Influence*, I highly recommend you do so. I was lucky enough to be a guest on an episode about the infamous Michael's parking-lot momfluencer (if you don't know the story, Google it. It's a doozy).

Jo said that when the OG mommy bloggers started doing banner ads and affiliate links, "it was just straight-up advertising."[35] An ad created by a brand without any involvement from the momfluencer on whose blog the ad appeared was an entirely different animal from today's momfluencer-sponsored content, which intrinsically relies on the momfluencer's personal brand and unique skill set to sell something.

Jo explained that when brands started seeing blogs as a way to gain new customers, they started sending merchandise to bloggers in hopes they'd do free advertising in exchange for high chairs or diaper cream or whatever. Ultimately, bloggers recognized that this model was inherently exploitative and started demanding compensation for their product reviews, which became known as sponsored posts. Eventually, Jo said, "as every single form of social media evolved, sponsored posts turned up on every single social media platform." Influencer marketing was born. Before she started consuming momfluencer content, Jo was never much of an online shopper, but she told me she "definitely" shops online more now because of momfluencers. "Now, I can see clothes on real human beings, moving around in the world," she said. "[Momfluencer content] actually eliminated my need to browse in a store. And I'm buying a lot more online, things like home goods, which I never would have bought without seeing them in a store. I sometimes have to kind of stop myself just because it's so much easier. Before, you had to, like, get up and go somewhere! Now, you just hit two buttons."[36]

Social media scholars Emily Hund and Lee McGuigan cite Grant McCracken's work on celebrity culture to explain one of the reasons influencer marketing is so effective. In a 1989 article on celebrity endorsements, McCracken writes, "The celebrity is an especially potent source of meaning for the marketing system and a guide to the process of self-invention in which all consumers are engaged."[37] Why did I buy my Care/of vitamins upon seeing Julie D. O'Rourke's Instagram story? Because my subconscious and conscious selves had a little conversation.

Conscious self: *Shit, there are those vitamins again. I do feel kinda tired and blah.*

Unconscious self: *Her hair is so long and silky. She seems so chill in front of the camera. How does she manage to make a fucking ad seem cool? She seems so self-possessed, and she's not yelling at her kids. Her kitchen sink full of dishes makes me like her even more. I want to be like her and joyously romp through the moss with my kids instead of feeling shitty about my own sink full of dishes.*

Conscious self: *RudyJude20 is the discount code. Nice. Should get my vitamins by Friday.*

Unconscious self: *Vitamins and a new lease on life. A new lease on myself as a reinvented mother!*

This fruitful conversation between my selves does not take place at the mall, nor in a twee boutique full of succulents and beeswax. It's made possible by engaging with momfluencer culture, which is like celebrity culture in that it invites us to think about ourselves—or, more importantly, the selves we want to become. And when it comes to shoppability, Hund and McGuigan argue, "visibility is necessary to veneration."[38] Instagram, arguably the most aesthetically loaded of all social media platforms, makes it easy for us to see what we should want (to be).

I'm currently trying to sell a $460 sweater on Poshmark, and, yes, I feel gross about even typing that sentence.* But, after years of willfully subjecting myself to a certain kind of momfluencer sweater porn, I bought a $460 sweater. The sweater was too big (I initially thought I could pull it off in a slouchy way, but I was mistaken), and I missed the return window. It is probably the most expensive momfluencer-induced purchase I've made, but it's by no means the only one. My face is currently coated in True Botanicals Pure Radiance face oil, I'm wearing a ticking strip linen romper, and I'm drinking water from a lilac-colored Hydro Flask, all purchased due to momfluence. Kitty-corner from my desk is a laundry basket, purchased from a momfluencer's home goods store. Somewhere in the mountain of clothes in said laundry basket is my daughter's Alice and Ames dress and my son's Winter Water Factory T-shirt, also purchased, at least in part, because of momfluencers. Because of Julie D. O'Rourke (of pine-tip ice cream fame), I have briefly considered buying my kids mini picnic basket lunchboxes, but I ultimately couldn't pull the trigger. Even I have my limits.

I often wonder if I would be so addicted to shopping as a means of self/life/home improvement if it weren't for momfluencers. I also wonder if all of us mothers shop more in general (addiction or not) because of momfluencers. Faith Hitchon thinks so. "Definitely," she told me. Faith might be considered an Instagram microinfluencer herself—she has a laid-back LA vibe and posts sun-shot photos of herself and her kids at the farmers' market wearing burnt-sienna-colored dresses and chunky clogs. She is outspoken about destigmatizing marijuana use (especially by women and moms), and her posts are candid and smart and demonstrate a clear awareness that motherhood need not be one's

---

*To be fair, I also am trying to curb my fast-fashion purchases, and, as someone who has knit a few sweaters in her day, knitting sweaters takes a ton of time and skill. So if this company wants to pay their seamstresses decent wages, the sweater has to be pretty pricey.

entire identity, that it can just be one side of oneself, not the defining role. She is also acutely aware of how motherhood and shopping go hand in hand; she has a highlights reel devoted to "Thingz I Buy" on her Instagram page, and she cites @africanboheme, @thevitamindproject, and @sarahshabacon as momfluencers that will "most likely convert [her] to sales or research." Most recently, she bought some breast-milk storage bags because of @african boheme, and she emailed to tell me she almost bought some fake lashes because of Jessica Oakes (@jessicaoakes). "But then I was like, wait, I don't even use anything besides BB cream on my face so when the fuck am I EVER going to use those?! Lol."[39]

Faith occasionally posts sponsored content for her twelve thousand followers, but I initially reached out to her to get her perspective as a social media and community director to better understand how marketers, advertisers, and brands view momfluencer culture and shoppability. The marketing expert connecting influencers to brands and vice versa? That's Faith Hitchon. It's her job to understand which momfluencers are best suited to sell which product to which audience, and she's really good at it. Faith was definitive in her view that "the mom market is the jackpot market in terms of hitting every product category." Having just conducted a totally unscientific survey of roughly one hundred women myself, this much is also clear to me. When asked what sorts of things they purchased because of momfluencers, respondents to my survey named everything from toothpicks (truly!) to clothes to beauty products to diapers to "shit for my house so that my house looks like other houses I see on Instagram lolsob."[40] As a shopping category, "motherhood" conveniently covers, well, almost everything one would ever need or want to buy.

Faith told me that within the "jackpot" motherhood market, "FTEs [first-time expecting mothers] are the über-jackpot." Which makes sense. When I was pregnant, I made copious lists of things I needed (or thought I needed) to get; I polled friends, I read blogs, I consulted books. Some of these FTE products are also extremely pricey—like $1,400 Bugaboo strollers or $1,200

Pottery Barn cribs. So brands work really hard to snag FTEs when they're most vulnerable to spending money, in the hopes that they can keep selling them various motherhood-centric products throughout their mothering years. This is why, Faith reiterated, FTEs are the "holy grail" target consumers.[41]

Faith also explained to me why momfluencers, versus other types of influencers, operate as such effective cites of shoppability. "Momfluencers are at the top of the game in terms of how they transform social media from a community-based kind of entertainment into, like, hardcore shopping and revenue for brands," she said.[42] Many of us don't start following momfluencers because we are consciously looking for shopping outlets; many of us start following them because we searched for "nursery inspo" on Pinterest, which led us to a momfluencer's Instagram, where she posts disarmingly endearing anecdotes about feeling insecure about her postpartum body. We connect to something about them, whether it be their personal style, their wit, the impressive health of their fiddle-leaf fern, whatever. Without the promise of community and/or entertainment, momfluencers lose their power as shopping destinations.

And when it comes to figuring out which momfluencer will sell the most blenders or handcrafted leather huarache sandals (I own a three-year-old pair from Nisolo, and would happily hawk some sponcon for them—these shoes hold the fuck up!), Faith says companies have plenty of metrics and data at their disposal. Third-party apps like Grin and Brand Ambassador help brands figure out which momfluencers will appeal to a budget-conscious mom in Ohio who wants to make nutritious, cost-effective meals for her family versus a Brooklyn-based mother interested in incorporating bee pollen into her kids' daily acai bowls. In 2019, Instagram offered people with at least ten thousand followers the option of switching to a "creator account," which allows both brands and influencers themselves to see where most of their followers live, how old they are, which types of post they tend to engage with the most, and so on. People like Faith familiarize themselves with various momfluencers' consumer demographics so as to create beneficial relationships between brands and content creators.

When we think about how momfluencers sell us stuff, and how marketers and brands view momfluencers' selling potential, the underlying importance of class and identity politics to shoppability is impossible to ignore. We wouldn't expect the picture-perfect mamas, in their sprawling "beach cottages" in the Hamptons, to sell us on the convenience benefits of a Happy Meal, just as we wouldn't go to a momfluencer selling sponsored ads for luxury lifestyle brand Jenni Kayne to share budget-saving hacks for Disney World.

In her book *(Not) Getting Paid to Do What You Love*, Brooke Erin Duffy, an associate professor of communication at Cornell University studying influencer culture, interrogates how the gendered labor of influencer work impacts influencers themselves. She told me that class aspiration has historically been instrumental in selling people all kinds of things, and that "the expectations for momfluencers vary across class lines."[43] As it always has. The upper-class white women who reigned supreme during the nineteenth-century Cult of Domesticity were valorized for their roles as domestic goddesses. But, while working-class women and women of color were held up to these same ridiculous, impossible-to-uphold standards, most advertisers were not prioritizing their shopping needs when it came time to sell Language of the Flowers books or corsets that promised "blissful dreams" (actual copy from a late-nineteenth-century ad for Warner Brothers corsets), or "snow white and deliciously fragrant" face cream (copy from a 1919 ad for Jonteel Combination Cream).[44] Class and race have always been critical metrics used by advertisers to understand how and what to sell to target demographics.

Brooke sees this expectation for momfluencers to essentially stay in their prescribed class lanes as something we expect of all women. But, she argues, for influencers in general, and momfluencers in particular, failure to adhere to audience perceptions of "who you really are" will not only be bad for business; it will also translate into criticism for not being "authentic." Momfluencers, Brooke told me, "are kind of expected to stay within particular economic configurations because when they don't, that's when they experience the backlash, the harassment, the hate, the negativity, the callouts."[45]

If I trust Julie D. O'Rourke to only serve me ads for organic, environmentally friendly, minimally packaged products, and then she suddenly presents an ad for a plastic Fisher-Price jingly-jangly nightmare of a toy, not only will I perceive this as being decidedly off-brand (I absolutely bought a $106 wooden marble run based on Julie's rec, but something made of non-repurposed, non-vintage plastic—*never!*), but I'll also be forced to come to the nasty conclusion that Julie's lying to me about liking this toy, solely to make a buck. As momfluencer consumers, we really hate being lied to, and we really hate feeling like pawns, which might have something to do with the fact that we're used as pawns in our patriarchal capitalist culture, which depends on our caregiving labor to maintain the entire system but denies us any compensation (financial or otherwise) for that labor.

We also hate to face the fact that our favorite monetized momfluencers are not sharing their lives and experiences of motherhood for solely community-minded reasons; we hate to acknowledge the role money plays in cherished parasocial relationships. We'll explore the psychological impact of momfluencer culture on consumers in more depth in the next chapter, but here it's important to remember that the illusion of perceived authenticity operates not just to create parasocial relationships between influencer and consumer, but to maintain healthy buying and selling relationships as well.

In her book, Brooke explodes the popular misconception that influencers make a ton of money simply by posting a few pretty pictures once in a while. While hard-and-fast numbers are notoriously difficult to find, Brooke reported in her book that only 8 percent of content creators "make enough money to live on." These numbers are critical to consider when we think about the gendered nature of influencer work in general and momfluencer work in particular. Brooke points out that much influencer work is done behind the scenes, and my interviews with momfluencers confirm this (remember Tiffany Mitchell's laundry list of tasks and skills needed to create a single sponsored post in chapter 1? And Myleik Teele's thwarted child-wrangling efforts for her Bounty sponcon?). And while successful, established momfluencers like Tiffany earn relatively reliable income from their influencer work, Brooke sees the labor of many aspiring influencers to be just that—aspirational, without any solid guarantees of becoming financially viable. And she sees the invisible precariousness of women's influencer work very much aligned with traditionally gendered "women's work" (like carework, reproductive labor, and domestic work). In her book, Brooke contends that these types of labor "remain invisible despite their central role in servicing the engines of capitalism."[46]

For momfluencers, this becomes particularly complicated because not only are they doing the unpaid invisible labor of motherhood; they're also attempting to monetize that labor by doing even more invisible labor (the aspirational labor of influencer work) and then ultimately making the labor of motherhood (or at least the performed labor of motherhood) visible on social media to (hopefully! Maybe!) earn external validation in the form of "likes" or financial compensation. Many of us might assume that doing what we'd do anyway (the work of motherhood) but monetizing it by sharing it online might be a perfect blend of personal and professional energy. Momfluencer work is also attractive because of its oft-celebrated flexible nature; many women I interviewed for the book and many women in Brooke's book as well cited flexibility as being one of the biggest pros of influencer work.

But the cost of (supposed) flexibility and (supposed) balance of work and home life comes at a high premium. Brooke agrees with Emily Hund and Lee McGuigan that, despite the dubious benefits of turning one's life into shoppable content, influencer work is full of unique perils for participants. In "A Shoppable Life," Hund and McGuigan argue that influencer work demands that content creators somehow combine their own personal metrics of success with those of the market. They must perform their identities as somehow authentic and recognizable, while also "meeting one's own standards of integrity and self-actualization. This carries profound emotional freight since it involves the very constitution of meaningful personhood for participants."[47] In thinking about momfluencers, this means they must first recognize themselves as being or representing a certain "type" of mother: for instance, the frugal mother, the fit mother, the "natural" mother, the nutrition mother, the urban mother, the fashion mother. This requires them to firm up their own core values and beliefs *while also* assessing how those core values and beliefs can be commodified.

Motherhood as a role is already tightly conscripted, and the idea of further solidifying my mothering identity as being only some things and never other things, makes me feel, well, bad! We contain multitudes, etc. But for momfluencers to gain traction, either with their followers or in the market, they must do the work of self-branding, which necessitates thinking of one's identity as something that can be bought and sold. Authenticity can only be translated into dollars if you leave your multitudes at the door. As Hund and McGuigan write: "To be recognizable to agencies and marketers as a legitimate, viable influencer typically requires some degree of conformity to this industry's ways of seeing and classifying branded personae."[48] This identity-shaping in service of the marketplace is the status quo for all influencers (imagine considering self-branding as a tween influencer!), but motherhood is one of the most confounding, life-altering identity shifts many women ever go through. Tying such an existentially complicated identity shift to a necessarily flattened, simplified, and commodified presentation of self wreaks a certain degree of internal havoc for those undergoing such labor.

As we've seen, the "industry's way of seeing and classifying" mothers hasn't changed much. Nineteenth-century mothers were either told to be domestic goddesses, or, if they weren't of the right class, didn't have the right skin color, or didn't possess adequate financial potential, they were overlooked by advertisers altogether. Mid-century mothers were tacitly told to ignore Betty Friedan's "problem that has no name" and to bake a cake instead. Now, Jean Wade Rindlaub's social media–savvy successors understand that mothers are burdened with huge amounts of stress, made worse by a global pandemic, during which mothers and caregivers were/are expected to uphold a broken system. No one is under any illusions that motherhood is a blissful walk in the park. But domesticity, and essentialist, gendered visions of motherhood still dominate momfluencer culture and traditional advertising.

In 2018, two years before the COVID-19 pandemic would plunge all mothers into what can only be described as a total shit show, Joe Pinsker reported on the annual M2Moms conference for *The Atlantic*, and his piece reads a bit like a dystopian nightmare. The conference, which still exists virtually, gathers advertisers and marketers to assess what exactly mothers want or need in their advertising in order to spend their money. Pinsker quotes one marketer as saying this to a crowd full of their colleagues, all focused on "getting inside [mothers'] heads": "Moms are the most powerful influencers on the planet," said one [marketer]. "She is caring for new life—she will buy anything for that baby," another said later.[49]

So many things bother me about this quote. There's the assumption that only mothers care for babies (where are the dads or other caregivers?) There's the equating spending potential with power. And there's the nefarious tone implied in the last statement: "She will buy *anything* for that baby" (my emphasis). It's as though marketers think that once women become mothers, all our reasoning and critical thinking skills fly out the window, and we can be sold anything at all, so long as the product is associated with our children's well-being or our fitness as mothers. These outrageous assumptions make sense in a culture that still prioritizes a fetus's life over the life of the person carrying that fetus. She will do anything for that baby because she *should* do anything for that baby, and, really, if she's a *good* mom, she better do *everything* for that baby. I'm equally irked by some of the titles of the presentations cited in Pinsker's article, "such as 'From Bras to Booze: The Principles of Marketing to Mom,' 'Decoding High Stressed Moms—How Brands Can Make a Difference,' and 'Do You Move at the Speed of Mom?'"[50]

I'm certain a marketer was instrumental in cementing the "wine mommy" as a cultural caricature.

Pinsker echoes everyone I talked to for this book in asserting mothers' importance in the market, writing that "American mothers are estimated to make the vast majority of household purchasing decisions and collectively spend more than $2 trillion per year. But claiming even a small portion of that spending requires getting through to moms, which in turn requires a great deal of—to employ one of the most frequently used buzzwords at M2Moms—empathy."[51] He goes on to detail the ways in which marketers discussed mothers' fears, doubts, and insecurities, all to elicit empathy, which would then be used to sell these poor harried souls more stuff.

Empathy goes hand in hand with the gold standard of momfluencer success, "authenticity": a word that, for all intents and purposes, has ceased to mean hardly anything at all in today's parlance. For momfluencers, it can mean vulnerability, as illustrated by sharing an Instagram reel of a home birth; it can mean righteous anger, as illustrated by an anti-racist infographic; it can mean depression, as illustrated by a #nomakeup selfie two weeks postpartum; it can mean joy, as illustrated by a "Meet Flora June!" newborn photo. Effectively, authenticity effectively translates to this for consumers of momfluencer content: "Whatever I think this stranger should be (for me) in any given moment." And, for marketers and momfluencers themselves, authenticity means becoming intimate with the particular needs and desires of a target demographic. This, as Duffy, McGuigan, and Hund all show in their work, can be impossible and emotionally and psychologically depleting.

Hund and McGuigan repeatedly emphasize the labor of performing authenticity for an audience who wants to shop your life: "Maintaining a successful, shoppable social media presence requires near constant self-assessment, self-discipline, and self-disclosure. Yet the seemingly required nature of disclosure added a layer of pressure—and complication—to carrying out their lifestyle/careers."[52] Many of the women and mothers Hund, McGuigan, and Duffy spoke to for their work find this constant effort (labor) exhausting, and most of the momfluencers I spoke to for this book echo this exhaustion. Shanicia Boswell, founder of *Black Moms Blog*, told me via email what she does to prevent that exhaustion from taking over:

> A great influencer (mom or any other type of influencer), learns the important lesson of letting your community feel like they are a part of your family while still keeping yourself private. There are certain things I don't share online. Things like my love life, my day to day activities, and even some of my business moves, I keep private. Every share is intentional and with purpose. I have considered all outcomes before posting so that I can keep myself from becoming shocked by any feedback that may come my way. I also give myself breaks from social media. I scan through the many comments to make sure there isn't anything harmful but I don't read them all. That in itself is overwhelming. And when it comes to helping women, I offer what I can, meaning, group events, blog posts, heartfelt captions. I am not a therapist, nor do I pretend to be one.[53]

This is not an insignificant amount of labor! And, really, this type of labor ceases to be merely labor and threatens to become something more pernicious, more potentially harmful to one's selfhood. How can the ceaseless work of contorting oneself to meet an external audience's needs not make it difficult to assess one's *own* needs? I overthink and rethink and second-guess nearly every one of my Instagram posts, and I can't begin to imagine how much of my brain/soul space might be wholly taken over were I ever to pursue a career as a momfluencer.

Bekah Martinez (@bekah) says her work requires "lots of boundaries and radical self-honesty . . . And the biggest lesson that I would share with anyone who's influencing or has an internet presence, is to *know when to get off your damn phone*. You *know* the point when you cross a line and get sucked into the vortex. And in those moments you need to literally delete the Instagram app off your phone and stop for the rest of the day and get back into real life."[54]

Tiffany Mitchell also told me how critical intentionality is to her mental health when it comes to performing authenticity as her job, which can also be likened to fulfilling others' needs at the potential expense of your own.

> I absolutely feel exhausted with the effort of performance. I think the main issue for me is digesting so much social media myself. It affects how I write and how I share, and I have to work to strip it back to what I really mean to say and who I really am. It's hard not to scroll through and see what's performing well for other people, then feel pressure to imitate what they're doing. But I know that robs from the heart and soul of why I'm even on Instagram, so I have to nip that in the bud and stick to my own story even if engagement plummets. In terms of momfluencing, I think I'm sometimes impacted by this because I see other moms who seem to really have it together, loving every second of a perfectly styled life with MULTIPLE kids, and I'm gasping for breath with just one. It's then that I usually share something on my stories about what I'm going through. To do some more vulnerability practice in those moments is very centering for me, and so many moms show up for the conversation, so we're all encouraged! For me to stay centered, that vulnerability practice is everything.[55]

Mitchell's self-awareness in this passage is striking: she both recognizes when she's not being true to her own sense of self (imitation of others on social media) *and* tacitly highlights how showcasing her vulnerability (which is authentic!) ultimately leads to more engagement ("so many moms show up for the conversation"), which leads to more potential brand partnerships, which leads to more shoppability. This is why authenticity and shoppability are the salt-and-pepper shakers of influencer marketing. One cannot exist in any meaningful way without the other. Hund and McGuigan write: "The shoppable life not only relies on the aspirational labor of social media users who hope to profit from presenting monetizable lifestyles, but the aspirational leisure of their followers: it works to convert abstract consumerist dreams into an immediately buyable reality, with various stakeholders shaving profits off every transaction."[56]

Historically, marketers and advertisers have deliberately catered to mothers' anxieties, both quotidian and existential, to sell us things. We buy momfluencer-sponsored FridaBaby snot-suckers and CCC Clean Corrective with Vitamin C Tinted Moisturizer Broad Spectrum SPF 30 from the Honest Company, to, yes, suck the actual snot from our "littles'" noses, and to moisturize/camouflage our ever-important skin (respectively!). But we also buy these things because the very existence of the FridaBaby snot-sucker tells us there is a right way to help one's baby with nasal congestion; the very existence of the Honest Company's CCC Clean Corrective with Vitamin C Tinted Moisturizer Broad Spectrum SPF 30 tells us there is a right way to age in a patriarchal society. And because momfluencers are just like us, but better (hotter, smarter, more successful, thinner, richer, cooler), buying the things they present to us gives us the illusion of forward momentum. We need to buy shit from momfluencers because if we don't, then what? What kind of mothers and women will we be?

3

Mirror Neurons
and Cringe Follows

Kelly Havens Stickle is a slim white woman with Anne Shirley–red hair. More often than not, on Instagram, as @kelly havensohio, she is pictured wearing homespun cotton dresses with her red braids pinned atop her head much like Anne Shirley herself might have done in her fictional nineteenth-century life. She lives somewhere vaguely rural (presumably Ohio), and her feed abounds in wistful musings on the natural world, the nobility of self-sacrificial motherhood, and serene acceptance of God's will. I've followed her for a while, and I'm sure my reasons for doing so aren't great. Mostly, I think, I follow her for shock value, so I can text friends about a particularly sanctimonious phrase or a completely decontextualized photograph. "Ugh, I can't," I'll text friends, accompanied by a screenshot of Stickle reading a book meant for adults while snuggling with her toddler son, both of them beaming. I'll copy and paste the words Stickle typed alongside the photo: "But dear mothers. Remember your roots. Remember your world. Your world is not your home, not primarily. God is your world. Do whatever it takes to preserve your secret world with Him, your secret garden with Him, so that you can be your little boy's world."[1] "I DON'T WANT TO BE MY KIDS' WORLD," I text scream to friends (and into the void). My friends text back red-face and vomit-face emojis. Expletives. Rows of exclamation points and question marks. But no one asks me why I don't just stop following her. Nor do I often ask myself.

I'm not the only one a little perversely obsessed with Kelly Havens Stickle. Maya Kosoff, from chapter 1, was inspired to pen an entire essay based on her preoccupation. And Kate Lindsay, writer and cocreator of the internet-culture newsletter *Embedded*, wrote a treatise on the allure of trad wives—women performing traditional gender roles online—for Embedded's predecessor, no-filter, in 2020. In "Screw It, I'm Going Full Trad Wife" (largely inspired by Stickle but never mentioning her by name), Lindsay writes about following Stickle's "life as a homesteading, apron-wearing, Bible-verse-quoting mother who I'd assume didn't even have working electricity, were it not for the fact that she posts all this from her phone to 30,000 followers [at the time of writing, Stickle has fifty-four thousand followers]." Lindsay reports that Stickle's Instagram makes her feel like "I'm seeing something I'm not sup-posed to"—to which I can absolutely relate.[2] There's something so intimately earnest in both Stickle's images and her words that it feels almost profane to be gawking at them from miles away, to be consuming such content mostly so I can . . . what, exactly? Make fun of her? Understand my own motherhood more clearly in opposition to hers? Both?

In her essay, Lindsay locates the root of her preoccupation with Kelly Havens Stickle and other Instagram trad wives in feel-ings of powerlessness and purposelessness triggered by a year of pandemic and political upheaval. In 2020, Lindsay (like so many of us) craved the illusion of escape; she fantasized about living in a different world as a different person with different priorities.

> The [trad wives] themselves refer to this as a slower, quieter way of life. To me it feels like the last remaining card I have

to play. I've gone through all the normal coping mechanisms. I volunteered. I donated. I changed jobs. Changed apartments. Started exercising regularly. This morning I drank hot water with lemon in it. I've even started doing trad wife things: growing herbs in my windowsill, knitting a pair of socks, making sourdough bread. And yet? Donald Trump is still president, we're still in a pandemic. What if I just opt out? What if just disappear and one day someone finds me upstate, married to a man named Ezekiel, and I have no idea who's president and don't care that I can't go to a movie theater or meet my friends at a restaurant or literally go anywhere because I have a chicken pot pie in the oven and three babies to bathe?[3]

For Lindsay, trad wives' all-consuming devotion to children and domesticity seemed like a nice alternative to the exhaustion of trying to keep one's head above the water of contemporary news cycles. During these pandemic years, Instagram has also facilitated the fantasy of escape for me, and, truly, believing in the potential of hot water and lemon as a panacea for all my problems is still critical to my well-being. It helps that I've never tried to put it into practice.

I reached out to Kate Lindsay because I wanted to know if she was still following trad-wife momfluencers, and whether or not she had any more insights as to *why*. If following someone like Stickle is only serving to delineate one's own life as stubbornly and painfully enmeshed in the brutality of now—versus Stickle's apparently context-free life, blissfully devoid of any stubborn reminders of despotic leaders, climate crises, systemic structural inequities, or anti-vax propaganda—why keep doing it? Aren't there other less psychologically complicated ways to numb oneself? Does the escapism of Stickle's whimsically crusted apple pies outweigh the doubt and dissatisfaction that might arise from wishing to care more about homemade pastry than almost anything plaguing contemporary life?

During our Zoom (which I did in my bathroom because it has good light and because it's as far away as possible from all child-related interrupters), I was thrilled to learn that Kate actually went to college with Stickle. She knew of Stickle before she was a trad-wife momfluencer, back when she was, in Kate's words, a "regular person."

Both Kate and Stickle attended Kenyon College, a small, liberal arts school in Ohio, where everyone more or less knew (or knew of) everyone else. Kate told me that, back in college, Stickle "didn't dress like that [in *Anne of Green Gables*-esque garb], so to see that change was so jarring but also weirdly intoxicating."[4] A friend initially introduced me to Stickle's Instagram account when I was ranting about the implausibility of Hannah from @ballerinafarms. And because I'm obsessive, and, you know, because I was doing *research*, I scrolled alllllll the way back to the beginning of Stickle's Instagram feed, and indeed, back before she became she is now, she dressed like any other mom who goes to Target on rainy days with her baby to kill boredom and to buy more diapers. A few years ago, for example, she posted a selfie in which she's wearing what appears to be a vintage collared shirt under a dark sweater—very 1970s thrift store vibes—and making a silly face at the camera, with the caption "'Anne Shirley! What have you done this time!??'—Marilla."[5] She's less the gracious domestic-goddess mama from *Anne's House of Dreams* and more the spunky, troublemaking *Anne of Green Gables*. There are badly lit photos of branded plastic smoothie-drink bottles.[6] There are badly lit photos of Chick-fil-A![7]

This is all to say that Stickle made deliberate choices about how she wanted to curate her feed (as we all do), and as someone a little darkly fascinated with that feed, it's interesting to chart the progression from a "typical" liberal arts college student (a philosophy major!) to someone who wrote about "purging" that college education in 2020. Kate directed me to a specific post that particularly haunts her, in which Stickle is pictured wearing a white linen dress with wooden buttons down the front. She's holding her baby in one arm and a bunch of Queen Anne's lace in the other.

She's in a field of wildflowers washed by the sunset (and maybe the Gingham filter?). She is wistful. "I used to be afraid of having a quiet mind," her post reads:

> I was afraid of family get togethers and having nothing to say. But by the 3rd year of college my mind was so full of theories and ideas and worries that I had to dump it all out. This purging took a full 2 years and carried over into early marriage. I would run down our gravel road and not think about the clouds, but gaze at them. I would pick flowers and not think about how the world had lost touch with them, but simply twirl them in my fingers. I must have looked so simple and possibly foolish to those who witnessed the change. No more lofty phrases like, "the amoralism of America has destroyed the impetus for action." Instead it was, "I'm happy because Fall is coming with its sweet and spicy breezes." A quiet mind.[8]

This passage is chilling for me because it seems to bear out the fact that Stickle—unlike me, unlike Kate—turned her longing for escape into reality. She deliberately turned away from the knots of modern life and twirled flowers instead. No matter that climate change threatens to destroy "sweet and spicy" fall breezes; with any luck, Stickle won't be around to worry about it. Kate says the mention of "sweet and spicy breezes" is what really got to her when she first read this post in August 2020, when the world was still gripped by an international pandemic and a hellish US presidential race. Kate wanted to experience the bliss of a sweet and spicy breeze, too, instead of everything else. "It's like, I was almost envious of the fact that her life as she presented it didn't seem to change [because of the pandemic or current events]," she said. "And I liked watching people bake things and make their own clothes. It was very soothing to me at that time."[9]

I understand this sense of soothing by escapism, but for me, it's not possible to consume Stickle's content without feeling accompanying rage. There's something almost indecent about her performance of serenity—but maybe this has more to do with my very unserene experience of 2020 and less to do with Stickle's Instagram presence.

Recently I came across one of my kids' "virtual learning" schedules from 2020 in a junk drawer and my entire body tensed up. One of my kids started her virtual learning adventure when she was in kindergarten, another when he was in first grade. I had grand plans for "homeschool" when real school initially closed down. I made a color-coded schedule. I designated a "recess" time. I tried to be cute and pack lunches in lunchboxes. This lasted maybe a week. Maybe less. My kids quickly realized I was just their mom pretending to be a teacher, and, once that happened, my façade of authority crumbled and we engaged in daily power struggles about . . . everything.

After the novelty of seeing their friends on computer screens wore off, both kids hated virtual learning. They resented me trying to get them to complete homework. They routinely disappeared mid-Zoom school to pee, request a snack, or play with their baby brother. They missed their friends.

At the time, my youngest was just shy of his first birthday, which meant he required constant one-on-one attention unless he was sleeping. My husband's job sustains us financially and is a traditional nine-to-five, so we prioritized his work time over mine; we had no other choice. He did his best to support me in caring for the kids as well as he could (and he 100 percent did the vast majority of housework during this time), but there was only so much he could do. So sometimes I begged one kid to "watch" the baby while I hid in my room and tried to work on the proposal that ultimately became this book. Sometimes I tried to write while the baby napped, but I was often so exhausted by noon, so drained from trying to cook, clean, mother, and teach, that I ended up just scrolling the internet with dead eyes. Sometimes I threw myself into bed. Sometimes I tried to read but ended up staring at a wall. I knew I was failing my kids every day. I knew I was yelling too much. I knew I was letting them watch too much TV. I knew my failure to enforce Zoom school would result in them "falling behind" academically. I was angry all the time. My jaw was always tight. Serenity was a fantasy I didn't even attempt.

Kate Lindsay told me the purity of her fantasy about Kelly Havens Stickle fell apart when Stickle posted photos of an indoor birthday party at the height of the pandemic with nary a mask in sight. She became "really grossed out" and felt like "following her and/or enjoying her content was making me complicit."[10] Complicit in what, though? Stickle's wholesale disregard for the suffering of the rest of the world? Or something more personal? I ask myself these same questions all the time. I usually don't come up with very clear answers. Or one of my kids demands Cheez-Its and I gratefully flee introspection for the relief of action.

Kate doesn't have any children, but she wants them someday, and she says part of the draw of trad-wife momfluencer accounts is the promise of priority shifts: of donning the role of mother in exchange for sloughing off other female roles she might be weary of inhabiting. Kate told me she's been thinking a lot about making life choices, not according to some invisible, external, mostly patriarchal gaze, but for herself. She cites struggling with making career choices based more on how they'd look to the outside world and less on how they'd impact Kate's day-to-day happiness. She, like so many of us, has been thinking a lot about what work means, and why we do it. To make money, yes, but also to be a certain kind of person, one who is valued by virtue of her job title. "It's like, if you want to say, *my life is looking after my children and living slower, like, living off the earth, taking joy in the simpler things*, for some reason, because of society, that feels acceptable because they have children."[11]

We talked about how if a childless woman decides something about work (working less, for example, simply because she wants to and can), judgment often follows; that woman is often deemed, either by herself or by external voices, selfish. Kate says her attraction to motherhood by way of momfluencer culture is wrapped up "less with the children, and more, in my brain, that having children gives you permission to live a bit differently. . . . Then I can stop, like, applying, or, like, I can stop worrying about what my purpose is? I don't know."[12]

To say I understand what Kate (who was twenty-six when we spoke) means in her nebulous desire to take a break from the exhaustion of becoming herself in a capitalist patriarchy is an understatement. Talking to Kate was like talking to my own twenty-six-year-old self (albeit a way more intuitive, thoughtful, critically aware version), and during our conversation, I found myself welling up. I was wearing glasses, so I don't think Kate noticed my very unprofessional display of emotion. But I SO GET THIS. I studied theater in undergraduate school, haplessly spent a few years "acting" (read: dog walking and temping), before haphazardly pursuing graduate school as a way out of my career confusion. I ended up with a terminal master's degree in literature after I realized academia is hell, whereupon I got married and launched myself into motherhood as a desperate way to embody some sort of role that would be seen as incontrovertibly acceptable—by both myself and the rest of the world. I was too terrified of facing my own reality, which was that I didn't know who I was or what I wanted. So I got pregnant instead.

During our interview, Kate explained, "The one reason I'm looking forward to the process of being pregnant is that I feel like right now my body feels very much something that is observed. And I wonder if it will feel like a relief. Like to have that be so not even a thing I'm thinking about because my body is like, doing something incredible. I always say, like, *I just want to be a mom in linen and clogs, walking around Cobble Hill*. Like, that sounds ideal."[13] After I had my first child, I experienced postpartum depression that was partially physiological distress and partially existential disillusion. Because instead of solidifying my sense of self, motherhood obliterated the wobbly foundation I had hitherto established and reduced me to a doer of mundane tasks. It did not make me a maternal goddess.

Despite my hard-won understanding that motherhood is a shabby placeholder for self-knowledge, part of why I scroll is still very much wrapped up in Kate's dream of the Cobble Hill mom. I've been a mother for nine years, and I've never managed to embody the Cobble Hill mom ideal. But seeing other moms do it (or look like they're doing it) on Instagram makes me hold onto the belief that some people must have found the pot of gold at the end of the maternal rainbow, allowing me to retain the dream that that pot of gold even exists—a sense of noble purpose coupled with baby snuggles and cool sack dresses.

Kate astutely acknowledges that much of the pressure she puts on herself to be a certain way has to do with her own ideas of who might be judging her identity and choices. "Social media has kind of caused me to invent this person who is viewing what I do in the most bad faith, or judgmental way possible," she said, "which I think is why I'm like, *Oh, motherhood would be acceptable to this made-up person, right?* As a reason to slow down."[14] I'm struck by how beautifully Kate is able to elucidate how we internalize the judgment of the external world according to our own particular personal insecurities. Ever since having kids and realizing I am neither one of those mamas who is able to laugh away the chaos of everyday life, nor one who is content to live solely (or even mostly!) for my "littles," motherhood has been and remains one of my greatest insecurities.

On Instagram, I shop not only for toddler forks and latte-colored BPA-free pacifiers, but also for a version of motherhood I want to embody—only, the act of buying things gets in the way of pursuing the happy, effortless maternity I crave. I often miss out on my own tender moments because I'm busy scrolling through someone else's. And when I'm thinking clearly, I know that even the women sharing these moments aren't always experiencing them either, since to share them necessarily means interacting with a phone, curating, staging, and playing with lighting and filters. But consuming those moments feels like an act of self-care, an escape, and a compulsion. Part of my wanting to write this book was to understand what exactly consumption of others' tender moments was doing for me, or to me.

Elizabeth Nathanson, associate professor of media and communication at Muhlenberg College, says the longing to scroll, despite knowing better, might be so powerful because momfluencers promise us an experience of motherhood that eradicates the modern need to balance work and maternity. "Momfluencers appear to have found an idealized solution to the impossibility of 'balancing' home and work—they collapse the two," she wrote in an email. "This can seem like an efficient solution to the constant challenge of juggling paid labor and caretaking work. The monetization of motherhood on social media can become an ideological as well as strategic mechanism for coping with the impossible expectation of 'having it all.'"[15] Many of us follow women whose performances of motherhood seem to exist in a vacuum because our own performances frequently do not. Kelly Havens Stickle, etc.

Of course, sometimes we follow momfluencers because we're in a weeknight dinner rut or feel like all of our clothes are sad, or we need to find snow mittens that won't fall off toddler hands. But the idea that we follow momfluencers solely for design inspiration and family-friendly meal ideas is far too simplistic. More often than not, what we are doing when we scroll is chasing an ideal, even when (perhaps especially when) we know that it cannot exist. Other times, we're looking for validation that motherhood is lonely and hard. Sometimes we look for communities of moms going through similar life experiences, sometimes we look for distractions, sometimes we look for momfluencers experiencing motherhood in wholly different ways from our own. Sometimes we hate follow. And each of these reasons for scrolling not only says something about us as individuals but also reveals something about motherhood as an identity marker. I interviewed nearly fifty women for this chapter—some mothers, some women who never want kids—and their reasons for following various momfluencers are as varied as the moms they follow.

Tomi Akitunde started her blog *mater mea*, and her Instagram account of the same name, in 2012, in order "to have transparent conversations with women about how they managed motherhood and their successful, demanding careers."[16] I love *mater mea*'s tagline—"Black Mom Google"—and the account is a rich mixture of humor, resources, interviews, guest essays, and more. There's no stifling sense of a painstakingly orchestrated "aesthetic," and a huge variety of perspectives are represented. If you want to educate yourself on how generational wealth impacts parental experiences, or how Black birthing people are empowering themselves in a system that has systematically worked against them, or how the experience of single motherhood is not "synonymous with struggle" (in an essay by writer Ashley Simpo), @matermea is the account for you.[17] There's also plenty of relatable memes and expressions of parental joy that feel energizing rather than confounding. It's a delightful corner of "mommy" Instagram.

When Tomi and I Zoomed, she was interrupted only once, by a bowl of oatmeal threatening to fall from her desk, and I was interrupted only once, by a child surveilling my whereabouts (caused by forgetting to lock the door, which was an unforgivable rookie move). Tomi said she started *mater mea* in 2012 because she noticed a gap in the mamasphere, which, she says, "still prioritizes a particular type of white women over women of other races and backgrounds," and her intent with *mater mea* was to "fill that void and counter the internalized stereotypes that made our community something to be fixed and not something to celebrate."[18]

When Tomi started *mater mea* in 2012, she was a journalist in her mid-twenties feeling adrift. She was at the age where she was no longer entry level but not sure how to move forward in her career, and where dating wasn't just about having fun but about finding a partner to have a family with one day. She'd read profiles and treatises on "work-life balance" to find some kernel of truth she could apply to the life she wanted, but observed that women's media, "despite being made for women, isn't really pro-women."[19]

Tomi saw two dominant viewpoints being expressed: lean in, or bemoan not being able to "have it all." And those narratives weren't inclusive: white women like Sheryl Sandberg and Anne Marie Slaughter, C-suite professionals who were at the "tippy, tippy top of their careers," were defining the conversations society was having about work and motherhood. "We didn't use this language at the time, but they [Slaughter and Sandberg] both had a relative amount of privilege to talk about this possibility of having help in a way that a lot of people don't have," Tomi says. "So, as I was reading these profiles of women in women's magazines, it was just the same narrative of *I just woke up in this beautiful New York brownstone with this beautiful man, and these beautiful, well-behaved kids who are very well dressed in my very-well-appointed home.*"[20]

Tomi's belief that the maternal imagery she was seeing online didn't reflect the full experience of *all* mothers led her to create *mater mea*, which, in its original form, was an online magazine featuring in-depth profiles of Black women across professions and experiences. The blog *mater mea* also countered the narrative that Black moms could only be one type of mother. In 2014, Tomi wrote a piece for *Huffington Post* about the pervasive racist notion that Black moms are either Claire Huxtable/Michelle Obama types OR abusive single "welfare queens." In the piece, Tomi writes: "Black mothers aren't the best or the worst—they're just simply mothers."[21] As Tomi explained to me, "I just wanted to have these real conversations with women who looked like me. Women who were transparent about how they became moms and how they created this life that I would like to have one day."[22]

It's worth noting that Tomi started *mater mea* as someone without children who instinctively realized the mother imagery she was being sold just didn't feel right. She wanted to learn and share what motherhood really looks and feels like for more than just one type of mother. I think there's an underlying assumption that most women and mothers follow momfluencer accounts because they want to engage in aspirational consumption, but, as Tomi points out, that is only one reason people scroll. Tomi deliberately stays away from the perfect mom in her perfect bubble because, for her, aspiration does not equate joy. So she partnered with photographers and graphic designers who helped her create the kind of social media experience she wanted to consume: community-driven, honest, and fun. In the early years of the blog, which was almost pre-Instagram (or at least pre-Instagram as it exists now), Tomi says the content focused on the inherent beauty of family, as well as the beauty of the various ways Black women parent. There were moms who were married, and moms who were single. Moms who completed their families through adoption and surrogacy, moms with large families, moms of only children. But, no matter their background, career paths, or family configuration, they had agency and were happy with their choices.

"And I know I needed to see that," Tomi confided. "When you spend so much of your career and your life in white spaces that don't reflect, you know, positive imagery about Black people, you start to believe the bullshit yourself. So getting to see women who I admired who had loving homes and partnerships was healing for me."[23]

Many people, when asked to describe a typical momfluencer, describe a white, cis-het, thin, conventionally attractive (which writer and podcast host Sarah Marshall has referred to on her show *You're Wrong About That* as "marketably attractive," a description that makes a lot more sense to me), married, nondisabled, upper-middle-class woman as emblematic of momfluencer culture. And this indicates that, while accounts like @matermea—accounts that dare to argue that motherhood is not one size fits all—are cropping up every day, the visibility of these accounts is still largely dependent on algorithms and one's comfort within a particular echo chamber. I think recognizing that a knee-jerk assumption that momfluencer culture is consumed for the same tired reasons (escapism, aspiration, and consumerism) by the same tired moms (a prevalent stereotype of a momfluencer consumer is a bored white stay-at-home-mom with nothing better to do) flattens both the breadth of maternal experience and also the output of content creators. Motherhood does not turn all people into a certain "type," and the reasons we follow momfluencer culture are just as varied as our experiences of motherhood. These reasons are important in unpacking why motherhood is a sour deal for many people in this country. Understanding *why* we scroll is critical to understanding how we're all impacted by momfluencer culture.

In response to a survey I sent out to thirtyish women who don't have kids, Katherine told me she isn't sure she will have children, but "sometimes, my uterus will awaken when I see a newborn baby posted on my feed and I think, *Oh, why can't I have that?*" While she isn't entirely sure her consumption of momfluencer culture consciously impacts her ambivalence about having kids, she says momfluencer culture does sometimes make her feel "incomplete" and wonders what "life will look like if I'm not chasing after little ones."[24] I think Katherine's observation also points to the fact that, more often than not, Womanhood with a capital "W" is represented by Motherhood with a capital "M." Social media abounds with thousands of representations of choosing a life with kids, but examples of lives made full without having children are less visible.

Sabia Wade, who is on Instagram as @theblackdoula, emailed me to explain that her consumption of momfluencer culture is largely connected to her work. "I wanted to see what my clients were seeing when they stepped into parent land," she wrote. "Understanding what they saw on social media helped me to understand their sometimes unrealistic expectations of themselves. I could also make suggestions on who to follow based on what my clients were looking for. Sometimes they seek a momfluencer of the same race, gender, parenting style, etc." Sabia is unsure about having children herself, especially since she's acutely aware of how challenging parenthood can be, but she feels secure in her knowledge that, if she does ever kids, she'll go into parenthood "knowing what REALLY happens behind the scenes" versus what is often portrayed on "perfect mom/child" Instagram. She also thinks her queer identity has protected her from some of the social pressure many straight women feel to have a baby at the "right" time in order to become the "right" kind of "good" woman.[25]

Both Katherine and Laura noted the parasocial relationships they've formed with some of their favorite momfluencers. Some of Katherine's faves include Naomi Davis (@taza), Kelly Larkin (@kellyinthecity), and Miranda Schultz (@thepluslifeblog). She says she "gets excited when they announce their pregnancies. It almost feels like a friend is having a baby." And Laura told me in an email that she "follows momfluencers because I feel attached to their lives." She cites both Julie D. O'Rourke (@rudyjude) and Hannah Carpenter (@hannahacarpenter) as "serious favorites. . . . I want to see their businesses flourish and want to see their kids grow up." Laura also mentions her consumption of momfluencer culture as a bonding activity with friends: "Often times we talk/text about our third 'friend' that has no idea who we even are. It's pathetic, but we aren't about to stop any time soon."[26] Um, yes, yes, yes. I follow a handful of momfluencers solely to keep up my end of various conversations, so I can text friends things like: "Will @rudyjude's flax harvest work out?" or "I am fascinated by the pageant stuff," or "PREGNANT AGAIN?!" To me, this doesn't feel necessarily petty or *bad*; it feels akin to community-bonding rituals by way of gossip, something human beings have done as a way to delineate one's involvement in various social groups since forever.

I've always hazily believed vilification of gossip was simply rooted in a patriarchal imperative to keep women and marginalized people from connecting with each other, but I wanted to have more than just a vague understanding of why it feels good to text my friends about a stranger's flax harvest. So I called Amanda Montell, a linguist and the author of two books, *Wordslut: A Feminist Guide to Taking Back the English Language* and *Cultish: The Language of Fanaticism*. She had a lot to say about why we feel compelled to scroll.

First, she says, people have always sought out "like-minded tribes of others, ever since the time of ancient humans." While initially finding like-minded peers was about survival (*We both want to not get eaten by that saber-tooth tiger—let's be cave-mates!*), she says community also just makes us feel good. "It makes us feel happy, it makes us feel like our lives have meaning. This is a profoundly human drive."[27] Taking a minute to text a friend about our inside-jokey following of @rudyjude's flax harvest makes me feel grounded in space and time, makes me feel seen, makes me feel like life is not just a random series of events to withstand. The specificity of our shared interest brings me joy. Plus, flax is bizarrely interesting.

Amanda also indicated that the avalanche of choices made available to people in contemporary life is another factor for following momfluencers in order to get a dopamine hit of communal belonging:

> There are just a crushing number of possibilities for the direction a person's life could go in. Not just *Are you a goth?* Or *Are you a jock?* It's like, you can have any hair color under the sun, you could pursue any job, you could fall in love with anyone—or at least there is the illusion of all these different possibilities, because we see other people living so many various lives online. And yeah, we are built to make so many independent decisions about who we are and what we think. We crave a sort of identity template, you know, we want somebody to give us a sense of identity, especially when we feel pressure to cultivate a personal brand. It's like planning a wedding when you have, like, six hundred flower options. It's like, *I don't fucking know, I just want a guru to pick one for me!*[28]

Yes! I don't fucking know about so many fucking things! I don't fucking know if gently coaxing my kid to join a team or a club without knowing anyone on the team or in the club is good for her sense of independence or maybe too anxiety-inducing to be beneficial. I don't fucking know if my purchase of a hand-dyed swimsuit cover-up is a legitimate act of self-care or a Band-Aid covering up some bigger soul wound. I don't fucking know if I want to get Botox. I don't fucking know. So it's deeply comforting to consume a momfluencer as a way to direct one's choices, to say to oneself: *I might not fucking know but she apparently does, so I'll just follow her lead.*

I also think motherhood is the ultimate *I don't fucking know* scenario for some people (me!), and Amanda, while she doesn't have kids, imagines that the impossible pressures of motherhood provide powerful reasons for moms to scroll. She thinks the inherently unbelievable nature of motherhood—we grow human bodies in our bodies, they come out of us, and we are responsible for them—makes momfluencer culture that much more appealing. "If I were to all of a sudden be, like, growing a human in my womb, I would be like, *What the FUCK*, like, *am I a kangaroo?*" Amanda thinks the "shock-and-awe factor" of motherhood is especially relevant when girls spend the majority of their adult years prioritizing career, financial independence, and becoming "a badass career bitch" and then are expected to pivot on a dime to be "connected to the earth and connected to the womb." Given how "existentially confounding" motherhood is (and when you stop and think about it, yeah, it really is), Amanda rightly thinks mothers are desperate for any sort of voice telling them how to do it, especially when tangible support like childcare and mental health resources are inaccessible for so many.

> Not everybody can hire a full-time fuckin' doula. But what is cheap is, like, following a bunch of momfluencers on Instagram. So, I think, you know, the combination of feeling existentially bewildered, physically overwhelmed, inadequate, because you invariably don't feel like you're living up to your standards for your entire gender, like, you're going to be a bad mother. And that's a bad woman. And that's a bad person. And you probably can't afford someone to be your, like, one-on-one mentor. The internet seems like a natural place to turn.[29]

People talk a lot about hate-following, and while I don't want to discount the fact that blogs like *GOMI* (*Get Off My Internets*) and Reddit threads exist for such purposes, I think most of us are more likely to do something Amanda calls "cringe-following." Amanda started to tell me about a particular person she and her best friend cringe-follow on Instagram and laughed when she realized that "she's kind of a mom," but not necessarily a momfluencer with a monetized account. "But, yeah, we cringe-follow her. And, yeah, it's, like, something to talk about over drinks. It's totally a bonding ritual."[30]

Our reasons for following momfluencers are myriad and complex, but perhaps one unifying reason people of all ages, races, and classes consume momfluencer culture is the fact that motherhood has been culturally packaged as something people must "do right." Returning to Susan J. Douglas and Meredith W. Michaels's understanding of the "new momism," in *The Mommy Myth*: "Motherhood is, in our culture, emphasized as such an individual achievement, something you and you alone excel at or screw up."[31] Screwing up is always scary, but screwing up at work or in one's romantic relationship is different from screwing up at motherhood, which implies you're not only screwing up according to social mores and expectations but also that you're potentially screwing up the pure material of a human soul. It's a lot! It's hardly surprising that, given the lack of external validation (or resources) we receive as mothers, and given the largely invisible nature of our work, we're eager for sources to inform us of the various right ways to *do* motherhood. And in 2010, Instagram obliged by offering a platform to thousands of certified and self-fashioned experts, on everything from breastfeeding to swaddling to diet to personal style. Instagram momfluencer culture is nothing so much as a way to understand one's own motherhood as held up against everyone else's.

In 2021, scholars Mara Moujaes and Diarmuid Verrier set out to understand how our cultural imperative to do motherhood right coupled with Instagram momfluencer culture impacts our mental health, particularly the mental health of new mothers with young children. In their paper "Instagram Use, InstaMums, and Anxiety in Mothers of Young Children," they use the lens of social comparison theory to assess how mothers' mental health is potentially impacted by the consumption of momfluencer content.

Social comparison theory, which was conceptualized in 1954 by psychologist Leon Festinger, basically posits that people have an inherent need to evaluate and understand themselves by comparing themselves to others. The social comparison process works in two ways: upward and downward. Both terms are fairly self-explanatory. Upward social comparison is when we compare ourselves to people we believe are somehow better (that is, richer, prettier, more maternal, etc.) than us and focuses on our desire to become more like them. Downward social comparison is when we seek out comparisons of people we believe might be failing in ways that we are succeeding.[32] I might be fairly accused of following Kelly Havens Stickle, for example, in order to feel better about my own sense of feminism, political agency, and general disinclination toward treacly iterations of self-sacrificial motherhood.

Moujaes and Verrier ultimately found that people who "lurk" on Instagram without participating, and thereby maybe missing out on some of the community benefits of momfluencer culture, "are more likely to experience negative mental health outcomes, while interactive users are the least likely to experience negative outcomes."[33] They also found that "social media use has been shown to be associated with more negative outcomes in those with higher social comparison orientation, lower life satisfaction, higher fear of missing out, higher tendency toward physical appearance comparison, and lower self-esteem."[34] On the face of things, this makes sense. If I continually consume content that confirms my own insecurities (in my case, that I'm not a fun, "natural," or joyful mother), I'm not going to feel great about my own motherhood! And, if I'm already prone to FOMO (fear of missing out) and have shaky self-esteem, I might also be more prone to feeling like shit when following beautiful momfluencers jetting around Europe and eating baguettes with their beautiful kids who apparently don't live or die by sleep schedules.

But it's not as simple as assuming that engagement by means of likes, comments, or conversations with other followers will lead to positive mental health outcomes. Moujaes and Verrier found that, for those with lower self-esteem (which can manifest in so many distinct ways), and "those with a higher tendency towards social comparison," consumption of momfluencer culture was "more likely to be associated with higher anxiety."[35] Of course, correlation is not necessarily causation, and someone prone to depression or anxiety might find themselves drawn to particular momfluencers intending to consume their content as self-care or entertainment, only to find themselves caught in the matrix of upward social comparison. And, while comparison against other parents is as old as parenthood itself, social media has given us way more people to compare ourselves against, potentially offering far more examples of ways in which we are failing to "excel" as mothers and as people.

One could posit that engagement with social media influencers of *any* kind might trigger potential mental health issues, but motherhood as an identity marker is so utterly fraught in our culture that I was frankly shocked that Moujaes and Verrier's study was the first to really focus on how mothers specifically are impacted. I emailed Mara Moujaes to ask her about what she and Verrier describe as the "highly emotive component" of maternal identity, and why this "emotive component" makes consuming momfluencer culture maybe a little different from consuming, say, fashion influencer culture or even exercise influencer culture.

Mara indicated that our cultural construction of motherhood plays a huge role in whether or not engagement with momfluencer culture might impact an individual in complicated ways:

> If [momfluencer consumers] imagine that they are not liv-
> ing up to the difficult standards of the pure, yet still sexually
> attractive, mother, mental health issues that were underlying
> can be exacerbated. In relation to perceived lower parental

competence, this seems to relate to how Instamums show how they live their life. They create an image of achieving everything a 1950s and 2020s mother should be able to achieve. They cook, clean, socialise, work, have enterprises, have healthy relationships with their partners and look fashionable and made up throughout. Being able to achieve the key aspects of motherhood, caring and nourishing the young life of a child, seem to no longer be enough. Feelings of incompetency can grow because the goal posts of what it means to be a successful parent have widened hugely.[36]

As mothers, we are encouraged to buy particular lip balms, kaftans, lunchboxes, nightstands, food storage containers, seed kits, books, camping equipment, menstrual cups. We are also encouraged to tick off similarly voluminous lists of personal attributes. We must be beautiful, sexy (but not too sexy!), nurturing, gentle, firm, smart, organized, good at home decor, good at cooking (ideally baking as well), well read, playful, patient, calm, effortless, and, and, and. The list of qualities we should embody is as limitless and all-consuming as the things we should buy.

When I consider where I'm absorbing most of these messages, it's hard to quantify. Not from my friends. Not really from other mothers I encounter in real life. But I'm hard-pressed to think of a single mother I know who truly does not give a single shit about how she's being perceived according to an arbitrary list of patriarchally mandated femme mom attributes. As we've seen again and again, Instagram momfluencer culture, despite being far from monolithic, is still very much wrapped up with communicating many attributes considered maternally good via external packaging.

It won't be surprising to any female-identifying person that the above list is littered with contradictions. Mara thinks these contradictory demands are placed on mothers essentially from birth: "[Girls, women, and mothers] must be attractive and well-presented but not overtly sexual. Their sexual habits define them in a way not seen for males. When or whether they choose to have children is debated openly and when they become a mother, the expectations placed on them only increase and further complicate things." Mara also spoke to the pressure many of us feel to be seen—either by ourselves, our peers, or a shadowy judge of all things—to be a good mother, and many momfluencer accounts succeed in part because they're feeding our need to see motherhood as black and white. *This type of sleep training is best. This type of meal planning will lead to the best kind of child nutrition. This is the best nursing bra and won't lead to clogged milk ducts, which will help you be "successful" at breastfeeding, which is the "best" way to feed your baby.* "Being part of the good mum club is something you have to achieve for yourself and fight to keep," Mara wrote. "Mother seems to know best but only if mother knows the rules of Instagram motherhood very closely." She said the inspiration for the study and ensuing paper came from witnessing a friend's rejection by a group of moms and seeing her friend struggle with feeling like she wasn't living up to expectations of "good motherhood" as dictated by social media.[37]

Dara Mathis, a journalist, sometimes-blogger, and a former staff writer for *Romper*, has covered the intersection of feminism and motherhood for several years, and thinks both her personal and professional experience has largely prevented her from seeking out perfectly rendered, heavily performative versions of motherhood online. Over the phone, Dara credited her upbringing in a conservative, fundamentalist Christian community with showing her early on what a good performance of motherhood should look like. "The physical site of a church is a performance for several different things at the same time," she told me, "and motherhood ensconced within womanhood is definitely one of them." Dara went on to recall certain women in her church as her first momfluencers. "Women dressed to the nines, with kids that had be perfectly, perfectly behaved and they better sit still on the pew, and they better not move to the left or to the right . . . and then bring the perfect cornbread to the potluck. The performance of motherhood in church was my very first sort of realization that, yeah, this is how you will be expected to conduct yourself once you become a mother." She thinks maybe this early understanding that motherhood is, on many levels, a performance rendered for public consumption makes her "less amenable" to the stereotypically perfect momfluencer with her perfect everything.[38]

But Dara did find support and community in momfluencer culture. Experiencing "ambivalence" about her postpartum body, she found the Fourth Trimester Bodies Project (@4thtribodies) to be a "very affirming space" for the disorientation she felt during the postpartum period. "If the pregnant body is hypervisible then the postpartum body can sometimes feel invisible, discarded . . . I appreciated that the project did not default to 'stretch marks are warrior stripes' positivity, but rather presented postpartum bodies as statements of fact and witness. Seeing other people voice a range of feelings (and share photos) about childbirth and their postpartum bodies helped me come to terms with my own."[39] Before we get into Dara's experience of finding validation via momfluencer culture, I want to take a quick detour to contextualize her mention of the "stretch marks are warrior stripes" trope. In 2015, Rachel Hollis went viral for posting a photo of herself in a bikini.[40] The photo itself is pretty unremarkable: Hollis is thin by most metrics, and her stomach has a little loose skin, indicating that her body has created and birthed another human being. I can't actually detect any visible stretch marks, but that's not (or at least shouldn't be) the point! Hollis is a white self-help guru whose platform was famously categorized as "Goop for red-state women" in a *Washington Post* article by Nora Krug.[41] She's also infamous for her toxic positivity/Protestant prosperity gospel approach to life, work, and relationships, and we'll dig into her "tiger stripes" version of community and feminism in more detail in chapter 6, which explores the massive role of whiteness in momfluencer culture.

Back to Dara and the Fourth Trimester Bodies Project. Because of Dara's life experience and her own degree of self-knowledge, she deliberately avoids momfluencer accounts predicated solely on glossy ideals of motherhood, but she did find real sustenance in an account that refers to itself as "Body liberating. Queer affirming. Anti-racist. Inclusive" in its bio. After perusing the @4thtribodies account, I understand why. There are photos of engorged breasts leaking breast milk, C-section scars, soft bellies, and, in nearly every photo, infectious joy. Accounts like these are affirming in every sense of the word—they provide much-needed representation of real mothers as well as resources and networking opportunities for moms in search of them.[42]

After talking to Dara, I was curious how far community by way of momfluencer consumption can go, how valid of a substitute it can be for more traditional versions of community, like church groups, neighbors, or family members who live down the road. Pooja Lakshmin is a board-certified psychiatrist specializing in women's mental health. Quoting from her website bio, her work focuses "on how broken social systems impact women's emotional lives," and she's writing a book about the many toxic ways we've been conditioned as women to think about self-care.[43] Pooja recognizes that many people follow momfluencers for aspirational reasons, which can lead to sometimes unhealthy cycles of comparison, but via Zoom she told me that many of her clients mention specific facets of their own maternal struggles as first articulated by momfluencers.

For Pooja, community is an empty word if it's made up exclusively of fleeting dopamine rushes initiated by hearting someone's earnest post about postpartum depression, for example, but finding online communities can be useful in starting conversations with IRL (in real life) friends and community members. That same post about postpartum depression you hearted might "make it easier for you to talk about it with your real friends. You know, you can be like, *hey, did you guys see this post?* Like, *this was really great, and I've been struggling with it, too,* or, like, *has anybody else struggled with this?* It's kind of like a conversation opener."[44]

Pooja's reframe of the power we might gain in recognizing our own particular maternal struggles within a momfluencer's feed really resonates for me. When I was experiencing my own postpartum depression, which I'll discuss more in the following chapter, momfluencers didn't really exist yet, and the mommy blogs I followed at the time were mostly sunny, Taza-esque narratives of motherhood. But had I followed someone like Heather Armstrong of *Dooce*, for example, who wrote in depth about her own mental health struggles as a mom, I think it might have inspired me to seek out help for myself sooner, rather than waiting to fill out that uniquely sad postnatal mental health questionnaire in my OB's office, quietly sobbing when encountering the question about laughter and numbly filling the "not at all" box. "In the past 7 days: I have been able to laugh and see the funny side of things: ☐ As much as I always could, ☐ Not quite so much now, ☐ Definitely not so much now, ☐ Not at all."

Most women I've interviewed say one of the reasons they follow momfluencers is as a form of self-care, and most of these women utter the phrase "self-care" with dripping sarcasm or put it in italics or scare quotes. I was eager to know Pooja's thoughts about this reasoning. Part of the trickiness in referring to the scrolling I do in my bathroom as self-care, Pooja says, is that, often, when we scroll, we're "doing other stuff," and consuming momfluencer content while supervising one's kids on the playground, or waiting for a pot of water to boil, or waiting in the school pickup line, isn't exactly "taking care of yourself." Pooja acknowledges that finding a momfluencer whose kid also won't eat any nonwhite foods, or a momfluencer who finally figured out how to get rid of her pregnancy-induced melasma, can "make you feel kind of supported or like you have this community because you can comment and share, etc., but that's still not actually taking time for you." The reason Pooja doesn't think this type of social media consumption qualifies as true self-care is largely wrapped up in the passive nature of scrolling.

Because in order to take care of yourself you need be taking something in *energetically*. Like, you need to actually be

making decisions, you need to actually be actively doing
something that is going to maybe free up more time down-
stream for yourself. So, you can think and feel and reflect
and, like, connect with the human being that you used to be
before you became a mom. . . . But when you're consuming content, you're consuming. You're not metabolizing or
reflecting or, like, putting out any energy for yourself. So, I
think it's different.[45]

This distinction between active and passive self-care makes a
lot of sense to me. There's a reason we can scroll away for hours
and feel drained and disoriented when we finally come up for air,
versus feeling energized and refreshed after going for a walk, knitting, talking to a friend, or just lying down in a quiet, dark room for
fifteen minutes. Even that last example indicates an active choice
to deliberately remove oneself from all stimuli and pay attention
to one's simple physical presence. Social media companies are very
much aware of the addictive, enervating effects of scrolling and
design their products accordingly, and in chapter 8 we'll get into all
the sexy, dystopian themes inherent to living within The Algorithm.

My conversation with Pooja illuminated a great deal for me,
but the consumption of another mom's tender moments in lieu
of consuming my own tender moments with my own children
still rankled. One would think I'd be more eager to summon my
wee cherubs to my side to help chop carrots after seeing a post
in which Kelly Havens Stickle waxes poetic about the beauty of
shared kitchen tasks, but, more often than not, I don't. Cooking
with kids is mostly annoying and messy. I craved more clarity, and
Nicole Beurkens, PhD, a licensed psychologist, gave me that clarity
by introducing me to the world of mirror neurons, after taking
a brief jaunt down phantom limb lane, which I'll get to in a bit.

Nicole echoed much of what Pooja said when it came to interrogating one's own particular reasons for consuming momfluencer
culture. She says momfluencer culture comes up a lot in her work
with clients, moms eager to "do motherhood right" but lacking

critical structural support. She told me over the phone that she sees a "lot of confusion and questioning, a lot of hesitancy, a lot of *I'm consuming all of this and I don't really know how to make sense of it.*" Nicole says one way to locate one's real self amid the noise of momfluencer culture is to assess how momfluencer content impacts your lived reality, and why. She cited a specific story of a client experiencing parenting angst while blueberry picking, which, yeah, been there. This story is lengthy, but I'm including it here because I think it's such a powerful example of finding oneself lost in motherhood without understanding how you got lost in the first place.

> So she's got three kids, one of whom has some behavioral challenges . . . and she's going on about this blueberry incident, showing me all these pictures, and I finally stopped her and was like, *explain to me why you were at the blueberry patch to begin with*, and, honest to God, it came down to, like, *Well, everybody does it. Like, this is something you're supposed to do with your kids in the summer, like, I see all these pictures and it seems like, Oh, that would be such a great, like, important great family thing to do.* And I was like, *Have you ever been blueberry picking before? Like, do you enjoy it?* She's like, *Oh, no.* And I was like, *So basically, you did this because a lot of other people that you see on the internet do this, and you thought, therefore, it was an important thing to do and, of course, none of it went well because you hated it. Your kids hated it, like, everybody fell apart, so I'm unclear that this is a problem with your child. And more than that, like, what were you doing at the blueberry patch to begin with?* Right?[46]

Nicole helped her client parse her fraught reasons for taking her kids to a probably doomed outing (she equated pretty blueberry-patch photos with proof of good parenting), and her client was left with a better sense of her own maternal identity and a clearer perception of how the momfluencer content she was consuming was impeding her own maternal self-knowledge. I love this story because, wow, why am I buying a frilly white blouse with a huge Peter Pan collar? Because I'm someone who has always liked frilly white blouses and can wear such things without getting stained or stickied by my 2YO's grubby paws? Or am I buying it because some momfluencer looks like she's enjoying motherhood while wearing a similar blouse and I want to enjoy my own motherhood a bit more and buying a white frilly blouse seems like a way to do that even if my true sartorial identity thrives in cotton T-shirts that need never be dry-cleaned?

But back to phantom limbs and mirror neurons and what they have to do with consumption of a stranger's tender moments. Nicole said that when I'm sitting on the toilet behind a locked door scrolling through Amanda Fillerup Clark's latest round of newborn photos, the neurotransmitters in my brain are being lit up by dopamine. And the reason I can leave the bathroom and go about my day as the type of mom who would usually rather listen to a podcast about MLMs than consume too many of my own tender moments with kids asking for stuff might have to do with mirror neurons, which are brain cells that allow us to visualize doing something, and regardless of whether or not we literally do that thing, help us *retain the feeling of doing it*. So, Nicole explained, if we meditate on a certain task for long enough, we can feel similar feelings of satisfaction and fulfillment even if we don't actually complete the task. "These are brain cells that react when we actually perform an action," she said, "but also when we observe it, or when we think about it."[47]

Nicole said we first discovered the powerful role mirror neurons can play in how we perceive reality when people were studying phantom limb disorder, which occurs when people who have lost a leg, for example, can still feel itching or other sensations in the missing leg. In the mid-1990s, neuroscientist Vilayanur S. Ramachandran did a series of experiments to figure out if mirror neurons might help doctors care for patients suffering from the disorder. In an article for *BBC News*, Stephanie Hegarty explains what happened. Ramachandran noticed that mirror neurons lit up when an individual with phantom limb disorder watched someone itching or moving their right leg. One of his patients suffered from a relentless feeling of clenching in his missing hand, so "Ramachandran put a mirror between Jimmy's arms and asked him to move both his phantom and healthy limb simultaneously, while looking at the reflection of the healthy limb—effectively fooling Jimmy's brain into thinking his phantom was moving in a normal way. Jimmy felt his clenched fist release almost immediately." Ramachandran explained that "the vision" of the moving limb was enough to cause the mirror neurons to make the patient feel as though his phantom limb had actually moved.[48]

While Nicole isn't sure how much mirror neurons and Ramachandran's discovery of mirror visual feedback therapy can be directly applied to my tender moment quandary, I think it's *very interesting* that consumption of visuals can have such powerful, direct effects on our own lived experience. And I really don't think it's that much of a stretch to believe that looking at pictures of a cute toddler wearing a handcrafted Montessori birthday crown is all I need to feel as though I contain the same maternal warmth and creative spirit as the maker of the crown without actually making my own cute toddler a cute felt crown.

When transcribing Nicole's interview, I had to skirt around the many "wows" with which I interrupted her. Because, *wow*. Nicole agreed that the connection between mirror neurons and phantom limb disorder has "really fascinating applications" and said there's current research being done into how we learn empathy and whether it's rooted in our mirror neurons. "I really think that that's a piece of what's going on there when you describe that tender moment scenario. It's like, the brain processes it as if you actually did it so it's like, *Oh, there's no need to actually do it. I already did it!*"[49] I made the crown. I let my kid cut some carrots. It was beautiful. I did it.

Lest anyone think my own momfluencer consumption habits have changed drastically as a result of this research, I'm here to assure you they haven't. Not much. I still feel mild despair when

I see a mom succeeding in ways that I perceive myself to be failing, and I still buy shit I don't need because I think it'll help (with
whatever). But on good days, increased awareness of the whys
help me feel a little less like I'm drowning—in my own motherhood, my own maternal desires, and the versions of motherhood
I consume. It's sometimes hard to know where I start and where
my embodiment of someone else's identity stops.

My cousin Hannah and I were texting about all of this one
day, and she said about a particular momfluencer, "I hate how
much I love her." So obviously I wanted her to expand. She cited
getting caught up in the creation of an aforementioned Montessori
birthday crown because of a particular momfluencer's influence,
but doesn't think that's necessarily bad. "Prioritizing those small
breaks from the heaping efforts of daily tasks, using my hands to
make something rather than clean encrusted avocado that smeared
on our floor. It's not bad at all." She feels genuine inspiration
from this momfluencer and can clearly see that she gains tangible
benefits from following her. But.

> But there are a few ugly thoughts that run through my
> mind . . . like she has the god damn monopoly on quilted
> jackets, Rosa rugosa petals, pressed cider, plaster walls, shou
> sugi ban wood, and mother fucking butter churning. I pore
> over her feed in the wee hours of the night hooked up to a
> breast pump because my baby can't breastfeed and I don't
> have the primordial dance of motherhood with a babe at
> the breast as I fish for mackerel from a dock on the Atlantic.
> The bitterness brews because she has good-looking messes.
> Because she still is fucking funny and "authentic." Because
> she seems to have it all and does it *mother fucking all*. I think
> the realization is not that I hate how much I love her. I
> hate how I am here . . . most of us are here on our phones
> trying to teleport out of our present moment somewhere
> else. Somewhere more beautiful, somewhere away from our
> screaming baby and last week's undone to-do list.[50]

Hannah *hates how she is here*. Here trying to figure out motherhood despite it not feeling or looking the way Instagram tells her it should feel or look. Here wanting to feed her kid in a way that looks a certain way despite knowing the way something looks doesn't matter as long as the kid is fed. Here being a mom still doomed to want to have it all even though she knows many cultural structures and systems make that utterly impossible. Here questioning what "it all" even means. Here trying to be somewhere else. To be someone else. We can intellectualize why we might be scrolling, and shuffle through how scrolling might be serving us and how it might not. And this is not nothing. Thinking critically about our own whys, and realizing that they are as unique as the momfluencers we follow, is necessary, because at the end of the day, our individual struggles are our own, and no golden glow from our phones can filter away that reality.

4

Pretty/Ugly

My mother wasn't the Betty Crocker type of stay-at-home mom. She was the kind of mother who pulled us out of school to go antiquing and get Reese's sundaes at Friendly's. My mom found yellowed botanical guides in dusty piles at secondhand shops. She carefully ripped eight butterflies out of the guides before placing them in gilt frames way before Pottery Barn and Wayfair would sell knockoff vintage butterfly prints to the masses. She set giant turquoise bowls of clementines atop the kitchen table's Pierre Deux tablecloth. She added butter and cream to every soup. She was always sending me and my siblings out into the woods to find moss or Princess pine for art projects; blue-jay feathers and dried Queen Anne's lace littered her craft table. We spent afternoons digging with her in an old bottle dump behind our nineteenth-century Massachusetts farmhouse, searching for treasure. If ever we found a cobalt-blue medicine bottle (which was almost never), she'd scream as though we'd struck gold: "It's the rarest color!" She told us only boring people got bored.

When I was six, eight, and eleven, my mother made tuna melts, sharp cheddar softening over ripe tomatoes and briny tuna. She laughed on the phone with her friends, she laughed in the car as we drove home from TJ Maxx at something the "dingbat" salesgirl had done, she laughed in a way that always sounded like she was laughing about something profane. She believed whole-heartedly in "mental health days." In a photo from 1984 that, for me, captures the essence of her motherhood, she is twenty-seven, her curly blonde hair is cut in a 1984 shag, her eyes are storm blue, her jawline sharp, and, even as she holds me, a tear-stained toddler, on her lap, my hand nestled in the hollow between her breasts, she is so regal, so singular, so entirely herself.

My mother made motherhood look like beautiful magic. As a kid, I never considered whether or not I'd become a mother because she showed me that there was nothing more exciting one could be. She made me believe that motherhood was a source of ultimate power that could be used to create a world in which you might be your best, truest self. Her performance was so big I got lost in it. Well before I would spend hours scrolling Instagram looking for newer, fresher maternal performances to inform my own—before I coveted Naomi Davis's (@taza) bold red lip version of motherhood, or before I had feelings about Hannah Neeleman (@ballerinafarms) and her seemingly endless font of sourdough-baking maternal energy, before I found Julie D. O'Rourke (@rudyjude) and her Wes Anderson–esque, handcrafted Hal-loween costumes—my views of "Mother" were informed almost entirely through what my own mom made of the role.

■ ■ ■

I'm thirty-two years old and "Mom" lights up my phone. "Sara, if you're driving, you should pull over." I swerve my blue Subaru station wagon into a scenic-view parking area that overlooks the Bellamy River, a New Hampshire tidal river that feeds the Atlantic Ocean. I wonder if anyone has died.

After I pull the Subaru over, I sit and wait, examining clogged pores in the flip-down mirror, noticing a few stray hairs between the otherwise clean arches of my eyebrows. I turn on the seat warmer and rub my hands together. I'm cold and I need to get home to the babysitter who's caring for my one-and-a-half-year-old. I'm six months pregnant with his sibling, who pushes a heel or a knee or an elbow against my bladder, reminding me I have to pee. Seagulls sail by in the wind, which forms whitecaps from the water of the Bellamy River. No one has died.

"I've written you a letter," my mother says. "Can I read it to you?"

She begins to read. Page after page. The crisp sound of paper being shuffled means new words, words that hack away at assumed truths. *I loved staying home with you kids, but did I ever get business trips to escape once in a while like your dad did? Did I ever get a break? Did I ever get to just live for myself or pursue my dreams?* It had never occurred to me to wonder about her dreams.

■ ■ ■

I wrote a letter once, too.

I was twenty-nine and my youngest brother had recently moved out of our childhood home after having lived there for a year postcollege to save money. My mom seemed depressed. Absent. She was eating what seemed like too many salty foods after recovering from a heart attack she'd had the year before and being told by her doctor she needed to reduce sodium intake; she had taken up smoking cigarettes after quitting ten years prior. She stopped going for long walks, for short jogs, which she attributed to a heel injury, but I attributed to a dearth of effort to "fix" the heel injury (I'm not sure why I thought it was OK to police her food or presume more knowledge of her own pain or bodily experience than she herself possessed).

When we visited, she holed up in her bedroom during family dinners, which my father cooked and often consisted of rice pilaf, some sort of grilled meat, and a salad devoid of my mother's culinary imagination. She did not join us for cocktail hour. She wasn't interested in listening to my sister's and my friend dramas. She went blank when we mentioned a name she would've recognized if she'd been listening. She didn't ask follow-up questions. She didn't seem to care.

I told my therapist that she remained impervious to our anxiety about her health, about her detachment. My therapist suggested I write a letter and read it aloud to her. I did, with my sister Megan. We called the letter our "intervention."

The three of us sat on the front porch of my parents' house, the heart-shaped catalpa leaves fluttering in the breeze above us. We told our mother we had to talk and that it was serious. We told her we loved her and wanted her to understand. We read the letter, which was full of desperation and longing for the *real her*. We told her we would find physical therapists for her plantar fasciitis. We told her we would find a nutritionist to recommend delicious low-sodium meals. We made a list of possible gateways to happiness for an empty nester.

Find a therapist.

Find a couples' therapist.

Volunteer at a dog shelter.

Volunteer at a wild animal rescue.

Volunteer at a mustang ranch.

Plan a European cruise with Dad to reconnect.

Join a bridge club (Grandma suggested this one—we knew it was bullshit).

Visit Megan in Boston.

Sell wreaths and topiaries on Etsy.

Find a spiritual retreat in California.

Take a class at the local art museum; dust off your box of oil paints.

Plan trips with girlfriends.

Read more books (like you used to).

We love you. We want you to change because we love you. We miss the person you were before. We are scared you will die. We did not say, *We want you to be a regular happy mom, like you used to be.* We did not ask, *Were you ever a regular happy mom?*

My mother's face was like granite. With every new "helpful" suggestion, rage etched itself more deeply into the lines around her mouth.

And the more we cried, the more angry I became. Why did her children sobbing and saying they feared she would die from another heart attack fail to move her? What was wrong with her? Why couldn't she figure her shit out? In the back of my self-centered mind, I imagined that I was empathizing with her during a disorienting period in her life. The last of her children was gone, and her work as a mother was no longer urgent. But we still wanted it, still felt we deserved it. We wanted her to keep on performing, to put on a glorious show when we visited, to make our favorite meals, to greet us with cheer and show us wreaths she'd made out of bittersweet vines. We wanted her to keep on performing the role of Mother, even if we were mostly no longer there to appreciate it. This is what we wanted, what we thought she needed. To be happy.

We finished the letter, and she snapped in response. "I'll do whatever you want me to do. I'll quit smoking. I'll eat only bland food. Fine."

Megan started ugly-crying. I dried my eyes and started yelling. My mom yelled back.

What did I imagine would happen? That she would take my hands, see my pain, and collect it in her arms like she did when I was little and fell from my bike? That she would tell me not to cry, that she would agree she needed to change? Did I imagine she would thank us for being so brave, so honest? That she would join a gardening club?

When I told my therapist about our failed intervention, she told me I needed to start working less on changing my mother and more on changing my emotional responses to my mother's actions. She told me I needed to start working on acceptance. But that my mother had given the best years of her life to her husband and children and had nothing to show for it wasn't something I was ready to accept. I didn't want to grapple with the grim knowledge that the identity she had so perfected no longer sustained her. At the time of our intervention, I was pregnant with my first kid, and I needed to believe in a motherhood that would never betray me, a motherhood that would fill me up, not leave me empty and searching. I wanted to be the type of mother my mom had been for us, but I didn't want to end up like her. A person stripped of the very identity that had made her shine so bright.

■   ■   ■

Amanda Watters has four children, the youngest of whom was born prematurely and hospitalized in 2020 for respiratory issues during the first months of the pandemic. The thought of dragging my ravaged postpartum body between hospital and home while juggling anxiety over my newborn's health and the world's health and caring for my older children makes me shiver.

But Amanda Watters glows.

I know this because I follow @mamawatters on Instagram, where she posts images of her children and her inviting, Shaker-style kitchen. Clean countertops basking in wide slants of sun.

In March 2020, she posted a selfie from the hospital, holding her tiny newborn. In it, she is wearing a floral-print blouse whose delicate pattern could easily be transposed onto vintage transferware china or a bolt of calico Laura Ingalls might have coveted in 1886.[1] Baby Matilda's eyes are closed, her downy head resting against the rust-colored fabric. Her little hand reaches up and rests against Watters's chest, which is bare, the shirt having been unbuttoned, I imagine, to facilitate breastfeeding and skin-to-skin contact, which helps bond newborn babies, and especially premature infants, to their caregivers. Watters's eyes are clear and blue and directed straight at the camera, but it's easy to forget that there is a camera, because she looks so full of reverence, joy, love, grace. So full. She and the twenty-seven-year-old version of my mom in that photo from 1984 share something ineffable, something capable of convincing the viewer that motherhood is not just a never-ending slog of diapers and whiny questions but the key to a greater understanding of life, of self, of everything. It feels central for me to believe this, rather than the alternative, which is that they might just be good at projecting emotion via photographs.

The only thing that mars this image of Madonna and child is the fact that the rest of Watters's face is obscured by a hospital mask and Matilda's by a breathing tube, but these signifiers of a frightening reality only serve to uphold Watters's selfless maternity, which is complete in its unification of otherworldly strength and softness.

One Monday soon after consuming Watters's hospital selfie, I spent an hour searching for English stoneware jugs because @mamawatters posted a photo of one on a bare bureau in her uncluttered entryway. The image soothed me like a tonic and assured me that the vintage jug would make me happier, make me a better mom. Or, maybe more accurately, it assured me that being happier and being a better mom are one and the same, and that beautiful objects might take me there. This was back when I breathed in momfluencer culture without stopping to consider the air quality or whether or not I was personally thriving by inhaling and exhaling it.

On Tuesday, I received a passive-aggressive email from a coworker informing me of a missed deadline, and I tried to convince myself that my kids, screaming in the background, would be better off without my intervention. My kids were *always* in my background in 2020, when they only spent two months of the school year in actual school. I returned to Instagram and scrolled way back on @mamawatters's feed, looking for I know not what, until I found a photo of her three children smiling through an unsmudged French door: "the season for laying babes on beds with sweet bonnets on heads has long passed, for now. life with three under seven is wild and loud and blurry and full."[2]

In that particular moment, I had "three under seven" of my own, and felt nothing but rage for the words "babe" and "bonnet" and even "sweet." My life was indeed "wild and loud and blurry," but I wasn't sure it felt "full." I chastised myself for feeling all the ugly things—envy, jealousy—and unfairly targeting a stranger when my resentment had nothing to do with her and everything to do with me. Or everything to do with a culture that both glorifies and neglects The Mother in the same breath—particularly in 2020, when parents (particularly moms) were praised for being heroic martyrs and then left to flounder.

On so many days, I want to find happy maternity in a stoneware jug. I want the performance to be real, because if it's real, then I have some hope of inhabiting it. On other days, I long to see my own motherhood reflected in the lives of these on-screen women. Julie D. O'Rourke (@rudyjude), whose Instagram presentation of motherhood most closely matches the way I've come to think of my mother's, recently threw an apparently devil-may-care birthday party for one of her kids in what looks like a mossy fairyland. There are streamers. There are whimsical touches. I think there's a scavenger hunt. And I'm reminded of the elaborate birthday parties my mother threw for us, when she sent us scrambling over the fields on themed scavenger hunts (the clues were clever and rhymed), and I am exhausted. Because I consistently fail to achieve the maternal grace I dreamed of as a child, I want confirmation that *all* moms are failing to achieve that grace, and I scroll to locate the place where the performance stops. I spend too much time scanning photographs of @mamawatters's living room for a glimpse of neon or plastic, a *Paw Patrol* toy hidden beneath the linen slipcovered couch. There never is any *Paw Patrol* toy, but I keep wondering if it's lurking just outside the frame. I want proof that I'm chafing against motherhood not because I'm innately selfish, impatient, and bad, but because motherhood makes me this way. Makes us all this way.

Typing out a bullshit excuse to my coworker about the missed deadline, I yelled down to my children that I'll take away dessert if they can't "figure it out," because I hadn't yet learned how fucked-up such diet-culture-dependent, food-related "discipline" is (now I simply threaten to take away screen time). I yelled at them to stop yelling, feeling a brief burst of catharsis immediately followed by dull regret for my hypocrisy and my parenting, which is ineffective at best and damaging at worst. My motherhood is often ugly.

When I bemoan my sometimes-miserable experience of maternity, my therapist asks me to recall the not-so-shiny moments of my childhood, to move past the fairy tales I've told myself about my mother. Instead, I rattle off the usual stories about her artistry and her laughter, her insistence that we learn the names of the flowers and the birds.

My therapist nods (she's heard it all before). "Did she ever yell at you?" she asks.

And I remember. How, actually, my mom moved through my childhood in a state of just-below-the-surface simmer. How she sometimes stayed in her gardens until it was dark, and my siblings and I would call out that we were hungry; how she clenched her jaw; how she swerved her car out of the driveway too quickly, cigarette smoke trailing her. She yelled often. She yelled when we were packing up the house to go on vacation, she yelled at us to "stop fighting," she yelled when I was sullen at breakfast, she yelled when I didn't respond brightly enough to the too-loud question "How'd you sleep?" She yelled at me for being "fresh."

I remember calling her a bitch as a kid, remember her hand gripping the back of my head like an iron vice as she shoved a cold, waxy bar of Irish Spring soap into my mouth, bits of it softening into the cracks between my teeth. I feel her rage in my bones sometimes when I slam doors, when I shove a shoe onto a squirming kid's foot because *we're running late just put your shoe on jesus christ!* When I yell at my kids to "stop fighting." When I yell at my kids as we're packing up the house to go on vacation.

As a teenager, I remember how I yelled back at my mom. Yelled that I hated her. We filled the space between walls with her quick, guttural eruptions and my shrill squawks. I could never predict what might make her explode. And, back then, I couldn't understand why. She was in charge of her world, and her world seemed beautiful. Didn't she have everything? Everything I thought I wanted?

. . .

Pregnancy wholly confirmed my decision to follow in my mother's footsteps. I was the glowing pregnant goddess of my dreams. My bump was always described as "cute." *Looks just like a basketball under your shirt*, grandmotherly nurses would say after checking my blood pressure during prenatal exams. I'd lay in bed reading before bedtime, feeling like the star of my own gorgeous mama story, smoothing my hand over the taut skin of my hard, round belly and marveling at my magnificence as my baby moved inside of me. Instagram wasn't a thing yet, but if it had been, I would've splashed my account with photos of myself wearing diaphanous white sundresses on the beach, looking every bit like the mother I wanted to be.

And then my son was born. During my labor, everyone told me I was so strong, and I believed them. Afterward, the nurses told me my uterus was shrinking wonderfully, and I felt proud.

We left the hospital and opened the door to my sister's camera. She wanted to capture the moment. I took the baby out of the car seat and nursed him. She captured the moment. After which I sat down carefully on the toilet with my peri bottle to change my blood-soaked pad and noticed a jam jar my mother had filled with the bright, clear pink of cosmos, the sunshine amber of black-eyed Susans. I switched out my pad, and, for a second, their beauty worked. My sister's photos are beautiful, showing me cradling the baby, his dark brown fuzzy head under my chin. When I look at those beautiful photos now, I think my eyes are the eyes of a cornered rabbit. I feel my chest tighten and shuffle the photos back into their box, out of sight. None of them are framed.

I left the bathroom to confront my family, the bouquet of sunflowers on the kitchen table, the smell of zucchini bread baking in the oven, and the brightly wrapped packages of small and soft baby things. I remembered a passage from one of the many

Dr. Sears books I had read while smug and pregnant, in which he writes about these first precious days at home during which mother and baby should focus solely on getting to know each other. He calls this critical bonding period "nesting-in."[3]

On the second day home, I perched painfully atop a pillow (my tailbone had cracked during childbirth) and tried to choke down a piece of buttered toast before nursing. My son latched on to my nipple, his heart beating into mine. I looked around at my living room, which my mother had helped me paint and decorate. The soft fawn leather of the couch and the strong indigos striping the linen throw pillows melted into Benjamin Moore Shaker Beige, but I saw things. Stuff. Covered-up plaster, a feather shaken loose from one of the pillows, and a clump of dusty insect carcass caught under the leg of the couch. I seemed to be the only one who noticed this. I wondered about when the feather first started growing from the flesh of whichever bird it was plucked from. I wondered how it hurt.

I stared at my baby and then at the walls of my world. Needlepoint Navy, Benjamin Moore Shaker Beige, Petersen Cream (my mother had dubbed it so because she had custom mixed it)—these colors that used to matter. I couldn't swallow the toast. My mouth was dry, and I had no appetite.

"Sara, sleep deprivation is hell. It's totally normal to feel like shit." My mother's voice made me look away from the walls.

On the third day at home, my sister tried to tell me about her life. "Omg, did anyone tell you about Lisa's super awkward situation with her dog walker? They're basically having a feud." Megan looked expectantly at me.

"No," I said. "No one told me."

Megan waited for me to ask a follow-up question, but the effort was too much.

Megan changed the subject to clothing and hair care. "Black drapey sweater or silk navy blouse? What do you think of my middle part?" She was going to a restaurant. With people. My envy felt like the pain of a phantom limb.

"I like the middle part." I tried to inject enthusiasm into my voice.

I looked past Megan at my son being rocked back and forth by a swinging contraption we called the Spaceship. I hated the soft whirring noise.

My aunts brought my grandmother to visit, and my aunt Linny cradled the baby, saying, "Newborns are my favorite." I probably tried to smile. She held him as though he were a miracle, and her eyes shone. She looked how I was supposed to look.

Night and day coagulated. My bed, once a haven of Egyptian cotton, became a milk-soaked, night-sweat-drenched, twisted-sheet torture chamber, from which I emerged after fourteen hours of non-sleep.

With burning eyes, I scanned Facebook and read birth announcement posts: "Welcome to the world, baby Emma. We're over the moon and so in love. Can't remember life before you."

When the baby was four weeks old, my mother watched me amble through the tickly dry grass in the front yard, wearing sagging maternity cutoffs and a stretched-out tank top. She opened up the door to the screened-in porch, where she was smoking weed and playing with moss and dirt to make something for people to enjoy looking at, and hollered at me, "Look at you! I kinda hate you for being so skinny a month after having a baby." She laughed.

These words were meant as encouragement. I smiled wanly and thought of the obliging speed with which my uterus had so quickly shrunk.

My mother told me to go for a walk, get moving, get some fresh air. I listlessly climbed the driveway, certain nothing could help. As I concluded my walk, I stopped at the final hump of maples before reaching the house—the beautifully painted house, so thoughtfully curated.

Skimming my hand over the vacancy of my stomach, my hot rock boobs, which leaked with inexorable ongoingness into the saggy tank top, my body reminded reminded reminded me. Always reminding me reminding me reminding me.

"How was that?" my mother asked when I joined her in the screened-in porch.

I started to cry.

"Honey, you've gotta call your doctor. You can't wait until your six-week appointment." My tears felt like breaths. My mother rubbed my back and told me I was just exhausted, just so exhausted. And I was. I was so tired and so scared I would never sleep again, so sure I would never be myself again.

My mother made me lay down with the baby and look at him, touch him. He was beautiful, but not enough to make the hollowness within me recede. I sobbed, my body limp. Usually, everything tenses up when I cry. My shoulders rise to my ears, my chest draws in, my back hunches. But these sobs felt like my body had given up even on the healing, cathartic power of tears.

"I'm supposed to be happy," I whispered through the wetness. I thought about how beautiful my mother had made motherhood seem, and then I let her hold me until I fell asleep.

My postpartum depression dovetailed with the dark certainty that I'd made a grave mistake in thinking motherhood was the most direct path to fulfillment and self-actualization. Zoloft helped with the despair, but I still hated much of that first newborn experience, which was mostly drudgery peppered with moments of bliss. Even now, as a mother of three, I'm typically happiest and feel most myself when working, when using my brain, away from my maternal responsibilities. Playing make-believe or feigning interest in how fast a Hot Wheels car can go drains me in a way that is hard to quantify. Most days, I'd rather vacuum the Cheerio crumbs under my baby's high chair than read a Sandra Boynton book to him. I'd rather scroll through someone else's tender moments than try to locate my own.

■   ■   ■

In the blue Subaru, I listen to my mother read her letter. The windows are fogged up with my breath, my heat, but I'm still cold. I stare at a small boat covered in lobster traps rising up and down with the movements of the tide, tugging at its buoy. I think about the crushing darkness following the birth of my first child. I'm terrified it'll happen again, and I need my mother to tell her story to someone else so she can show up and be a supporting character in my own.

At the end of the letter, my mom says that she has spent her life pleasing others and that now it is time to please herself. I think of her body, which fed me, held me, raised me up. I think of her cool hands holding damp washcloths to my forehead. I think of her sitting with us in spring snow, piling great mounds onto overturned stumps, handing us old toothbrushes, screwdrivers, gardening trowels, and showing us how to make snow unicorns with skinny pinecones as horns. I think of the way she taught me to weave fairy lights through gradations of resiny pine to build a magical Christmas tree lit from within. She taught me how to tuck the wires out of sight.

Maybe my mother's performance was less for our benefit and more for her own, because the beauty she created convinced her that she was good, that she was necessary, that her work mattered. Beauty is tangible in a way that teaching children to say thank you is not. Beauty elevates the invisible work of motherhood into something one can point to and say, "See, see what I have made." See how what I've made has made me?

My mother is quiet on the other end of the phone.

"So you have nothing to say?" she asks. "After I pour my heart out like this—nothing?" She spits the word "nothing."

"Not really," I say. Everything inside of me feels dull and numb.

"I thought out of everyone *you* would understand, Sara. You know what it's like to be stuck at home all day with a baby—you *know*. But it must be nice to only care about yourself."

We both hang up without saying goodbye.

■　■　■

My writing career does not sustain my family financially, and when the pandemic hit and schools closed it took a backseat to childcare and housework. A babysitter comes four mornings a week to help with my toddler now, but, during lockdown, I eked out paltry writing and editing hours during naps and early in the morning. The effort of sustaining the illusion that I could think critically and turn that thinking into writing while being used up by the demands of domestic life was exhausting. On the days I tried to protect my writing time, the counters were sticky and the kids' hair unbrushed. Whatever writing I did was in small, unsatisfying chunks and felt stilted and superficial. I would fall asleep certain I'd tried to do everything and achieved nothing.

Amanda Watters writes frequently about how home nurtures her creative spirit. In an Instagram post of pink tulips in a cream-colored jug and a record player on a simple pine table, the caption describes folding laundry and a podcast in which Elizabeth Gilbert defines the creative impulse as "making something more beautiful than it has to be." Watters writes:

> Right then i stopped folding and my soul perked up and was like, 'yes! yes, girl! that's exactly how i see homemaking. doing those few extra details that really leave you feeling comforted and alive and grateful and safe and warm.' considering how we make our homes, especially now that we are all staying home (as we all should!) invites us to take the time to fold this sentiment into the work we do there. it's work that's important and valuable. it's also deeply personal as it is life-giving when things feel rather bleak or hopeless. i challenge you this weekend to do something to make your home—the space that nurtures you—more beautiful than it has to be. yesterday the kids and i made sun prints and we hung them around the house this morning. what joy! feel free to share your beauties below.[4]

In 2020, I read this in the bathroom, feeling bleak as hell, while my husband was wrangling the kids for bedtime. I heard a dull thwack in the distance (the sound of a kid falling) and my body tensed. My daughter burst in. "Mom, Si's crying and he wants milk." I sighed and cursed under my breath that I can't even remove my menstrual cup in peace. I wanted so badly to do work that is "important and valuable," but this didn't feel like that. I kissed my baby's head-bonk and nursed him, his hiccuppy sobs slowing into the steady rise and fall of his chest against my own, and I resolved to live the next day in the spirit of @mamawatters, to go all in. Because seething in bathrooms wasn't working.

When I woke up at 6:43 a.m., I lit a candle. When I got dressed, I chose my fake-vintage Levi's, even though they're not comfortable when I sit down, and a sweater that looks hand-knit. I smeared organic face oil onto my face and called it a "calming ritual." I stuck to some semblance of a homeschool schedule, googled "Magna-Tile activities," took meat out of the freezer at noon, and wiped the counters after every meal. Laundry was sorted, started, dried, folded, put away.

We made potato prints, but my daughter painted hers over with garish neon pink glitter and my son made a cartoony cat. Both of them fucked with negative space in uncool ways. The only print that made it to Instagram was mine, which featured minimalist arcs. I felt a little guilty for not showcasing my kids' ugly art, but mostly I felt angry at myself for placing value on their art in the first place and treating it like a reflection of my motherhood. Instagram makes it easy to believe that beauty is part and parcel of the work of mothering. If you're not trying to make it pretty, what's the point?

Somehow the baby stepped in ink and the resultant mess set back dinner prep, which made the kids hangry, which made me yell. By the time my husband emerged from our home office, I hated him for his uninterrupted hours upstairs. I thought of @mamawatters and, willing myself to find a way to make my space "more beautiful than it has to be," stooped down to pick up Polly Pocket's tiny plastic chair. I hated that tiny plastic chair, too. It was twenty-seven minutes past bedtime, and I could hear one of my kids having a fit because her favorite PJ bottoms were in the wash. I felt an overpowering urge to get in the car and just drive. I was too consumed with my own rage at the time, but, reading this now, while two of my kids are at school, and the other is at a petting zoo with his babysitter, I can see myself in my mother as she careens out of the driveway, cigarette smoke trailing. Desperate to escape.

I'm capable of creating beauty. I'm capable of hiding plastic toys away in bins and endlessly wiping down countertops. But I can't see past the mind-numbing work that goes into it. And the monotony of that work doesn't often equate to the momentary feeling of calm produced by neatness and order. The bud vase of violets will only be pretty if the streaks of toothpaste have been scrubbed from the sink, if the dark-yellow urine spots sprinkled across the toilet seat by a first grader with poor aim have been scoured. And if I take a picture, then what? Who will see the fruits of my labor if I don't post it on Instagram? If I don't (or even if I do), who will care? And even if someone does care in a passing *Oh, that's pretty* type of way, how will that translate into me having a better/easier/prettier experience of motherhood? If anything, won't my bud vase of violets just make them remember their own toothpaste streaks getting in the way of something better?

Amanda Watters recently opened a home-goods shop called Homesong Market, where she sells vintage copper measuring cups, hand-painted wooden toys, and an implausibly beautiful laundry basket. The basket, made of "100% organic naturally harvested reed," is marketed on the website as being able to fit one "very large load of laundry."[5] I know this is true, because I bought one. I had been lugging our laundry from the dryer to my bed using a ratty old laundry bag I must've had since college, and the process was not sparking any joy. When the pale blond basket arrived in the mail, I was delighted to discover that it was both incredibly light and sturdy. It was accompanied by a handwritten note signed by Amanda. I can't remember what it said, but it was warm.

I don't really believe that I'm a bad mother; I don't believe there's anything so simple as a good mother or a bad mother. I know an argument could be made that the time it takes to craft idealized images of one's house and children for the consumption of strangers in order to maintain a lifestyle brand would be better spent engaging with those children IRL. An argument could also be made that @mamawatters and other Instagram mother-artisans are getting far more out of motherhood than I am, so good for them.

Sometimes I throw the laundry basket against my hip and imagine myself existing within a neat square frame, wearing some sort of Nap Dress instead of old American Eagle sweatpants, and in this way the basket allows me to envision myself as someone else, as a different mother made happier and better by different things, one who can coax her children into gingham frocks and prevent them from blowing out the candle that's casting golden light on an empty wood table. Sometimes I choose to believe in the laundry basket. I choose to believe in the inherent goodness of beauty.

■ ■ ■

My parents split up recently, and my dad lives in my childhood home, where my mother's ghost lingers in every corner. My longing for my childhood mother is strongest there. This is where she belonged—where I want her to belong.

She moved to a rambling house in New Hampshire near my own and shifts her furniture around, reorganizes, redecorates, as much as she wants to. Every room is a work in progress, every space holds the potential of something new. Her mantel is covered with chunks of creamy granite she found in the woods, stones flecked with the glitter of mica. Crumbling bits of dried moss and lichen litter surfaces and I remember how many beautiful messes she made during the first couple months of my first child's life, when she stayed with me to hold me together, when I didn't care about how things looked because the rawness of new motherhood rendered appearances obsolete. I remember spending forty-five minutes to get my son to sleep before running out to the screened-in porch, which my husband and I dubbed "Cin's opium den." I remember how she validated my feelings that motherhood felt like a scam sometimes, I remember walking by her side as she smoked and I sipped an IPA, and she showed me what she had done in the gardens while I had nursed, pumped, rocked, shushed in an infinite loop. I remember when she finally left, her suitcase in the backseat, and feeling OK only because she promised she'd come back if the blackness returned. I remembered how she mothered me.

At her new house, she welcomes frogs in the swimming pool, and makes my husband move boulders to the edges so they can easily hop to freedom. She paints the house an inky black but can't decide on the color of the front door. For weeks the door is covered in a patchwork of red and yellow blotches. She still cares about how things look, but she seems to have found a way to care that doesn't necessitate an audience.

She's not a typical grandmother, by which I mean she isn't content to disappear into a life of gentle background servitude (and a typical grandmother is a social construct just like a typical mother is). She doesn't offer to change diapers, and she is never shy about telling us to hit the road when she's tired of our chaos. She does not knit, and she provides grocery-store-bakery cornbread muffins instead of home-baked cookies. If we beg her, she'll still make us tuna melts and hodgepodge soups, but when she's alone, she likes to eat popcorn for dinner. With lots of butter, salt, and Parmesan cheese. She doesn't apologize when her kitchen sink overflows. I like popcorn for dinner, too.

I asked her recently about those years immediately after we all left home, asked her if she felt any sense of relief once the heavy lifting of mothering was done. "It's a blurry line between relief and loss," she said. "When I was a kid, I was chubby and never felt pretty. But I grew up with two gorgeous, naturally thin older sisters, and it seemed like they had it so much easier. So, after high school, I made myself skinny and knew that everyone would be happy if I got married and had kids. They were. And I was happy to make people happy. I placed a lot of value in myself for being able to provide comfort, and in creating a beautiful childhood for you three. And then there was nothing left to perform, no one left to perform for once you all left."

I know that the performance was never for us, because I know that the performance is never for my kids, even when I pretend that it is. They're kids, after all, and by nature completely self-obsessed. I only exist as a background to the foreground of their own experiences. The performance is for me. It is for us, who were trained to perform for the male gaze and whose primary value as sex objects no longer holds so much currency. We perform mothering online as a way of accessing meaning when, most days, the work of motherhood doesn't seem to mean much of anything according to the many men legislating against paid family leave, universal preschool, and childcare subsidies.

We perform motherhood for ourselves. We mother for others.

On a still summer day, bored and aimless, I pile the kids into the car to go to Grandma Cin's. When we arrive, my mother is wearing a linen smock, sort of like the ones Instagram moms favor, except it's soaking wet. She's barefoot, and her feet are a mess. Calloused heels, horny nails.

"Hey!" she yells, directing a hose into one of several birdbaths. "Kids! Come see!"

"Why are you covered in water?" my son asks, his eyebrows raised incredulously.

"I'm hot!"

The kids giggle.

She points to a little wooden house nestled among ferns and moss. A tiny stone path leads to its door.

"Lift up the top!" she instructs.

Five stone owls of varying sizes sit inside.

"It's a family!" my daughter shouts. "There's the baby, the big sister, the big brother. There's the daddy. And that's the mommy."

5

Minimalist Moms, Cool Moms, and Unfiltered Moms

M y mom introduced me to the aesthetic power of motherhood. The way motherhood looks (or the potential for how it can look) is what grips me most tightly in my current consumption of particular momfluencer accounts. From vintage water jugs to punchy red lips to linen slipcovers, the potential of aesthetics is impossible to ignore in momfluencer culture. Particularly on Instagram, an app that was intentionally created to influence consumer behavior (and the stories we tell about ourselves) through imagery.

At this point, I've lost track of how many times I've exchanged knowing laughter with an interview subject about all the white paint, all the beige furniture, and all the wooden Montessori toys that dominate a particular momfluencer aesthetic. The mere invocation of, for example, an organic cotton swaddle or a farmhouse sink evokes a particular image of a particular type of mom.* One whose home is bathed in natural light, whose furniture is

---

*I have a farmhouse sink (and I love it), but it has not made me any more nurturing, any more accepting of dirty dishes, or any less likely to yell at my kids. By which I mean that the farmhouse sink has not delivered on any of its tacit momfluencer promises.

Scandinavian-inspired, whose belongings are carefully curated, and whose children are dressed in hand-knit woolen garments. This mama (she's never a mom or mommy, and rarely even a mother, since her linguistic choices are just as important to her aesthetic as her home goods choices) eschews bright colors in favor of serene control. Over her body, over her domestic space, and presumably over her children. She is minimalist, she is natural, she is simple. Her Instagram feed's cohesive aesthetic communicates not only *good taste* but assurance that her way (her look) is incontrovertibly right.

This particular momfluencer aesthetic is, of course, only one aesthetic among many, but I want to explore how it came to be the dominant one, and how alternative aesthetics almost always seem to exist in opposition to it. Why did white, ecru, ochre, and rust become synonymous with Instagram motherhood? And why does nearly every mother, whether she consumes momfluencer culture or not, feel this aesthetic influence in her life, as either something to emulate or something to rebel against?

I think it's helpful to ground this conversation by examining first how Instagram considered aesthetics as an integral feature of the app, something that would differentiate it from other social media platforms like Facebook and Twitter. According to Sarah Frier's invaluable business analysis of Instagram, *No Filter*, aesthetics and the drive to communicate values through imagery have always been at the forefront of Instagram's mission. As Frier writes, "By looking at the way commercial spaces, products, and even homes are designed, we can *see* Instagram's impact, in a way that we can't as easily see the impact of Facebook or Twitter."[1] And by examining the aesthetic significance of momfluencer culture, it's equally important to understand how the structure of Instagram in particular has contributed to more firmly aligning visual presentation alongside the performance of motherhood online.

Frier's book charts the evolution of Instagram from the very beginning, when one of its founders, Kevin Systrom, discovered an affinity for art history. He loved the Renaissance especially. Systrom's first attempt at building a social media app was called Burbn, sort of a cooler, hipper, better-looking version of Foursquare, its intent being to let your friends know where you were going and what you were doing. According to Frier's research, coolness seemed hugely important to both Systrom's sense of self and to the look and feel of Instagram. Frier writes of Systrom: "He was the kind of person who would say that he wasn't good at something he was actually good at, or that he wasn't cool enough to do something he was actually cool enough to do, toing the line between being relatable and humblebragging."[2] Frier's assessment of Systrom, formed from dozens of interviews, speaks to the fact that the appearance of relatability, the illusion of not having to try very hard to demonstrate innately authentic taste, ended up being synonymous for how we think, disparagingly or not, of #relatability and #authenticity on Instagram today.

Before launching Instagram, Systrom and his cofounder, Mike Krieger, knew they wanted content to look good, first and foremost. They wanted users to use Instagram filters to discover beauty within their shitty iPhone pictures (which were, at the time, truly shitty in terms of quality). To ensure that aesthetics played a formative role in how people approached using the app, they handpicked users they thought would create content that communicated a certain aesthetic. As Frier writes of the founders' intentions, "Instagram posts would be art, and art was a form of commentary on life. The app would give people the gift of expression, but also escapism."[3] This strikes me as particularly prescient given what we know about many mothers' reasons for engaging with momfluencer culture. The desire to amplify our experiences, so often rendered invisible, and the desire to escape our spit-up-stained realities by way of momfluencers living cleaner, prettier, better maternal lives.

Frier explains how Systrom and Krieger determined what type of people they wanted spearheading the first rounds of content:

"The founders picked their first users carefully, courting people who would be good photographers—especially designers who had high Twitter follower counters. Those first users would help set the right artistic tone, creating good content for everyone else to look at, in what was essentially the first-ever Instagram influencer campaign, years before that would become a concept."[4] While "the right artistic tone," as imagined by Systrom and Krieger, is never explicitly described, Frier indicates that certain values and aesthetics were prioritized over others. The founders wanted images that *felt* honest, that communicated imagistic good taste (whatever that means), that didn't seem overly contrived, and that made consumers feel like they were looking through windows into more exciting, more aesthetically interesting lives than they'd previously had access to on other social media platforms.

My own reasons for reluctantly downloading Instagram back in 2013 were solely to do with access to the "cool filters" I saw my friends using to make their photos (and their lives) look better than mine. I wanted my sunset photos to pop, wanted to find art within baby silhouettes. At the time, my life was comprised of Music Together classes with my one-year-old and muscling through wooly spells of fatigue caused by the first trimester of pregnancy with my second kid, and it was gratifying to look back on those days through the lens of Instagram, which made everything look less vanilla, made my reality feel sharper, more imbued with importance. As Frier notes, helping users see their lives reflected back to them as a little shinier, a little prettier, a little more worth examining, was the entire point. "Instagram's early popularity was less about the technology and more about the psychology—about how it made people feel," she writes. "The filters made reality look like art. And then, in cataloguing that art, people would start to think about their lives differently, and themselves differently, and their place in society differently."[5]

Did I look at my responsibilities as a stay-at-home mother differently because of Instagram? I'm not sure. But I do know that snapping pictures of my son sitting in a patch of violets subtly shifted my perception of myself as a mother. Not only did it give me something creative to do for a few minutes (find the patch of violets, plop him in the patch of violets, consider violet-to-baby ratio), but it also allowed me to see the work of motherhood as more than filling snack cups with Goldfish. It made it easier for me to see, visually, the beautiful moments of my own life. Frier notes how Instagram fostered this new sense of visual appreciation among users, making it easy for anything to become beautiful and, by extension, important, worthy of being looked at:

> Now Instagram users found that basic things, like street signs and flower bushes and cracks in the paint of walls, all of a sudden were worth paying attention to, in the name of creating interesting posts. The filters and square shape made all the photographs on Instagram feel immediately nostalgic, like old Polaroids, transforming moments into memories, giving people the opportunity to look back on what they'd done with their day and feel like it was beautiful.[6]

Mothers know that motherhood is an active endeavor. It is comprised of tasks rather than abstract imagery. But Instagram allows moms to lay their individual claims on the visuals of motherhood, long culturally upheld as more powerful, more compelling, than the active labor of motherhood. It's nice to get a slice of archetypal Madonna and child for oneself, to feel as though one's work matters because of visual representation.

In *No Filter*, Frier doesn't delve too deeply into what exactly the "Instagram aesthetic" is, but I think most of us know it when we see it. White walls. Fiddle-leaf ferns. Blond wood. A *this is luxe but I'm not trying too hard* vibe. And when the Instagram founders decided to allow advertising on the platform, they chose their first partners strategically (Lexus and Burberry were two of those early collaborations), ensuring a certain level of luxury was conveyed by both the actual brands featured, and also by the aesthetics of the brands themselves. Frier writes:

> Systrom and his business team decided that if advertising was going to work on Instagram, promotions needed to look like Instagram posts, and be *visually pleasing, casually artsy, without trying too hard to sell*; there could be no writing or price tags on the image itself. It was important, as Systrom had said the prior year, that any post from a brand "*comes across as honest and genuine*," Instagram modeled the look off Vogue magazine's: high-end brand advertising showcasing products in a subtle matter, as just one element of the lives of beautiful, happy people.[7]

The italics in the above-quoted paragraph are mine, because it's so clear that, from the very beginning, Instagram cared a lot about appearance, and cared just as much about that appearance communicating specific values. The most compelling of those values seems to be lack of effort. Beauty that exists without strenuous effort functions to communicate both authenticity and innate goodness. Think of our culture's obsession with the beautiful woman who doesn't know she's beautiful: her beauty is heightened by her lack of effort (I could write a tome about no-makeup makeup trends).

In Instagram's case, beautiful ads make consumers feel like they're not being marketed to, that companies who care about beauty somehow care about making money less. And for mothers, our maternal goodness, our maternal rightness, is often illustrated through a lack of effort entirely dependent on gender essentialism, the belief that people are born with certain qualities or characteristics by sheer dint of our sex. Mothers' much lauded maternal instincts, our innate need to nurture, our softness, our gentleness—all these qualities can be communicated more easily through imagery than mundane action. Instagram is where the archetypal mama thrives.

To understand which visual maternal archetypes stick (and why), I want to examine a few distinct aesthetic trends in momfluencer culture: the "cool mom" aesthetic; the "aesthetic of truth" (lots of nipples, lots of C-section scars); and, of course, minimalism, or the "all-white-everything" aesthetic. There are many, many more, but I've chosen these as representative of larger conversations about which mothers are deemed worth looking at and through which lenses we are looking.

Before researching this book, I think my hazy understanding of minimalism was like how I understood the Instagram aesthetic, a bit like the design equivalent of the infamous "eat food, not too much, mostly plants" Michael Pollan quote: "Simple objects, not too many, mostly white." When I think of minimalism, I think of white walls, pale wood, and empty spaces. I don't think of burgundy plastic robots purchased from Walgreens, throw pillows smeared with cream cheese, surfaces stained with crayon, or any other visual indicators of a child's presence. I don't have the space (or desire) to do a deep dive into the history of minimalism here, but my understanding of how the minimalist aesthetic operates in momfluencer culture was hugely informed by two books: Kyle Chayka's *The Longing for Less* and Christine Platt's *The Afrominimalist's Guide to Living with Less*.

In *The Longing for Less*, Chayka acknowledges that minimalism, as a concept, as a lifestyle, as a set of interior design rules, has myriad roots, and can mean entirely different things depending on which roots one chooses to honor. Minimalist art, for example, could be described as metallic, brutal, and heavy, whereas the minimalist lifestyle as undertaken by Henry David Thoreau is defined by discipline, restraint, and intellectual rigor. Minimalism as understood by a certified KonMari consultant could be understood as ridding one's life of objects that "don't spark joy," and minimalism can be purchased at Target in the Hearth and

Home by Magnolia aisle in the form of Joanna Gaines–approved mass-produced mugs that are meant to look hand-kilned.

Chayka notes how disparate ideas of minimalism coalesced into something easily replicated by dint of white paint largely through the blogger boom in the early aughts, which gave way to the #Instagrammable aesthetics later on. "What the bloggers collectively called 'minimalism,'" Chayka writes, "amounted to a kind of enlightened simplicity, a moral message combined with a particularly austere visual style. This style was displayed prominently on Instagram and Pinterest. . . . Two social networks that encouraged the accumulation of aspirational digital artifacts, if not visual ones."[8] Chayka's mention of "the moral message" inherent in cultural understandings of minimalism cannot be overstated, and it's something he returns to again and again in his book. He notes that minimalism requires "discipline," and that it operates as a "brand to identify with as much as a way of coping with mess."[9]

Minimalism is attractive to mothers in particular, I would argue, *because* it requires discipline, because it promises a modicum of control over the inherently uncontrollable experience of parenthood, which is anything if not chaos. I personally am utterly tantalized by the promise of some sort of stringent, disciplined lifestyle shift transforming my reality (exercise, lemon water, meditation, fucking clean countertops), and now that Instagram offers inspiration and aspiration paired with shoppability, the combination feels irresistible. I'm only buying shit because this particular shit will allow me to extract myself from the hamster wheel of consumerism; this particular shit will usher in a new era of calm as exemplified by floor-sweeping linen curtains.

Chayka also situates our current understanding (and desire for) minimalism within a particular historical context. He notes that following the 2008 recession, people not only had less money to spend on stuff but they also craved more control, since so many aspects of life felt out of control. Marie Kondo (and her best-selling book *The Life-Changing Magic of Tidying Up*) found her foothold in the cultural consciousness, as did a "back to basics" mentality:

Shopping at thrift stores became cool. So did a certain style of rustic simplicity, the kind epitomized by the lifestyle magazine *Kinfolk*, which was founded around the time of the crash and took root in Portland, Oregon. As the magazine's soft-focus photo shoots demonstrated, perhaps too well, hosting an outdoor picnic with your friends, decked out in DIY peasant shawls, didn't cost very much. Brooklyn was filled with faux-lumberjacks drinking out of mason jars. Conspicuous consumption, the ostentation of the previous decades, wasn't just distasteful, it was unreachable. This faux-blue-collar hipsterism preceded the turn to high-gloss consumer minimalism that happened once the economic recovery kicked in, preparing the ground for its popularity.[10]

Reader, I save fancy jam jars and use them as wineglasses. By which I mean my critiques of minimalism, which might also be called the millennial aesthetic, which can also be called Instagrammable, which can also be called the *Kinfolk* aesthetic, are very much entangled in a desire to emulate that aesthetic. The jam jar wineglass is a particularly apt example of how aesthetics encompass morality. Not only am I enacting some sort of environmental consciousness by reusing my old jam jars; the jam jars also act as a visual representation of that environmental consciousness. And I guess they look good because *Kinfolk* signed off on them looking good?

Before we continue our minimalism journey, I do want to pause to discuss *Kinfolk*, because so many momfluencers embody this "faux-lumberjack" aesthetic. Julie D. O'Rourke (@rudyjude), who seems to come up in every chapter whether or not she's invited, is a perfect model (although, to be fair, she and her partner, Tony, are legit building their new home with their own two hands, so "faux" lumberjacks they are not!). And, in fact, her Rudy Jude–branded jeans themselves could accurately be described as part and parcel of a certain *Kinfolk*-esque momfluencer's uniform. In Lisa Abend's *Vanity Fair* article on how *Kinfolk* has influenced

Instagram millennial aesthetics (as well as the larger culture), she offers the following summation of why a small, arty, niche magazine is worth paying attention to:

> *Kinfolk* is famously about intentionality, about a kind of wholesome slow living that exults in deliberately curated moments, carefully selected objects, and, as its twee tagline once read, "small gatherings." Like all lifestyle magazines, it traffics in aspiration, and if, in the past eight years or so, you have found yourself craving a precisely sliced piece of avocado toast, or a laundry line from which to cunningly hang your linen bedsheets in the sun-dappled afternoon, you probably have *Kinfolk* to thank for it. But the seductions featured on its pages have always been aimed as much at the soul as the body. Through intention, *Kinfolk's* austerely beautiful pages whisper, lies not just a pretty room or a lovely outfit, but a truer expression of the self, something more meaningful, more, as the marketers now put it, authentic.[11]

Kinfolk was founded by a Mormon couple, Nathan Williams and Katie Searle, and its first issue was published in 2011, only a year after Instagram was founded, so it seems fitting that the *Kinfolk* aesthetic, as it would come to be known, was also an aesthetic people loved to showcase on their Instagram accounts. Abend notes this happy marriage between an aesthetic and the social media platform:

> It wasn't long before millennial feeds were filled with the *Kinfolk* aesthetic; even with images of *Kinfolk* itself. "Somehow—I don't know how—the magazine became popular for social media," Williams says. "Taking photos of it on a coffee table, in a café, on the bookshelf—it just exploded. We started seeing lots of signature *Kinfolk* photos—like the cone with flowers coming out of it to look like ice cream—pick up traction and also go off on social media."[12]

When I first took up writing, I didn't know where my proclivity for written self-expression was going, but I definitely dipped my toe into establishing my maternal brand as being aligned along *Kinfolk* lines (albeit with a sense of humor). If you scroll way, *way* back on my Instagram feed, there are serene photos of tea, of felted animal toys, close-ups of wood grains. Adopting this aesthetic seemed as good a way as any to communicate my values, although what values I thought I was communicating through well-lit expensive toys, I can't say.

In an *Elle* profile of Katie Searle (the other cofounder of *Kinfolk*), Leslie Jamison says the following about what the *Kinfolk* aesthetic so often inspires: "It's the same envious resentment we bring to Facebook pages and Instagram feeds, the triple punch of projection, aspiration, and repulsion we often fling at lives that appear more ideal than our own."[13] I scarcely need point out the clear parallel between what this aesthetic can make people feel and what certain momfluencer accounts can make people feel. And when the *Kinfolk* aesthetic (which Lisa Abend brilliantly delineates as "an aesthetic so sharply defined, you could slice sourdough with it") is paired with motherhood, it seems especially inevitable that "projection, aspiration, and repulsion" will thrive.[14] Motherhood is an identity ultimately defined by labor—labor that is mostly messy, often chaotic, and nearly never aesthetically "sharp," so there's something discordant about *Kinfolk*-inspired momfluencers that never account for this unavoidable disconnect between visual idealization and lived reality. And it's this discordance, made visible through a lack of ugliness (ugly kid toys, ugly processed foods, ugly reminders of modernity), that gets under my skin. And yet *Kinfolk* momfluencer accounts continue to thrive.

Chayka surmises that the cultural burnout with American maximalism might be at the root of both *Kinfolk*'s popularity and the various iterations of minimalism made popular by Instagram. Minimalism suggests that simplicity, and the ability to consume and own less things, will release us from the existential weariness evoked from living in a "society that tells you more is always better."[15] Minimalism's promise that "less is more," and that "less" can be both aesthetically and morally superior, is an enticing one—particularly for mothers, who are barraged with an onslaught of "buy this now" messages as soon as they start googling anti-nausea teas in their first trimester of pregnancy.

According to Chayka's research, "The average American household possesses over three hundred thousand items. Americans buy 40 percent of the world's toys despite being home to 3 percent of the world's children. We each purchase more than sixty new items of clothing a year, on average, only to throw out seventy pounds of textiles per person."[16] We know that mothers are marketers' dream consumers, and our culture's drive to own more stuff (and to put that stuff in increasingly bigger houses) cannot be divorced from how patriarchal capitalism views mothers as potential buyers, as drivers of the economy. I think minimalism is particularly appealing to mothers, because being at the receiving end of countless ad campaigns and countless articles detailing which toys are best for which stages of development and why, is exhausting. As is the belief that our drive to consume, and the objects we accumulate, are making both our physical and emotional worlds more cramped.

But while it makes sense that moms crave lives made freer from stuff, the commodification of minimalism as an aesthetic has often simply encouraged us to keep buying stuff, so long as it's the *right* stuff. Chayka writes:

> No single English-language word quite captures this persistent feeling of being overwhelmed and yet alienated, which is maybe why "minimalism" has become so widespread. I began thinking of this universal feeling as the longing for less. It's an abstract, almost nostalgic desire, a pull toward a different, simpler world. Not past nor future, neither utopian nor dystopian, this more authentic world is always just beyond our current existence in a place we can never quite reach.[17]

Chayka also speaks to the way minimalism, both as a practice and an aesthetic, gives consumers the illusion of control, if not of the world, at least of our domestic spaces. "It's often an internal, individualized process rather than an external one," he writes. "Your bedroom might be cleaner, but the world stays bad."[18] This notion of fixing one's immediate space/life versus attempting to fixing larger societal problems reminds me of how Jean Wade Rindlaub, our intrepid mid-century advertising maven from chapter 2, wrote copy that urged mothers to stop worrying about global concerns out of their control and simply "bake a cake" instead. The medium is different, but the message is the same: the world is a mess, but if you buy the right things (Betty Crocker cake mix and perhaps linen-covered drawer organizers), you can consume your way to a good life.

The insular nature of minimalism—at least as it pertains to buying the right salvaged wood coffee table or the "only winter coat you'll ever need"—is also inextricably bound up in race, class, and the "psychology of ownership," something Christine Platt, on Instagram as @afrominimalist, writes about in her book *The Afrominimalist's Guide to Living with Less*.

Christine and I slated a half hour to talk about aesthetics and momfluencer culture, but as soon as we connected on the phone, it was clear a half hour wouldn't be enough. Christine laughingly said as much in the first five minutes: "Two moms tackling all this stuff? A half hour?" Truly. When I first asked Christine about how race and class factor into our conversation about aesthetics and minimalism in momfluencer culture, she said her book could've been five hundred pages long because these issues are so "nuanced." Even the cover design of Christine's book butted up against dominant beliefs about how minimalism is "supposed" to look. The book cover is a bold tomato red and features a small drawing of cotton blossoms. Christine said she had to "fight" for that cover. "They [the publishers] wanted, you know, everything kind of traditional," she told me. "They were like, *Look at this, it's a softer almond color,* and I was like, *It's* . . . [she took a long pause] *white.*"[19] Because so often, we think of minimalism as white, both literally white (white paint, white furniture), and figuratively as a design concept *for* white people.

As Christine points out in her book, people from the African diaspora must consider their relationships to consumerism and aesthetics from the perspective of white supremacy. "Ownership is an especially complicated matter for people of the African diaspora," she writes. "From our ancestors being stolen and once owned as property to our need to have things so that we feel in control of something in our lives, Black people have a different, deeper relationship with our belongings."[20] She argues that Black people, made to feel unsafe in so many spaces, are bound to "seek comfort in things" and the false sense of security that comes from ownership.[21] She notes that the drive to consume can jeopardize Black peoples' ability to build generational wealth, "run[ning] the risk of not only remaining victims of systemic oppression, but even worse, contributing to it."[22] I want to highlight Christine's point about why and how some Black moms might be driven to consume as distinct from, say, the desire of wealthy white women to buy stuff to quell ennui. This is a singular example of why it's so critical to examine all facets of momfluencer culture from very specific angles, to never assume all moms are behaving in the same ways for the same reasons.

Christine also notes that social media compounds our psychological need and desire to buy stuff to feel control of our domestic spaces: "The need to show people our lives has only been amplified by our online presence, resulting in many costly false narratives."[23] Again, mothers in particular are subject to this pressure to display our (good) taste on social media because (good) mothers are supposed to create good-looking homes. We are supposed to *naturally* know what looks good just as we're supposed to be *naturally* nurturing, *naturally* maternal, *naturally* feminine. It bears mentioning that all these so-called natural qualities are impossible to concisely define. What feels like nurturing behavior from one mom might be something totally different for another. Just as what looks good to one person looks drab and dull to someone else. Gender-essentialist beliefs that there is one way to be a woman, one way to be a mother, are necessary to considerations of momfluencer aesthetics.

Christine discovered that her own history of consumption was rooted in a misguided idea of self-care, that she deserved to buy herself things, even if the purchasing of those things was only providing a momentary endorphin rush (much like how some consume momfluencer content) and failing to bring her any meaningful sense of well-being. This is so relatable! For so many mothers I've talked to (including the one writing this book)! We *do* deserve to feel less exhausted, less overwhelmed, less frenetic. But, as Christine found, a bath full of luxury bath salts wasn't cutting it. "I would get all the bath bombs and oils and things, like, *you are going to relax, mommy!* And then I would get out the bath and my skin was soft, but I was still overwhelmed because basically all I did was take a bath, right? And, like, that is not enough for us."[24] A nice bath will not give you the peace of mind created through affordable quality childcare, for example. Soft skin will not replace equal employment opportunities, and pumiced heels cannot make up for having to go back to work while still bleeding from childbirth. A bath is not enough.

If you peruse Christine's Instagram account @afrominimalist, you will see a mint-green desk, a giant sculptural fork hung on the wall, mud-cloth pillow covers, lots of plants, and nary a piece of blond furniture in sight. She's passionate about educating people about minimalism as a practice, rather than solely an aesthetic, and thinks many corners of momfluencer culture make minimalism as a practice "inaccessible" and bewildering in the stark absence of kid-related detritus: "It's a lifestyle that is only accessible to white, wealthy people who also seemingly have no children, because I'm always like, *So you're just gonna put that one white couch in the middle of your five-thousand-square-foot living room?* There are no baskets or bins. These homes don't look lived in."[25]

Christine says she often gets messages from mothers trying to find some semblance of peace in their homes who get tripped up by the bombardments of capitalism. She told me a story of a particular mother who bought a T-shirt folder from Amazon before realizing she could've just used a clipboard instead of buying yet another *thing*:

> I think as moms we're so hard on ourselves and we're so critical and we so want to make sure that we are doing things right for our kids, even if it's having the right living space where they feel calm and peaceful and serene. And all of these materials and products and unnecessary things are marketed to us indirectly and subtly. It's like, you look at that picture of the perfect home on your phone and then you look up and there's, like, a handprint on your wall, there's a stain on the whatever, and you're like, *I suck*.[26]

In what is becoming a theme of this book, Christine believes that the more we understand about the culturally dominant voices telling us what an aesthetically ideal home/wardrobe/life should look like, and where the inspiration for perfection comes from in the first place, the more we can learn to trust ourselves instead of falling prey to the culturally constructed need to buy our way into happiness. As is clear from chapter 2, marketers and advertising agencies deliberately capitalize on mothers' (culturally constructed) feelings of inadequacy in order to convince us to buy stuff, and when it comes to establishing a domestic aesthetic that feels good or comforting, we've been indoctrinated to believe that it's a mother's *natural job* to be adept at creating beautiful domestic havens, and that doing so is another way to display our fitness as mothers. Christine says that the capitalist powers that be "understand our vulnerabilities as consumers. They are fully, fully aware that mothers do not have the support that they need, whether they are at home, or working outside of the house."[27]

I'm writing this a few days after four students were killed by gun violence in a Michigan school, highlighting yet again that our country cares more about gun access than it does about children or the parents who love them. I'm writing this as the Supreme Court debates whether or not people should be able to make individual choices about their own reproductive destinies, highlighting yet again that our country cares more about controlling non-male bodies than it does about mothers or children. It's been an incredibly depressing couple of weeks. And when Instagram shows me a photo of a happy mother snuggling with her kids on a cream-colored couch, I want nothing more complicated than that same happiness by way of a clutter-free, cream-colored existence. It is far easier to add a few pretty Swedish dishcloths to my virtual cart than it is to deal with my deep, deep despair when I consider what it means to be a mother in the United States.

And Christine says it's OK to buy those dishcloths and call that purchase (or even the clicking of the "Add to Cart" button) a reprieve from the news cycle nightmares that never seem to end. It's OK to indulge in the fantasy of everything being OK by virtue of attractively packaged reusable cleaning products. Christine writes quite a bit about the importance of forgiveness in her book and says that same forgiveness can be granted to the act of aspirational scrolling because "it feels good to stroll, it just *does*." During our call, she recalled a moment pre-Instagram when she got a Crate and Barrel catalog in the mail, which a friend of hers referred to as "mom porn." She described flipping through the perfect interiors and feeling a sense of calm despite never intending to buy "a single thing."

> It goes back to shaming, right? We're made to feel like all of our time should be spent focusing on our children or our homes, right? I know looking at the square is so ridiculous. My life, and probably very few people's lives will ever emulate and reflect the square, right? But look at the cute babies and

they're all dressed alike, and look at the moms and look at the pretty home. I mean, it's *fun*. It's fun and there should be no shame. No shame. We are allowed to have those moments.[28]

Christine advocates for extending ourselves "grace" and allowing ourselves to "redefine what you want for yourself." As an example of daring to embrace what feels right for oneself (despite the noise of social media), Christine referenced a friend who "is just very happy being messy." That friend might not be as organized as Christine, "but they have everything they need, and their kids are happy." After all, picking up after kids is one of the most grinding of domestic grinds. It's constant and feels futile (at least for me) most of the time. It was with a sense of revelation that Christine told me about a friend who "just doesn't want to pick up, *or* go through the rigmarole of having the kids pick up all their toys. Yeah, why pick up every evening, when the toys are all over the floor the entire next day?" She told me that one day, her friend "just stopped because it drove her crazy. Like, when we talk about tapping into our authentic selves, this is that! Like, *yeah, this living room looks great in this picture, but it's just not gonna work for me. I don't care about the toys being all over the floor; the kids are good.*"[29]

I love this so much. I also am horrified that it feels so subversive, so radical, to hear a story about a parent who made the decision to simply get off the toy-cleaning-up treadmill. She just *got off.* It boils down to distinguishing function from aesthetic. Viewing aesthetically ideal domestic spaces on a momfluencer's feed through the informed lens of entertainment is different from making a deliberate choice about what functions best in one's own domestic space. It can be fun to scroll through someone else's clean home, but if we can divorce that sense of pleasure derived through consuming content as entertainment from a pressure to emulate someone else's supposedly perfect domestic space and aesthetic, we might be better off.

By now, we're all familiar with (and many of us likely bored by) the white momfluencers with their white couches in their white homes. But there are so many momfluencers rejecting this aesthetic, as reflected by photos of their domestic spaces, and also in the overall aesthetic style of their Instagram feeds. Valerie Metz is one of those momfluencers. She has more than eleven thousand followers as @mammafolk, and her feed feels like biting into a juicy orange, feeling the saltwater crisp up your hair after a day in the sun, or listening to your kids' laughter ebb and flow with the crash of waves. Her feed feels, in short, like a day at the beach. So it's only fitting that, when we spoke, she phoned me from the actual beach. Which I was impressed by, especially given the fact that she was able to offer me insightful feedback about momfluencer aesthetics while also keeping a baby and toddler from eating handfuls of sand or throwing said handfuls at each other. #Momgoals.

Valerie's background is in photography, and she thinks part of her success as a momfluencer lies in her unique aesthetic as well as her Latina roots, which make her stand out from herds of white moms in white homes. She thinks brands like WildBird (which makes baby slings in sun-washed colorways) seek her out to create sponsored content because she "looks different." She said, "Like, I look one-hundred-percent Latina, and I think brands like that I'm not the typical mommy Mormon blogger from Utah with long extensions." She says she's "not into trends" (which could certainly include minimalism, cottagecore romance, or the prevalence of neutrals). When she reflects on her use of color, both in her home and on her feed, she sees that as a rejection of momfluencer-approved aesthetic trends:

> I just looked at how I was raised in my culture, and, like, growing up, our house had bright yellow walls and bright flowers and my mom had plants everywhere. And in my living room, I have a huge Latinas-in-music vintage art piece that my friend found at a flea market for me. And I feel like a few years ago I would've been like, *No!* It's got guys in Cumbia bands wearing, like, mariachi hats with guitars and

stuff, and it's one of my favorite art pieces. So now, I just try to focus on what feels more natural to me, and what feels like my culture and reminds me of my childhood versus, like, *Is this macrame wall hanging just super trendy right now and am I gonna eventually hate it?*[30]

This questioning of self that Valerie does in order to hear her own voice amid the din of momfluencer culture is a lot like the questioning of self that Nicole Beurgen suggests people do when faced with similar noise (remember the blueberry-patch mom?). Patterns!

Valerie sees a rise in momfluencer accounts that don't rely on presets or filters to cast their lives in the light of perfection. "I think there's this fresh newness of, like, no filters, no presets, just be yourself, post what you want. I guess playing with more freedom, and I think that that's going to continue."[31] She credits much of this aesthetic shift with people's burgeoning awareness that the many "rules" we've been taught to adhere to about creating and maintaining our social media selves, are not rules at all, but merely trends typically created and maintained by people and companies invested in us spending money.

Stacey-Ann Blake (@designaddictmom) also attributes her predilection for color to her cultural background. We chatted in December, when her feed featured a carnation pink Christmas tree set up against a backdrop of lapis blue paint and cheery bookshelves organized by color. It's like a Pantone party in the best way. Stacey is Jamaican and says a love of color "goes with the territory. I was born into it. It's innate. Maybe not all Jamaicans love color, but I've yet to meet one who doesn't." She finds all-white, all-beige spaces "blinding," and believes color has the power to "amplify one's mood." She's been blogging for over a decade, and, in the early days at least, she felt like sort of a lone wolf in terms of her aesthetic, but has recently noticed more color-loving moms taking up space on Instagram. Still, she often gets messages from fans calling her feed a "breath of fresh air," expressing their fatigue with the all-white-everything momfluencer look.[32]

I first became acquainted with Bethanie Garcia's work through an interview she did on Jo Piazza's momfluencer podcast *Under the Influence*, which emphasized her somewhat unlikely meteoric rise to success as a content creator, despite not possessing many of the privileges that can be prerequisites for carving out financial success in the influencer economy. When we spoke via Zoom (along with her delightful manager, Tami Nealy), Bethanie told me she started blogging as a young mother pregnant with her second child. "I was just so overwhelmed," she said. "I had a baby, I was pregnant, we were so broke that we couldn't even buy formula. And in the middle of the night, I started a blog called *The Garcia Diaries*, because I just needed a creative outlet or somewhere to put all my thoughts and emotions and just something that was just mine."[33]

Bethanie had several things to say about her own experience of adopting the "right" aesthetic as a momfluencer. From the very beginning, her lack of access to generational wealth impacted the look of her blog and Instagram feed. When she decided to get serious about monetizing her blog, she wanted to elevate her photo quality with an app called Lightroom, but didn't have enough money for a computer, so she rented one from Rent-A-Center. "Like, I couldn't afford to have a designer come in and do my blog. I learned to do it on YouTube. I couldn't afford to do any of the loop giveaways. There's this one girl, we had the same amount of followers in 2015. She has a million now. And she gives away, like, two thousand dollars on her stories every week."[34] Loop giveaways, which are rampant in the influencer economy, enable influencers to quickly increase their follower counts, provided they have enough buy-in money. Stephanie McNeal, who covers influencer culture for *BuzzFeed*, explains in a piece she wrote in 2020: "A group of influencers host the giveaway together, and in order to enter, you have to follow all of the participating influencers. This boosts all of the participants' follower counts, which help them get bigger ad

deals and partnerships. The participants either split the prize between themselves, or they pay a third party to play. They are often
framed as a way for influencers to give back to their followers."[35]

Bethanie told me that that loop giveaways, in addition to requiring up-front investments, are also, at least in part, organized
according to type. A Peloton loop giveaway, for example, will
likely be hosted by fitness-centric influencers, and a Snoo (a high-
tech baby bassinet) loop giveaway is more likely to be hosted by
momfluencers; a Pottery Barn Kids loop giveaway is more likely
to be hosted by a certain subset of momfluencers. White walls.
Blonde extensions. Etc.

After working as a momfluencer for a few years, Bethanie knew
she couldn't compete with extravagant loop giveaways, because
she simply didn't have the money. She also made the point that
of course people will always follow "rich people with nice clothes
and nice homes" for aspirational reasons, and she acknowledged
that that type of aspiration was never going to be why people
followed her.[36]

Despite her awareness of her own skill set, Bethanie kept
trying to keep up with what she saw around her on mommy Instagram. Around 2016, she partnered with a photographer friend
from high school who was trying to build up her portfolio. At
the time, she thought it was "the coolest thing" to have access to
professional-grade photos for her blog and Instagram. There was
only one problem: her kids hated it. Which makes perfect sense to
anyone who has ever attempted to take "nice photos" of their kids,
with or without a professional. Bethanie says she also started to sort
of hate it, because "the pictures didn't really reflect my style."[37] So
she stopped, and has been using her iPhone for photos ever since.
This decision seems to have paid off—so much so that when she
and her family were sent to a resort as part of a paid promotional
deal, the PR people from the resort specifically requested she not
use a professional photographer to document her visit, because
they wanted the photos to maintain Bethanie's aesthetic.

And what is Bethanie's aesthetic? It's decidedly not perfect, but it's also not #perfectlyimperfect, one of the more infuriating of momfluencer aesthetics, which features objectively well-lit and well-composed photos of both people and places under the premise that such photos are not orchestrated or staged, that such photos reflect "authentic" moments from real life. I did a quick hashtag search, and a good example features momfluencer Mel (@unconventional_acres) grinning up at her flaxen-haired baby, who's perched on his dad's shoulders. The dad is making a goofy face, which I guess makes the picture "imperfect," but the photo quality is pristine, the family is bathed in the glow of golden hour, and, because someone else presumably took the photo, it's clearly orchestrated to some extent.[38]

Bethanie's aesthetic is not that. Her Instagram profile picture as @thegarciadiaries, where she has 238,000 followers, features her sitting in a dark bra and underwear. Her arms are tattooed, and her bio reads: "Real, raw motherhood."[39] There are photos of her kids in matching jammies, but at least one kid isn't looking at the camera, and everyone is wearing grins unique to that harried *look at the camera and say cheese!* moment most parents are familiar with. There's nothing precious about it. When you scroll through her feed, you see earth tones, rich umbers, and moody ink blues. Not a lot of marble, not a lot of white.

Bethanie thinks the perfect mom/perfect home aesthetic will always exist (especially among momfluencers who are "naturally rich beyond any influencing money they make"), but agrees with Valerie Metz that it's abating as a trend to emulate. "I've always kind of liked a moodier vibe," she told me. "It feels more like home to me to look at a picture that is more, like, brown and orange and yellow. But that was already like my clothing style. And so, I kind of just started emulating that in my photo style as well." You'll find some photos of her kids in curated knit sweaters on her feed, sure, but Bethanie has always been transparent about the fact that such photos (and such kid outfits) are representative of effort. Like most kids, Bethanie says her children "like to wear the ugliest shit ever. Like character stuff and whatever. So, like, I'm not gonna force them. If I'm taking a picture, and I want them to dress nice, I'll bribe them and then they change out of it into their Spiderman onesies. But they're kids!"[40] Yes! One of my kids has a fleece *Frozen*-themed pajama onesie situation I can only describe as truly heinous, and she. loves. it. Because she's a kid and thankfully is not yet burdened with adopting an aesthetic to conform to some external force's idea of "good taste."

When Bethanie recently moved into a new house, she received a lot of commentary about her lack of perfect mom interior design prowess coupled with class-based assumptions about her income:

> People were like, *Your cabinets are brown; they're so ugly, like, blah blah blah, are you going to paint them, blah, blah.* And I'm like, *Well, we're renting so we're not going to paint our cabinets.* And people were like, *You're renting? Why can't you buy a house?* Well, because even though I make good money, we have shitty credit because when we were seventeen, eighteen years old we had no financial advice. We got credit cards, we got a car we couldn't afford, because we needed a car to bring our baby home from the hospital. And so we're in not such a good situation financially, even though we make good money now. And people are like, *What?!* and I'm like, *Well, just because I have followers on Instagram doesn't mean we can afford a home, right?*[41]

Bethanie received "hundreds" of messages from people thanking her for being transparent about her financial history, and for having the audacity to not really care about home decor as much as mothers are taught they should. She told me a story about purchasing an island with a brown countertop from IKEA. She "loved it," but was barraged with DMs from people chastising her for choosing a countertop that "doesn't even match" her cabinets. She told them what she told me: "I don't care. That's not important to me." And for every one of those DMs presuming interior design authority over a stranger, Bethanie also gets DMs from people thanking her for simply "showing your home lived-in and not, like, perfectly decorated like a Pinterest house. We live in a three-bedroom, twelve-hundred-square-foot house. We're not living in a mansion. And it's just a house. And it's messy because I have five kids! Let's be real."[42] The assumption inherent in DMs complaining about her countertops not matching her cabinets is one tightly tied to both class and gender, and another example of who gets to have "good taste" (i.e., people with access to wealth, as well as to class, race, and gender privileges).

Stephanie Land wrote the 2016 memoir *Maid*, a memoir about poverty, parenthood, and the author's experience cleaning wealthy people's homes, and Land wrote about the classist elements of minimalism for the *New York Times*. She explains how, when she and her daughter moved to a four-hundred-square foot studio apartment out of necessity, she was forced to get rid of a lot of "stuff." But this "stuff" wasn't "stuff" to her; these items held significant emotional value, things like "a painting I'd done as a child that my mom had carefully framed and hung in our house, a set of antique Raggedy Ann and Andy dolls my ferret once chewed an eye out of when I was 15, artwork my mom had collected over the decade we lived in Alaska. Things I grew up with that brought me back to a time of living a carefree life."[43] Land points out that, for some, the urge to declutter and rid their spaces of stuff is a privileged choice, and, for others, the necessity of giving up one's belongings can be a painful reminder of one's very *lack* of choice.

Land's essay illuminates how fraught the idea of "choice" is when we talk about maternal domestic aesthetics. There are so many sneaky value judgments implicit in the choices we make (and who gets to make those choices). We are good mothers if we create a dedicated space for our children to paint, to construct Lego castles, to dance freely with organic silk scarves. But what about the mothers who don't have extra space in their homes to devote to child-centric activities? What about the moms who can't afford organic silk scarves? Are they less good as mothers if their kids' Legos spill into the kitchen, if their kids' bodies cannot move quite so freely due to a dearth of space? Obviously the answer is no, but the visual presentation of motherhood as exemplified by how moms adorn their spaces, in the choices they make regarding those spaces, would have us believe otherwise.

Aesthetics encourage us to make moral assumptions. Imagine a scene. We're in a Shaker-style kitchen. The cabinets are painted in some creamy shade of Farrow and Ball white (let's get specific and go with Dorset Cream!), the teakettle is made of brass and has an elegant goose-neck spout, and a vintage Persian runner lies in front of the farmhouse sink. Who do you see in that kitchen? What are they doing? Obviously, we're all free to see different things. But I see a woman. I see a mother. She is conventionally attractive, and her abundant hair is loosely tied up atop her head in a bun. Tendrils fall in a pretty way that I've *never* been able to achieve. Maybe she's holding an eight-month-old. Maybe a toddler with golden curls plays at her feet. Her countertops are clean. She is happy. She is calm. She is a good mom.

Why is she a good mom?

This imagined scene is a static image. It's not a video. There's no audio. We can't hear how the good mom is speaking to her kids, we can't even know what she's feeding them for dinner. But she's a good mom because her space is clean, uncluttered, and aesthetically pleasing. Why is her space aesthetically pleasing? Because many of us have been programmed to equate clutter with moral ineptitude, to equate soft, pale colors with soft, subdued femininity. Brightness can be loud, jarring; brightness can make us feel uncomfortable. Mothers should not be loud, jarring, or unconcerned with the comfort of others.

The concept of good motherhood is so impossible to quantify that many of us have become accustomed to searching for signposts or clues to determine whether it exists or not, even if those clues have absolutely nothing whatsoever to do with the blood-and-guts labor of mothering. I guess what I'm saying is that aesthetic rightness is wholly wrapped up in the deified noun: Mother. The mess of life—the graham cracker crumbs that creep into every crevice, the chipped olive-green paint chosen by a prior owner, the plastic (BPA-free? Who's to say?) *CoComelon* bus that makes your kid cry because it's missing JJ—these are the things, the images, the stuff, that make up Mothering as a verb. Will you fixate on cleaning up the graham cracker crumbs, or will you take a minute to hold a heartbroken kid, to whom the missing JJ is everything? Will you spend extra money painting over the green chipped paint, or will you spend that same money getting a meal with friend to fill up your proverbial cup (to be a better mom, sure, but mostly to be a whole person)? This is not to say one choice is better than the other, or to downgrade the importance of living in a space that feels good to you, but neatness, clutter-freedom, and adhering to a specific aesthetic style has nothing to do with mothering.

Before we move on, let me quickly describe my kitchen. It's Shaker style. The cabinets are painted in Farrow and Ball Strong White (I tested at least eight other whites before landing on Strong White and ended up feeling good about Strong White not least in part because interior designer/influencer Emily Henderson chose Strong White for one of her homes' kitchens). The knobs and handles are unlacquered brass, which means they start out shiny brass and end up patinaed in a way that looks pretty to me. I had the privilege to make all these choices about my kitchen because my husband's job affords us the income to waffle about paint swatches. My own job does not. We were able to buy our house because my parents helped us financially. Both my husband and I have access to generational wealth. My race and class have everything to do with why I think my kitchen is pretty and why I made the choices I did about how to decorate it.

As I write this, in the kitchen, one of those playmat things for kids to drive cars on spoils the visual serenity with its garish shades of Home Depot orange and royal blue; I will likely trip on any number of Hot Wheels vehicles when I get up to make some peppermint tea. The jam jar from breakfast is still out and the cap is missing. Dirty clothes hastily removed by a kid are strewn on the pale wood island. There are two hairbrushes there, too. Crumbs and stickiness abound. Clutter is everywhere because I am miserable if I spend all my time and energy trying to maintain domestic perfection. I know this because I've tried! Many times! Because the desire to achieve an aesthetic domestic ideal is as deeply ingrained in me as anything else that pertains to my motherhood. But I'm a cranky, depressed person when I devote myself to clutter. My husband is the opposite—he's cranky and unsettled until he clears away clutter. I'm not a better parent because I can live with clutter and Brett isn't a less involved parent because he can't! But for *me*, I'm a better mom (and by "better" I mean I am more patient, more relaxed, more able to feign interest in my son telling me a convoluted story about a particular baseball play) when I allow space for the mess of life, when I don't spend every second trying to scrub it out of existence.

None of us should be imprisoned by arbitrary standards, aesthetic or otherwise. And I think, when it comes to motherhood (as opposed to parenthood in general), moms are more likely to define themselves against arbitrary standards than dads. Which sucks. Determining a mother's supposed goodness via her aesthetic choice is particularly ridiculous because the choices we make (or can't make) are so bogged down by external influences and factors, often outside of our control. I like how my (Strong) white kitchen looks and the liking of it brings me joy. But this joy has nothing to do with my mothering.

Valerie, Stacey, and Bethanie all offer antidotes to the all-white-everything aesthetic we collectively associate with momfluencer culture, and we know the general rise of minimalism—as an aesthetic and a practice—is part of why the all-white-everything moms grew to such prevalence. But, according to Kathryn Jezer-Morton, who is writing her doctoral dissertation on momfluencer culture (the working title of which is "Affective Expertise Among Momfluencers on Instagram"), there might be a much more prosaic reason behind white's totalitarian grip on the aesthetics of momfluencer culture: branding. Kathryn has been writing and thinking seriously about momfluencer culture before most of us, and has a column all about motherhood and domesticity for *The Cut* called "Brooding," which I can't recommend highly enough.

We Zoomed (and emailed and phoned) several times during the writing of this book, for which I'm so grateful. Kathryn offered this simple explanation for why whites and neutrals continuously cause our eyes to glaze over on mommy Instagram. While researching her dissertation, Kathryn interviewed someone who works at a Canadian agency called Momfluence that specializes in connecting brands with influencers and vice versa. When Kathryn asked the agency woman if the cult of neutrals would ever die, she said, *"Well, I mean, you know, it makes a lot of sense. Because it's easy for the brands to stand out. Like, it creates a neutral backdrop, in front of which you can do your sponsored content. And I was like, Really? Like, That's why? And she was like, Yeah, like, you can't have a busy aesthetic. It doesn't look right. And the brands don't like that."*[44]

I mean, neutrals as a neutral backdrop *do* make a lot of logical sense in this context. Think of a jar of raspberry jam (not that a ton of momfluencers are selling raspberry jam, but whatever). Think of the deep pop of magenta against an all-white kitchen versus that same pop of magenta against a *countertop that doesn't match the kitchen cabinets*. The resulting image becomes less focused, the eye more easily distracted, the consumer less likely to buy. Muted perfection as a background against which to sell products allows the consumer to just see the product, and, hopefully—free from the troubling confusion of mismatched countertops and cabinet—purchase the product. What the brands want, I suppose they get.

Kathryn and I discussed the most famous of all the neutral-shunning momfluencers, Naomi Davis, but agreed that pulling off Davis's bold, bright aesthetic depends on a lot more variables falling into place. Not everyone can make an entire room swathed in vine-green paint work, ya know? White is a lot harder to screw up. As Kathryn pointed out, taking risks with aesthetics also "takes more work." She added, "And it has to be more beautiful and more expensive. Otherwise, it looks garish. So, like, Taza is fucking rich, and, like, everything she has is super nice. So she can have crazy colors in her home. And it looks opulent. Whereas if I did, it would look like I was just a chaotic person."[45] Same.

While the revelation that marketplace function and practicality are at least partially responsible for creating the all-white-everything aesthetic trend, I asked Kathryn how much the all-white appearance of "having good taste," and communicating one's possession of good taste (which is tacitly connected to good motherhood) through Instagram, has to do with so many people seemingly conforming to the all-white mandate. "I think there's a feedback loop, for sure," she said. "Because now it's like, *Well, I want a house that looks like I'm a tasteful woman.* And 'tasteful woman' equals minimalism. Or whatever."[46]

When I had my first kid, back in 2012, I was not able to buy him a "tasteful" pacifier because it did not exist. Or a baby-saucer activity center thing in any shade other than Hideous Neon. I didn't know that Simply White by Benjamin Moore was a cooler (in tone) white than White Dove by Benjamin Moore, nor that Super White by Benjamin Moore was cooler still. But my third kid (he was born in 2019) gets his diaper changed on a changing pad cover that could be framed and hung on the wall. And, as my summation of my (Strong) white kitchen indicates, I know a lot about white paint. It's sometimes shocking to consider how much the expectations of mothers' aesthetics have changed in only a decade. Kathryn pointed out that so many of these expectations have woven themselves into popular mom culture with scarcely anyone even noticing. She cited Holiday Card Culture as an example of a clear biproduct of momfluencer culture, with its historically unprecedented emphasis on the "visuals of family." She said, "There's the expectation that you're going to have an image that's beautiful and shareable and, and, like, people do shoots for these things. I know, like, regular people that don't even *do* Instagram, but I will receive a card from them. And, like, it's professional. And they did it in October, you know?" Kathryn thinks we need to pay attention to these relatively new cultural norms (professionally photographed holiday cards!) and ask ourselves whether we want to participate. "I'm like, *Guys*, like, *this is all new, it's new, new, new, new. It's not old.* And we need to just acknowledge that people weren't being subjected to these expectations until quite recently. Now, we just take them for granted."[47] YES. Also, I'm writing this on December 9, and I have not created or ordered holiday cards and feel obligated to do so even though I know me feeling twinges of guilty obligation *is bullshit.* Such is the power of aesthetic expectations.

Laura Norkin, an editor at InStyle.com, has witnessed the many sea changes in momfluencer culture firsthand. These changes have impacted not only her experience as a woman and a mother but also her career. She thinks millennialism (and the millennialist aesthetic) are huge factors in how many momfluencer aesthetics were born. In 2014, Laura was an editor at *Refinery29*, which at the time was explicitly devoted to reflecting and exploring the experience of millennial women. She was one of the first people at *Refinery29* to broach the subject of motherhood as an editorial concern, and she told me all about it over the phone.

She remembers that at the time, motherhood content was seen as sort of niche, as sort of only meant for publications and websites solely devoted to parenting (like *Parents*, *ScaryMommy*, or "mommy blogs"). So often, Laura pointed out, motherhood coverage in the early 2010s "wasn't about the mom. It was about the babies. And I think so much now is about the mom." And in 2014, she was thinking quite a bit about whether she wanted to become a mother herself, and how that decision might impact her life and career. She was shocked that more women's media sources weren't covering the huge question of motherhood, since it indisputably was something many millennial women were bound to be thinking about. Laura thought women's media outlets like *Refinery29* had to start "acknowledging the elephant in the room that millennial women are aging into motherhood."[48]

She figured that women who consumed mommy blogs were likely already mothers, and she wanted to propel conversations forward for women considering motherhood, women who maybe didn't want to become mothers at all, and/or women who wanted kids but didn't know how kids would fit into their lives. When Laura initiated conversations with senior editors, she was "definitely met with some resistance."

> It was like, *Pregnancy and motherhood isn't cool.* At that time, *Refinery29* really represented the "cool girl," and we were experiencing, like, just enormous growth in every direction. Video was huge. Social was huge. Our newsletter was huge, like, everything was winning. And they [the senior editors] were kind of like, *Do we need to be competing in the mommy space?* And it also became kind of personal. The editor in chief was like, *Well, why do you want to talk to me about this? Are you interested in getting pregnant and having kids?* It was this weird moment where I felt like I had to decide like, *Am I a cool girl or am I going to be a mom?*[49]

Laura dodged the question, saying something about just thinking that essays and articles about motherhood might perform well as content: "It just was not seen as, like, a cool-girl thing to do. And the brand was cool girl."[50] The distinction Laura made between "being cool" and "being a mom" doesn't exist anymore—or, at least, not as an either/or binary. This is at least in part because of momfluencer culture, which has made motherhood, and all its attendant accessories, a legitimately cool endeavor. If you buy the right stuff. And look the right way.

Laura told me the workplace at *Refinery29* was very inclusive, and many different types of people could, "quote unquote, fit in, but 'mom' was not one of those types." She noted that the brand was invested in pushing progressive conversations forward, but the "motherhood conversation hadn't occurred to anyone as a progressive issue in any way at that time."[51] Again, I can't underscore enough how much has changed in such a short span of time. I've cobbled together an entire career prioritizing the progressive issue of feminist motherhood (as have many, many others), but in 2014, *Refinery29* deemed motherhood, the entire realm of motherhood, which encompasses race, class, socioeconomics, politics, technology, and so much more, as "niche."

So how did the cool mom aesthetic come to be? And what is it exactly? Laura remembers people like Jessica Alba, Kristen Bell, and Mila Kunis representing a certain class of celebrity mom, which was definitely aspirational, but not necessarily "cool." She said, "These celebrities were more 'cute mom,' and then the fashion girl moment and the mommy blogger moment kind of fused and became one thing. It was like this inflection point when blogger culture and fashion culture kind of merged creating this zombie superhuman, whose influencing power could not be contained."[52]

Laura cited fashion editor (and now social media exec) Eva Chen as a primary example of a fashion person who made motherhood seem like an identity that could be adapted to an already cool lifestyle, rather than something that eradicated that cool lifestyle. She remembers viewing Chen's pregnancy as "different and interesting," and as something of a curiosity. "Like, what is she going to wear while she's pregnant? What clothes are available to her? There was a kind of entrepreneurial spirit among the cool girls who were getting pregnant. Like, *Guess what, guys? I'm cool and I'm pregnant. Therefore, pregnancy is cool.*" It's important to remember that this was before baby carriers could be just as representative of your personal style as handbags, and when millennial cool girls started getting pregnant, and didn't simply disappear into the uncool land of minivans and soccer-mom hair, brands took note. In Laura's words: "Like, *Oh, we can target these influencers in this moment when this whole age group of people has basically nothing available to them. We can make baby and maternity stuff that feels as cool and unique and, like, zeitgeisty, as the stuff they had two months ago. Before they were pregnant.*"[53]

I scrolled way back to scope out some vintage Eva Chen pregnancy photos to get a better sense of what Laura meant. *Refinery29* actually covered her first pregnancy announcement, which was made on August 20, 2014, on Instagram, of course. At the time, Chen was famous for posting photos of her feet propped up in the backseat of a car; the photos showcased her always fabulous shoes (and sometimes bags) while also emphasizing Chen's active, metropolitan, aspirational lifestyle. That day, Chen posted a photo of her crossed feet, decked out in chic, black New Balance sneakers. Nestled against her feet were a classic black quilted Chanel purse and a tiny pair of matching baby New Balance sneakers. The caption simply states: "#evachenpose: like mother, like future (winter 2015!) daughter edition."[54] The look of the photo eschews the stale pale pinks and baby blues of "cute" motherhood, and instead stays true to Chen's trademark fashion-forward aesthetic. Gina Marinelli of *Refinery29* said the following of the announcement: "And, if the mini quilted Chanel in her photo is any indication, this kid is well on her way to being the best dressed tot in a town car we've ever seen. Sorry, North West."[55]

Early momfluencers like Eva Chen made expression of one's personal aesthetic through one's children possible in a way it simply hadn't been before, at least on a large scale. For a woman whose Instagram feed had been made notable by her photos posing alongside Jenna Lyons or Anna Wintour prior to having kids (and after), Chen made cool motherhood seem not only possible but also something to aspire to. Given Chen's insight into communicating cool mom vibes through the aesthetics of fashion and social media, it seems fitting that she made the following announcement on July 17, 2015: "👶😀💁🎀🐶👯🍼💃💆✔️🔝🔜💯! Beyond excited to announce that I'll be joining the brilliant team at Instagram as head of fashion partnerships! (Today being #worldemojiday is the best coincidence, yes! 😆)."[56]

While Eva Chen and plenty of other cool-girl moms certainly didn't throw away their careers once having children, Laura thinks the *aesthetic* of the cool mom allowed for a new generation of mothers to view motherhood as not simply an addendum to their lives, but as something that could be "a day-filling endeavor." The repackaging of motherhood as something one could devote oneself fully to—and still remain connected to one's creativity and coolness—has everything to do with aesthetics. Instagram momfluencers were the first to showcase the latte-colored pacifiers or diaper bags that complemented rather than ruined outfits. They also showed how the consumption of such products, and subsequent chronicling of how those products enhanced one's aesthetic lifestyle, could be a full-time pursuit. "It's just like, now one hundred percent of my time could be spent wearing ochre-colored Nap Dresses that coordinate with my child's onesie and feeding her out of this bamboo, organically sourced little bowl on our patio or whatever. It's not just that motherhood became cool and worthwhile, but the fact that it could be your *everything* is a big part of the story."[57]

"Cool," of course, is a nebulous concept and entirely subjective. For me, right now, at forty, moms with an irreverent sense of style feel cool, moms that somehow look good even if they're wearing a nightgown, carpenter jeans they designed themselves, classic L.L.Bean boots, and a bobbly knit sweater (yes, I'm talking about @rudyjude *again*). Moms that screw up and make messes and, in lieu of cleaning up the mess, make something (and, in doing so, make themselves happy) instead. The apparent lack of effort coupled with otherworldly confidence is what "mom cool" is for me. To look good and feel good while also not giving a fuck what other people think. The dream!

Speaking of those bobbly knit sweaters (yes, I'm talking about Misha and Puff), I was able to interview Anna Wallack, founder and creative director of Misha and Puff, about why she thinks the aesthetic of Misha and Puff (saturated colorways, bold shapes, distinctive textures) is so attractive to moms in particular.

Over the phone, Anna told me that once she had her first baby, she noticed the singular phenomenon of the "disappearing woman." After becoming moms, she said, "some friends just made the decision that they would disappear. Everything centered around their kids."[58] Yes, yes, yes. Nearly every time we tack "mom" onto any other word as a prefix, we're speaking to a certain kind of erasure. Before they were cool, "mom jeans" essentially meant jeans that erased one's sexuality. We avoid "mom hair" (which means we basically don't want boring, generic hair), and we know exactly what someone means when they say, "She looks like a typical mom." Nothing interesting, nothing that stands out, nothing that expresses individuality or a personal sense of style. A body that exists to serve others. A person who exists as a benign background to her children's central subjectivity.

Anna says motherhood made her explicitly want to define her personal style as something wholly her own, something that had nothing to do with her status as a mom. "The focus is not me anymore," she said, "but I *want* it to be me still because I still feel like a relevant person with a body in society, you know? That has really empowered me to push my personal style. . . . Our versions of ourselves are still valid."[59]

I kept interrupting Anna during this portion of the interview with loud moans of agreement or by bleating phrases like "That's so profound" because *it is*. It's reductive to oversimplify our desire to pursue personal style as small-minded or just more proof that we're pawns of capitalism; personal style is also one way we can reject erasure. In this way, aesthetics can be radical. Especially for moms. "I need to have my boundaries of myself be also defined in my body," Anna told me. "As much as I, you know, loved all the time spent at home with my babies, I remember thinking, like, *I am not going to be blurred forever between my kids and my actual autonomous self*."[60] Anna's designs defy being blurred! Her clothes are unapologetic, sometimes loud, often fun. It would be impossible to see someone wearing, for example, Misha and Puff's Retrospective Crochet Jacket (in Peacock) and make the assumption that the wearer was "just a typical mom." Cut in a blousy, boxy fit, the jacket has a '70s vibe, and is made up of nubby crocheted stripes of peacock green, oxblood, and marigold, all trimmed with sky blue. You might love it. You might hate it. But you'll notice it.

Laura Norkin knew she needed to find the "cool way into" conversations about motherhood once her motherhood vertical was eventually greenlighted at *Refinery29*. She commissioned and edited pieces a lot like Anna's clothes: bold, quirky, designed to be noticed. Pieces about Frankie Shaw's Showtime show about single motherhood, *SMILF*; pieces about how pregnancy could be sexy; pieces about how Lena Dunham's character chose to have a baby (versus an abortion) in the HBO show *Girls*. "I do remember this almost iconic moment of her in overalls pregnant and, like, happy," she said. "It felt like counterculture."[61]

Ultimately, Laura thinks it's impossible to consider the current aesthetic trends of momfluencer culture without considering how millennialism has shaped our understandings of consumerism, aesthetics, and selfhood.

> I really do think the inflection point was just millennials aging into motherhood, and millennials had already connected so much of our generational identity around coolness and a certain aesthetic, or the *pursuit* of the aesthetic period. Like the whole concept of, like, millennial pink and everything. This is what it is to be a millennial. You consume things and show them off to show who you are. And that's what makes you cool. And so then, when that generation became old enough to want to have kids and then to start having kids, it was just, *Well, what does that look like for us?*[62]

The pursuit of an aesthetic feels so critical to understanding momfluencer culture from a visual performance angle, and it resonates on a personal level for me, the mom who constantly falls victim to the misguided desire for products as a shortcut to maternal satisfaction. Both the cool mom aesthetic and the pared-down minimalist mom aesthetic appeal to my desire for a certain level of peace, both internally and externally, and the pursuits of such aesthetics are continuously confounding because of the innately unpeaceful experience of parenthood. Children are messy. And loud. And disruptive. No amount of white paint or photos of cool baby sneakers can erase that truth.

And the truth of mothering, and all the bodily fluids it entails, is what the "unfiltered" mom aesthetic seeks to uncover. Think photos of engorged breasts, runny noses, or surrealist images of a mom's back scrawled with marker courtesy of their kid. Karni Arieli started the Eye Mama Project during the first days of pandemic lockdown, with the intention of viewing motherhood through the eyes of mothers themselves, not a filtered patriarchal gaze. The result is an Instagram account bursting with images of quotidian life made magical by the skill and attention of artist mothers. One contribution from Amy Woodward features a photo of a baby reaching for their mother's breast; the nipple is spurting milk water-gun-style in a way immediately familiar to anyone who has breastfed. The spurts of milk feel playful, powerful, beautiful, in a way that has nothing to do with aspiration and everything to do with inclusion. It's a photo that draws the viewer into an intensely personal, specific experience of motherhood. It's a photo of a tiny moment usually swallowed up in the action of the day but slowed down in film to render the small labors of motherhood awesome.

Karni and I Zoomed about British pub culture, structural support for caregiving, and, of course, the aesthetics of truth inherent in the Eye Mama Project. She explained that in the UK, one is less likely to encounter the pretty Nap-Dress-wearing mama and more likely to find beer-drinking mums who glory in profanity and bright colors. "They drink a bit more beer," she said. "Nobody's really high-end in the UK unless you're, like, a princess. Everyone's a little more scruffy. We're quite down and dirty, you know, so you compare it to the US aesthetic of, like, detoxing green juice."[63] Karni's invocation of "princesses" seems particularly apt when we consider the aesthetic of the domestic-goddess mom, who, if nothing else, looks like a pretty princess in a pretty castle. And obviously I adore the fact that "green juice" popped into Karni's mind when imagining a typical US momfluencer. I mean, truly.

While I'd take a beer-swilling pub mumfluencer over a perfect all-white-everything momfluencer any day of the week, Karni points out that, despite the aesthetic differences, both archetypes are still, after all, types. They are imagistic ideals of motherhood that flatten the lived experiences of most moms into neat, tidy squares, as addictive and easy to gobble up as potato chips. She's quick to acknowledge that it's impossible to talk about motherhood aesthetics without falling into generalizations, but she does think some momfluencer consumption feels like the consumption of junk food or gossip mags: enjoyable, delicious, but not necessarily provoking any particularly meaningful sensations. Which is fine!

Karni started the Eye Mama Project because she was fatigued with flattened visuals, particular during the "crazy, intense period" of quarantine. They made her feel "kind of bad about mothering and motherhood." Karni said viewing her life through a distinctly artistic lens made her feel "empowered," and like she wasn't "lost and the end of the world was coming." Once Karni started documenting her own motherhood the way an artist might approach a subject, it became a "crutch" to get her through lockdown. "So suddenly you get this really professional gaze at motherhood that isn't produced, that isn't fake. . . . It's just you, right? So it's this kind of pure gaze that the more real it got, the more fantastical it was."[64]

"Fantastical" is an apt word for an Eye Mama Project contribution by Claire Dam, which features four seemingly disembodied arms pressing against a white shower curtain.[65] The image is haunting even though the reality is likely pretty humdrum—two kids showering (and maybe squabbling or wasting shampoo) as viewed from their mother's perspective. There's another image contributed by Mairéad Heffron that shows a low-lit kitchen (there are unattractive plugs, toys on the floor, evidence of life-based clutter) through which what appears to be a maternal ghost and her ghost baby flit.[66] I asked Karni how such an image is technically achieved, and she told me that it's with a tripod and long exposure. The image somehow captures the sometimes out-of-body experience of motherhood, when one's needs and corporeal reality seem to fade in the face of ceaseless doing. Karni mentioned Maisie

Cousins's work as a good example of the Eye Mama Project's aesthetic: "She takes all the dirt of motherhood and zooms in on it and then we'll just have, like, a filthy egg cup with spilling yolk, but it looks like a masterpiece."[67]

In addition to the Eye Mama Project, other momfluencers leaning into an aesthetic of maternal truth include Pia Bramley (@piabramley), whose line drawings of domestic, mom-centric scenes are rife with humor, grit, and humanity; Bri McDaniel (@moonandcheeze), whose lush, moody photos of her family hanging out in wildflower fields will upend any preconceived notions you might have of momfluencer flower field photos; Hanny Bobanny (@hanny_bobanny), whose stark photos of her pregnancy honor the truly unbelievable process of gestation; Estelle (@myprettyfam) whose glowing photos of her postpartum experience shone a spotlight on a phase of motherhood that often feels awkward (maybe because mothers have been socially conditioned to feel shame toward their postpartum bodies), and render it sublime; and so many more.

Karni believes artistically rendered images that zoom in on the raw truths of motherhood feel so transformative and radical because they are images of motherhood taken from the female gaze, the maternal gaze, rather than the male gaze, the gaze through which she believes many momfluencers operate. "It's the male gaze which makes us want to be cute and white and sexy," she said. "That's the male gaze. And handling everything, being OK with everything. That is not the female gaze. You got it wrong."[68]

Karni also thinks the other element present in all the Eye Mama Project images is the admittance of failure, pain, or labor. Every photo, in its own way, shows a version of motherhood that feels true because it allows for complexity and nuance. Photos of mothers cradling their newborns communicate the timeless beauty of maternal love, but they don't allow the viewer to ignore what always exists alongside that love. Maybe it's a Super Heavy menstrual pad worn inside disposable postpartum underwear. Maybe it's a C-section scar. Maybe it's the undereye circles, the exhaustion etched in every line of the face. And making the struggle of motherhood visible, making the struggle the point, is what, in Karni's view, makes these images beautiful.

I think looking at pain and failure is beautiful. Yeah, like, that's the trick. Looking at beauty is not beautiful and powerful. Looking at pain, and heartache and overcoming struggles, that's the real beauty, that's the real power. And it's a really complex, interesting, in-depth, meaningful journey that you have to go through to realize that. You have to kind of have been a mom and been through pain and through failures to really recognize that beauty, actually. You know, the enlightenment of realizing that, *Oh, lighthearted stuff is not the really incredible, beautiful stuff.* That's just, like, the icing, you know? What about the real stuff?[69]

And the aesthetic of truth, as communicated through @eye mamaproject and others, is part of a larger movement toward nuanced, unflinchingly honest narratives about motherhood. As Karni told me, it can be freeing to realize that "beauty doesn't have to be motherhood. It could be an adventure. It could be dirty, sexy, weird. Messed up. Like, so many adjectives." Once you start viewing motherhood as a conduit for aesthetic potential, rather than a straitjacket, meant to make us all conform to patriarchal notions of feminine, maternal beauty and grace, Karni said, "There's actually no way back. I can never ever look at superficial stuff again. Because I've seen the light."[70]

6 | Good (White) Moms

On June 23, 2021, @roseuncharted posted a giveaway on Instagram. To be eligible, one simply had to follow Rose Henges and another momfluencer (who was contributing a photo session to the giveaway), and you'd be eligible to win a "postpartum recovery tonic," a "mood support golden hour tincture," "wild child body oil (safe for both mom and babe)," a Haaka breast pump, and more. The photo features two braided baskets full of goodies that I, for one, would love to receive as a pregnant person. I used the Haaka with my third kid, and it's great for collecting milk from engorged breasts more gently than a traditional pump. Anything that evokes golden hour sounds delicious, and, hey, I love an oil.[1]

Not only does Rose have a lovely aesthetic very much in keeping with popular momfluencer vibes (ochre, petal, ecru) and a knack for creating pretty, botanically themed infographics, but she also promotes what seems like a feminist message of protecting one's bodily autonomy during pregnancy and childbirth. On May 21, 2021, she posted a photo of herself along with her thoughts about seeking an empowered birth. Wearing a soft-looking, rust-colored dress, she's seated in a relaxed pose against a backdrop of a white sheet and dried flowers. Her dark-blonde hair flows in waves down to her waist. Extreme maternal goddess vibes. In the caption, she explains her reasoning for choosing home births and avoiding unnecessary medical intervention, and includes the following quote, which she attributes to *Midwifery Today*: "Although the popularly desired outcome is 'healthy mother, healthy baby,' I think there is room in that equation for 'happy, non-traumatized, empowered and elated mother and baby.'"[2]

Most of us are familiar with the abysmal state of maternal healthcare in this country, particularly for Black mothers, Indigenous mothers, and people from other marginalized communities.[3] Moms whose lives are impacted by income inequality are at a higher risk for preterm labor and mental health complications, and they often struggle to access quality maternal healthcare due to geographic hurdles.[4] Black mothers are three times more likely to die during pregnancy or childbirth than their white counterparts, and Indigenous mothers are twice as likely to die as a result of pregnancy or childbirth than white mothers.[5] Moms in larger bodies are often told to lose weight before given access to fertility treatments.[6] And many moms, regardless of economic status or race, experience gaslighting, patronizing, and dehumanizing treatment in the context of pregnancy and childbirth, so it's always nice to see someone advocating for something better than the bare minimum of a "healthy mother" and "healthy baby."

In addition to posting about her children's clothing (in shades of flax, mustard, and terracotta) and promoting her new online wellness shop, Sunfolk, which sells beautiful hand-dyed tea towels, moisturizing creams bottled in old-school apothecary jars, and plenty of teas, Rose also shares her "truth-seeking" journey, which veers a little off-path from organic cotton baby swaddles and inspiring messages about advocating for your own maternal health.

On October 15, 2020, she posted a well-lit picture of a postcard being held aloft in front of a macrame wall hanging. The postcard advertised a "call to worship" in Kansas City, Missouri, led by Sean Feucht. In her caption, Rose includes the following quote, which she attributes to Feucht: "Let me be very clear, our fists are not held up in defiance; our hands are lifted in praise. Our voices are not raised in shouts of hatred, but our songs of hope and prayers for revival are piercing the darkness around us. God is not finished with America yet."[7]

Who is Sean Feucht, and why does it matter if Rose the momfluencer is inviting her followers to join her at a Feucht function? Sean Feucht has 293,000 followers on Instagram, and his profile photo shows a white man with long blond curls wearing a black T-shirt with a cross on it playing a guitar and singing into a microphone on a stage. He looks kinda like a guy from a '90s hair band. In a *Politico* profile on Feucht in 2020, Julia Duin referred to him as "a Trump-aligned guitarist and failed congressional candidate" as well as "a millennial face of the religious right in the Covid era." According to Duin's reporting, Feucht lives in California, where he is an active member of the Christian megachurch Bethel Church. He has recorded an album called *Wild* and written a book called *Brazen*, with a foreword by Mike Huckabee.[8]

According to Duin's piece, in the spring of 2020, Feucht started "a series of concerts he called 'Riots to Revival'" in response to COVID-19 restrictions. In June 2020, he held one of these concerts in Minneapolis, fifty feet from the site of George Floyd's murder. Duin notes that, "while Feucht has said, 'Yes, Black lives matter,' he also has called the BLM movement a 'fraud' and criticized it on Facebook for being pro-abortion rights and for supporting what he called 'radical gender theory and the complete denuclearization of family.'"[9]

In August 2021, Alejandra Molina wrote a piece about Sean Feucht for Religion News Service that outlined a growing concern from organizations that monitor hate groups about Feucht and his followers. Molina quotes an August 8, 2021, tweet from Feucht that featured a photo of Feucht and his security team and reads: "'If you mess with them or our 1st amendment right to worship God—you'll meet Jesus one way or another.'" Molina notes that Feucht's security team includes members of the white nationalist group the Proud Boys, both ex-military and ex-police officers, and a man charged in connection to the January 2021 Capitol insurrection. One of Feucht's gatherings in Portland, Oregon, that year "resulted in clashes between left- and right-wing groups."[10]

It's not just that @roseuncharted is a proponent of Sean Feucht, who, if not the most explicitly insidious flavor of white nationalist, certainly seems to run in dubious circles. It's also that many of her posts indicate involvement with QAnon, one of the more slippery conspiracy theories of our time, often aligned with white nationalism and the alt-right. Rose has posted various photos and captions that serve as dog whistles for QAnon, hashtagging #savethechildren and #WWG1WGA. (The hashtag stands for "Where we go one, we go all" and references QAnon supporters' belief that Donald Trump is the only one who can save us from the clutches of the "deep state.")

QAnon, which emerged in 2017 as a conspiracy theory about a group of shadowy elites bent on pedophilia and Satanism, and, like, blood-sucking hijinks, co-opted the hashtag #savethe children as a recruitment tool. While QAnon started in the relative social media underground of 8chan, leaders deliberately sought to proliferate their messages on more mainstream platforms like Instagram and Facebook by distorting concerns about human trafficking as a way to gain soft power. "The idea, in a nutshell," writes Kevin Roose in a piece for the *New York Times*, "is to create a groundswell of concern by flooding social media with posts about human trafficking, joining parenting Facebook groups and glomming on to hashtag campaigns like #SaveTheChildren, which began as a legitimate fund-raising campaign for the Save the Children charity.[11] Then followers can shift the conversation to baseless theories about who they believe is doing the trafficking: a cabal of nefarious elites that includes Tom Hanks, Oprah Winfrey and Pope Francis."

While QAnon has long been associated with anti-Semitism, Mia Bloom, while researching her book *Pastels and Pedophiles: Inside the Mind of QAnon*, found that racism is also integral to the group's messaging. Out of 240 QAnon images paired with #savethe children messages on social media, Bloom and her research team discovered that despite the fact that "the vast majority of children who are trafficked originate from the global south . . . the images of the children in the QAnon campaigns were almost uniformly white, usually female, and often badly bruised, bound, or bleeding." The reasoning, according to Bloom, is that images of white children would appeal to white moms in a way that images of children of color would not. QAnon often circulated images of a child being grabbed from behind, an adult hand placed over the child's mouth, and while the child in these images was white the vast majority of the time, the adult hand was Black or brown 90 percent of the time, leaning into age-old racist stereotypes vilifying Black and brown men as inherently violent and predatory.[12]

Keep scrolling past Rose's photos of wildflower fields, crystals, and beaches, and you'll find a millennial-pink infographic that identifies mask-wearing as a "path paved to fascism and hell on earth."[13] Rose doesn't just believe in the benefits of bioenergetic essential oils; she additionally believes that the most important tool a mother can use to protect her family is a gun, and that Donald Trump ran for president because he "was tired of seeing how certain races/countries were being constantly abused."[14] When I first started researching Rose, @roseuncharted had 120,000 followers. As of this writing, she has 193,000.

In a post on July 8, 2020, featuring Rose wearing a blush-colored tie-dyed "truth seeker" T-shirt stylishly knotted around her waist, Rose received these two comments, which beautifully elucidate why momfluencer content that blends aspirational wellness trends and aesthetics with incendiary disinformation can be so quietly dangerous. From @quiver.full.of.arrows777: "Hi Rose I was just wanting to let you know that I direct messeged [sic] you. I had a question about the Qanon stuff and was hoping you could help me understand something. I really, really would love to chat with you. Please 🙏😊 God bless." Directly under this comment, @kirsten_watson_wrote "@roseuncharted do you mind me asking the brand of organic mattresses topper you got for your kids was?

I remember it in your stories but never wrote it down. Could you pass along the info please! 😊"[15]

Rose is not a snarling, oafish white man screaming incoherently about "white rights" or about Hillary Clinton running a child-sex-trafficking operation. Such a figure would be a hard sell to moms eager to raise their kids free from toxic mattress toppers. Rose presents a calm, sane impression of simply "asking questions," and, most significantly, she presents herself as a loving mom, a good mom. A pretty mom. A white mom. And in this culture (and many other Western cultures), we've been taught to trust a good (white) mom, to never question her authority if it stems directly from her (good [white]) motherhood. If we trust her to recommend safe mattress toppers, maybe we should open our minds to trust her about other things as well? Like "QAnon stuff."

Social media, and the various algorithms impacting how we all want to look and how we all think, have made it easier and easier for "nice white moms" like Rose to embrace and spread disinformation and conspiracy theories. In her book *Sisters in Hate: American Women on the Front Lines of White Nationalism*, Seyward Darby shows how one mom, Ayla Stewart, used social media to document her transformation from a progressive, hippie mom to a powerful female voice in the white nationalist movement, noting how social media enabled Ayla to not only consume messages about white hate but also to repackage those messages for her followers: "Algorithms recommending what to watch or read next, feedback loops reinforcing certain viewpoints, talking heads making specious connections, memes reducing complex ideas to logical fallacies."[16]

In the early weeks of researching the subject of this chapter, the algorithms at large seemed to notice a shift in my usual internet amblings and started offering me targeted ads to accommodate my new interests. One such ad featured a thin white woman with beachy blonde waves wearing a T-shirt that reads: "5 Things You Should Know About My Husband: 1. He is a freaking awesome husband. 2. He loves me to the moon and back. 3. He's also a

GRUMPY MAN. 4. He has anger issues and a serious dislike for stupid people. 5. Mess with me and he'll make your death look like an accident."[17] While the ad is not an ad for white supremacy per se, it's not *not* an ad for toxic masculinity, a long-held bastion of white supremacy.

In addition to QAnon momfluencers taking up space in what momfluencer expert Kathryn Jezer-Morton calls the "mamasphere," there are also #bossbabe momfluencers, wellness mamas, and trad moms, whose accounts celebrate and romanticize a return to traditional gender roles.[18] Sometimes these momfluencers assume characteristics from all four groups, and sometimes they overlap with only one or two circles of this particular Venn diagram.[19] The single characteristic that seems to align all of them, however, is whiteness.

The significance of the relationship between whiteness and culturally constructed ideals of motherhood cannot be overstated. There are countless books and articles about how the idealization of white mothers has harmed mothers with intersectional identities (as well as their children), and this chapter is in no way a conclusive summation of this particular troubled history, or current reality. I've included a recommended reading list at the back of the book (which is also not conclusive) for more comprehensive coverage. This is all to say that whiteness and motherhood have been strange bedfellows for centuries, and this chapter is necessarily limited to a few case studies in hopes of revealing how impossible it is to consider the way we culturally construct motherhood without considering the impact of white privilege and white supremacy.

Like Rose, Rebecca Pfeiffer (known on Instagram as Bec @luv becstyle) seems like a momfluencer type familiar to many. She doesn't have Rose's earth goddess vibes; she looks more like a typical fashion influencer, and, indeed, many of her posts feature her outfit choices paired with #LTK (Like to Know It) links. Momfluencer expert Jo Piazza—who did quite a bit of research on the various apps and platforms that enable momfluencers to monetize their content (check out Jo's "Shoppable Life" *Under the Influence* podcast episode for a much deeper dive)—explained to me in a text, "Like to Know It is an application that allows consumers of your content to easily shop links on your Instagram. Through that you can get paid for products through Rewards Style."[20] Rewards Style was one of the first companies that figured out how to make it easy for influencers to link to shoppable content, and they really revolutionized the way we shop for things via Instagram. I would argue that pairing with a major agency like Rewards Style confers a sense of legitimacy to momfluencers—which might make users more likely to assume other, non-fashion-related content is also legitimate—so it seems relevant to point out in this case.

On December 3, 2021, for example, Bec posted a photo of herself in a white marble bathroom. She is a thin white woman with long beachy waves. (If a drinking game were played while reading this book, the term "beachy waves" would definitely be involved. Just saying.) She's wearing a vintage-looking T-shirt, a black beanie topped with a fuzzy pom-pom, black jeans, black Converse sneakers, and a red flannel shirt tied around her waist. The text alongside the photo is standard momfluencer shopping copy: "This holiday season, I'm committing to far less social gatherings. But I sure luv a cozy night in, getting festive with the kids. 🧨 ♡ Linking these cozy basics that I'm absolutely LUVing and more in my stories & the link in my bio (for anyone still here for this kinda stuff 😊). No seriously? Taking a poll—who's still actually here for this kinda stuff? 🪔 🤳 👇 Follow my shop @luvbec on the @shop.LTK app to shop this post and get my exclusive app only content! #liketkit #LTKHoliday #LTKSeasonal #LTKsale alert."[21] Nothing to see here, right? Just a momfluencer trying to make a few bucks.

Only a couple of weeks prior to posting this run-of-the-mill shoppable content, Bec posted a simple infographic. Across a background of baby blue and powder pink reads the hashtag "#whereareallthechildren" popularized, in particular, by QAnon moms. Bec's post reads as follows:

I created this graphic back in early 2020 and asked y'all to share it. It went viral then, as well as this hashtag I created. Which 1nst@ ended up hiding. And then eventually d3l3ting my 160k f0110wers. Why? They say a purge is possible here again tomorrow. (Follow my backup @luvbeclive just in case.) So maybe I should get quiet and hide. But neh. That's not my style. Instead, I'm bringing it back to where I started. WHY I started. The timing now lends a different perspective for so many, as the masses have awakened since I first shared this. Let's make it go viral again. 😎 Share. Start the conversations. Let the tyr@nts know we will ALWAYS f1ght for truth! Nothing is more important than the children. Not social media. Not followers. Not career opportunities or even our precious reputations! (Gasp!) Let the world know you are not resting until the truth is revealed that answers where they all go . . . wh3r3 are all the ch1ldr3n?! 🖤[22]

Bec's post has all the trademarks of a classic QAnon momflu-encer post. She confirms her own authority by mentioning how her original post "went viral" by virtue of a hashtag she "created." She misspells certain words to get past Instagram's guidelines against posting dangerous misinformation (see her spelling of "deleting," "followers," "fight," and even "tyrants"). She directs her followers to a backup account, something many conspiracy theorist influencers do as an insurance policy in case their main accounts get flagged by Instagram. And, most importantly, Bec draws attention to her motherhood as a moral imperative to be unthinkingly trusted: "Nothing is more important than the children." Who could ever argue with that?

While there are thousands of viral voices spreading QAnon conspiracy theories online, I'm interested in why mothers in particular have become some of their most visible spokespeople. QAnon is an infamously complicated conspiracy theory, the tentacles of which extend into everything from pizza to Wayfair furniture to movie star cannibalism, but, just so we're all on the same (confusing) page, I'll share Anne Helen Petersen's definition in a piece she wrote for *Elle*.

> A common thread among many of the QAnon theories is that there exists a group of "elites"—George Soros, the Clintons, and other enemies of Donald Trump—who are responsible for horrible deeds, and [Trump] is working covertly to stop them. Perhaps the most extreme example . . . is that those elites are kidnapping children and drinking their blood. During COVID, Q has expanded to include false theories about the virus (it isn't real, masks don't work, the vaccine is dangerous and should be avoided at all costs) and George Floyd (a crisis actor). Just to be absolutely clear, there is no evidence that any of these preposterous notions is true.[23]

Petersen points out that QAnon has often been associated with unaesthetically pleasing men who yell a lot. Not exactly momfluencer territory. But, as we've seen with both Rose and Bec, mothers (white mothers in particular) have successfully repackaged Q to appeal to regular moms who also might want to buy a cute beanie with a floofy poof on top. Petersen tracks how conspiracy theorists' co-opting of hashtags took place because of social media platforms' initial crackdowns on misinformation. For example, #SavetheChildren, prior to being taken up by QAnon conspiracists, was once a legitimate hashtag created by a child welfare organization. Petersen writes that the appropriation of new hashtags that initially seem innocuous and altruistic "inadvertently created a new radicalization pipeline around #SavetheChildren, which circulated freely in the aesthetically pleasing, female-dominated corners of the internet, appealing to moms who, amid the upheaval of the pandemic, just wanted something to believe in."[24]

I deeply understand and empathize with this longing to both be a part of something and to believe in something worth being a part of. Again, because of the politically and culturally disempowered role many mothers play in our culture, we are specifically vulnerable to groups and messages that promise a sense of purpose, promise us something that feels bigger than reminding our kids to do their homework or to eat their vegetables. Petersen points out, of course, that white women might look elsewhere for causes to join or work for, but she thinks the reason white women are less likely to participate in the Black Lives Matter movement, or start canvassing for local politicians, or donate their time to Planned Parenthood, is due to a fear of politicism. Referring to Black Lives Matters specifically, Petersen writes: "But many of them disagree with its goals, like defunding the police, or don't think of themselves as 'political,' a word that's often used as a placeholder for 'someone who talks about race.' They're faced with few options: put up 'Blue Lives Matter' or 'All Lives Matter' yard signs, which still doesn't feel like a movement, or remain silent. And that silence, especially for white women used to having their voices heard and respected—used to being included—can feel like suffocation."[25]

There's another reason white momfluencers might be more likely to spread Q conspiracies or preach about "toxin-riddled" vaccines than to align themselves with a conventional social justice or political group, and that has to do with motherhood. The implied moral goodness of (white) motherhood allows them to easily latch onto Q's fear mongering specifically related to harm toward children. After interviewing attendees of a "Freedom for the Children" QAnon-centric rally in London for a *New York Times* article about motherhood and QAnon, Annie Kelly determined that maternal protectiveness was at the root of many white mothers' participation. "Very few brought up QAnon's connections with President Trump, Hillary Clinton or the anonymous 4chan account known as 'Q' that started it all," she writes. They were here, they said, for the children. . . . Today, much of the original Facebook content relating to QAnon consists of videos posted by mothers—visibly furious, sometimes in tears—about the alleged sinister messages used to 'brainwash' their children through toys or Disney movies."[26] Kelly explains that the nature of our social media landscape is critical to understanding not only the appeal of QAnon but also the ease with which it spreads among mothers who have been traditionally restrained from access to male-only conspiracy groups. As Kelly notes, "QAnon, by contrast, has looked for converts anywhere it can find them, making the slogan 'where we go one we go all' (usually abbreviated to the hashtag #WWG1WGA) its rallying cry."[27] Kelly also points out that, while QAnon was initially based on niche platforms like 4chan and 8chan, the fact that it spread to Instagram, so dominated by women and mothers, made its attraction to that demographic almost inevitable. "And when majority-female anti-vaccine groups on Facebook began suggesting dark forces were at play in the COVID-19 crisis and expanded into anti-mask, anti-lockdown sentiment, QAnon eagerly folded all of these conspiracies into its own master narrative."[28] Ultimately, Kelly argues in her piece, the "unexpected aesthetic" of QAnon on Instagram has "obscure[d] a toxic ideology."[29] Millennial-pink infographics paired with a mother's love makes almost anything palatable for the masses, even if Bec is telling you that "all the world is a lie," or Rose is claiming that the "mama bear revolution" will protect us from the "inner workings of the elite" and reveal the "underbelly of dark things."[30]

It's easy to label moms trafficking in conspiracy theories as silly or crazy, but doing so not only negates their very real influence and power and also prevents us from understanding what drives white moms to Q and the alt-right in the first place. So I am enormously grateful and indebted to Seyward Darby's reporting in *Sisters in Hate*, which devotes one-third of the book to a comprehensive, in-depth analysis of white nationalist mom Ayla Stewart. While QAnon does not always intersect with white nationalism (explicitly, at least), both QAnon believers and white nationalists have successfully recruited white mothers to spread and sanitize their messages on social media in ways that come across as nonthreatening. And both groups also prey upon mothers' disenfranchisement in a culture that relentlessly erases caregiving and domestic labor, much of which is done by mothers. Ayla's story is incredibly useful in disentangling how and why some momfluencers end up using their platforms to spread disinformation, conspiracy theories, and white supremacist rhetoric.

Darby's Ayla chapter begins, aptly enough, with an analysis of maternal imagery. Citing Beyoncé's now famous pregnancy photo, in which she appears in a diaphanous veil surrounded by riotous flowers and wearing Virgin-Mary-blue underwear, Darby writes: "The aesthetic was inspired by art dating back centuries: Beyoncé was Raphael's Madonna, Botticelli's Venus, the Virgin of Guadalupe. She was a black woman inserting herself into a canon that so rarely depicted figures of color, much less glorified them. 'She appears as not one but many women—or, instead, maybe the universal woman and mother,' an art history professor at New York University told *Harper's Bazaar.*"[31] In other words, Beyoncé's aesthetic performance of motherhood dares to imply that her motherhood—her Black motherhood—can and should be adored and idealized, just like a certain kind of white motherhood has been in this country for centuries.

Ayla Stewart, a white Christian mother of six, took issue with Beyoncé's self-presentation as archetypal mother and shared her thoughts with her social media followers. In her analysis of the situation, Darby writes: "She juxtaposed the photo with a painting of the virgin Mary and an infant Jesus, encircled by gilded haloes. Ayla captioned the side-by-side comparison 'Tubillardine Whiskey (1952) vs. Kool-Aid.' Mary was the vintage; Beyoncé was the fake stuff."[32] According to Ayla's logic, Beyoncé, as a Black woman, could not lay claim to maternal authority like a white mom could. Ayla, whom you can find on Instagram as @wifewithapurpose, maintained an active, engaged social media presence throughout the 2010s and has garnered plenty of negative press coverage highlighting Ayla's role in both participating in hate groups and disseminating their messages via her various platforms. Annie Kelly, for example, covered Ayla's "white baby challenge" (a challenge predicated on encouraging followers to "match" Ayla's six babies and "beat" her) in 2018 for the *New York Times*.[33]

And while Ayla's racist undertones (overtones?) are impossible to miss in her post about Beyoncé's "fake" performance of maternal agency, Danielle Kwateng-Clark points out in a piece for *Essence* that within forty-eight hours of Beyoncé posting her pregnancy photo to Instagram, white writers were already sharing their own hot takes about how the aesthetics of her shoot were "tacky" (a word seething with race and class assumptions), and how her joy might make other women feel bad. Kwateng-Clark points out the hypocrisy inherent in descrying Beyoncé's Instagram announcement as somehow insensitive while staying silent about a plethora of similar white celeb pregnancy announcements. "So is it that Beyoncé is doing too much with all the photos?" she asks. "Is it because Beyoncé has surpassed Selena Gomez for the most liked in Instagram photo? Or is it that a Black woman, who's praised for being unapologetically proud of her blackness, is getting glorified by her community?"[34]

I'd also ask: Did public objections to Beyoncé's photos arise because a Black mother had the gall to lay claim to a celebration of motherhood historically associated with whiteness? Is it because white supremacist culture has historically mandated that a Black mother is unworthy of the collective cultural gaze, of our admiration? Is it because Beyoncé dared to communicate with her photo the assertion "I am a mother and my motherhood is beautiful." Ayla's renouncement of Beyoncé's pregnancy photos illustrates how the ideals of white motherhood intersect with overt racism, but Kwateng-Clark's analysis of how white writers critiqued these photos illustrates how the ideals of white motherhood intersect with more passive assumptions of race and motherhood. Both versions of whiteness and white supremacy at work are important and both versions abound on mommy Instagram.

If you scroll through Ayla's mostly dormant Instagram today, you'll see knitting photos, pie photos, cute kid photos. You'll also see a photo of her wearing a peach-colored dress, a tan shawl, and white gloves, smiling demurely at the camera alongside a long post about her belief in the sanctity of homeschooling. "Don't let the 'w4ite supremacist' phrase scare you," she wrote on May 19, 2019. "Talk to your neighbors, your co-workers, your family and friends. Have the guts to deal with the far Left radicals who will try and make your life hell in order to preserve your right to teach your children about God, about family, about love, and about real life."[35]

As is clear from Darby's reporting in *Sisters in Hate*, Ayla claimed to never understand why her devotion to "white culture" and her dedication to heteronormative, traditional Christian values made her critics accuse her of "w4ite" supremacy. No matter that she was the only woman slated to speak at 2017's white supremacist Unite the Right rally in Charlottesville, Ayla has always maintained that all she's ever tried to be is a "good mother." Darby writes: "In the hate movement, many women have found agency and purpose in this role [as wives and mothers]. As wives and mothers, they support loved ones while also serving a higher racial cause. When someone criticizes their politics, they express dismay. 'I don't cuss,' Ayla assured her online followers. 'I don't attack people. Nothing.'"[36] Ayla ultimately opted not to attend the rally, citing safety concerns, but on her YouTube channel, she delivered the speech she'd meant to give there, emphasizing her innate goodness as a woman and a mother, as well as her belief in endorsing "wonderful traditional values." Darby writes, "That's what people at Unite the Right really believed in: family and nation. The Nazi flags, the racist slurs, the violent things said on Discord—none of that mattered in comparison to white birth rates and loving your own kind. What could possibly be controversial about that? 'Tell me, please,' Ayla demanded. 'It's ridiculous.'"[37]

According to Darby, Ayla always wanted to become a mother, even as a young girl, "the kind of mother other women would look up to"; she viewed motherhood as a "a unique and special calling."[38] And, before embracing white nationalism, Ayla held alternative hippie views of motherhood that might have led her to become a very different kind of momfluencer: she practiced yoga, preached about free birth, health ("Ayla's version of it"), and alternative vaccine views. She started a master's program in women's spirituality and described herself at the time as a "radical, primal mama."[39] Ultimately, though, she felt alienated by mainstream feminism, invalidated by her choice to devote her time and labor to childcare and domestic pursuits. She wrote on her blog about being looked down upon for embracing traditional gender norms in her family, and for having so many children. "It's my choice to be led," she said.[40] She believed that "being a homemaker was sacred," and that "she had not felt the truth of that in the progressive perspective, in the feminist perspective."[41]

As someone who spent her first few years of motherhood solely devoted to childcare and domestic work, I understand Ayla's perspective. Care and domestic work is critical to capitalism (and more importantly, to life!), but because many mothers and care workers don't earn wages for that work, our work is denigrated as less than. We don't earn bonuses. We don't receive external praise. There are no "40 Under 40" lists celebrating our accomplishments, and, if we've been taught to view feminism as #bossbabe hustle and grind culture (more on that later in the chapter), of course we're going to feel like such a version of feminism is not only not for us but also doesn't see us or care about us. So for someone like Ayla, for whom "articulating her identity was a vital project," someone who seems to have thrived on being known as an authority figure, assuming the mantle of mainstream feminism was not likely to give her the type of outlet or the type of attention she might have needed/wanted.[42] The fact that social media allowed her to find an audience for her ideas and even make a bit of money from some of her domestic skills (she sold tea towels embroidered with the words "tradlife") must certainly have provided an extra jolt of validation she simply couldn't get from identifying as a mainstream feminist.[43]

Ayla told Darby that mainstream feminism "didn't support me as a traditional mother. . . . It didn't consider my needs valuable."[44]

But white supremacists *did* consider Ayla's role as a mother valuable and applauded her for it, in keeping with white supremacist groups from history, which have long recognized white motherhood as playing a critical role in hate movements. White women are not just responsible for literally perpetuating the white race; white mothers are responsible for instilling white supremacist ideology in their children, ensuring that white supremacy lives on in the next generation. And, given the gaslit reality of motherhood in America, where we are celebrated for our supposedly innate maternal goodness while wholly unsupported in meaningful, structural ways, it's not entirely surprising that a movement that gives mothers plenty of laudatory lip service paired with the illusion of power might prove enticing. Darby notes how white supremacist groups have historically utilized mothers' specific vulnerabilities:

> White nationalism pledges to esteem mothers and treat the issues they care about with the utmost concern. . . . Raising children might keep women busy at home, but white nationalists argue that this seems limiting only to someone who underestimates the political importance of the domestic sphere. Home is the microcosm of the nation; mothers are its teachers, keepers, and defenders. And nurturing children and warding off polluting influences, mothers are modeling a better world. Across time, white nationalist propaganda has been littered with images of women holding infants are surrounded by broods of children. The women appeared joyful and stalwart. They are always beautiful. Some images depict mothers as goddesses or warriors, ready to rise and righteous defense of their progeny if necessary. The language used to describe motherhood is equally glorifying.[45]

Homeschooling is critical to white nationalist moms, as is having as many children as possible to strengthen the race, and their literature often upholds the sacrificial ideal of motherhood along with white mothers' strength, resilience, and nobility. Above all,

Darby explains, white nationalist groups excel at "emphasizing women's agency as mothers."[46] This is a brilliant strategy when applied to a group of people who often feel robbed of agency in political and market spheres. One of the most poignant and explicit examples Darby offers is of Nazis handing out medals (!!!) to white German mothers according to how many children they had (!!!).[47] Alongside Darby's mention of this disturbing fact in my copy of her book is the word "vomit," which I scrawled and underlined with all the savagery my kids' magenta colored pencil could muster.

On her blog and social media platforms, Ayla frequently upheld her family's traditional roles as an example of simply playing to (gendered) strengths, and as a celebration of her (gendered) ability to nurture, educate, and homemake, not as an example of oppression. Darby ties Ayla's story to a history of white women adopting a "separate but equal" stance on gender roles in which men are acknowledged to be superior at providing for families by working outside of the home, while women are superior at childbearing and homemaking. She cites Andrea Dworkin, author of *Right-Wing Women*, as positing that (predominantly white) women have embraced anti-feminism for a variety of reasons, one of which might have been "self-preservation in the face of male oppression."[48] By hitching their carts to white supremacist patriarchy, white women might be oppressed by sexism, but they would have access to protections made possible by their complicity in upholding and perpetuating white supremacy.

Darby writes that during the American suffrage movement of the late nineteenth century, "women who opposed suffrage tended to be married, wealthy, and white."[49] And during the women's movement of the 1960s and 1970s, when feminists were lobbying for the Equal Rights Amendment, anti-feminist women mobilized by women like Phyllis Schlafly founded their activism on "their faith, their community, and their fear that change might compromise their interests." Darby notes that "black women tended to favor the amendment," while "white supremacists, including female ones, saw a complex threat [in the ERA] that they intended to stop."[50] Schlafly's anti-ERA campaign was called STOP (Stop Taking Our Privileges), a slogan that, as Darby explains, "alluded to the particular privileges of being a white women, situated in the social hierarchy above racial minorities and within favorable distance of white men."[51]

White nationalist momfluencers and white momfluencers who don't explicitly align with white nationalism draw on this history of proximity to white patriarchal power today, by praising traditional gender roles and eschewing feminism as a force that has made women allegedly unhappy, confused, and unfulfilled. Kaylyn Mead (@excellent_motherhood) posted a family photo recently in which she appears with her husband and two children and offers new followers an introduction to her platform. The post includes plenty of conspiracy theories about Big Pharma and "the truth" and ends with a commitment to traditional gender roles: "I am here to encourage, inspire and connect with other young mothers and wives and I will always unapologetically speak truth, even if it's hard to hear! I am anti-feminism and pro femininity. I believe that masculinity isn't toxic and that we need more strong, masculine leaders! There is a war against the nuclear family that we must fight to end!"[52] Mead's message is similar to Ayla's, who was passionate about creating content that promoted her idea of a "good life," which Darby describes as "a life where family was paramount, men were men, women were women, and feminism had no place."[53]

Both Ayla and Kaylyn self-identify as following a "trad" lifestyle, which we've discussed in prior chapters. Remember Kelly Havens Stickle and her Anne Shirley braids? I've written a bit about how nostalgia for simpler times is tied to whiteness (and white supremacy, whether it's explicit or not) before in a piece for *InStyle*, but I want to devote more time and space to it here. According to Darby, "As a hashtag, tradlife dates back to at least 2015. . . . To be trad is to seek a wholesale return to the social norms and gender roles of the past, when life for women was supposed better, safer, and stronger."[54] Darby also points out that one's idea of #tradlife might look different (in aesthetics, in practice) than someone else's. There are trad wives like Kelly Havens Stickle, who fully embody an aesthetic more aligned with the nineteenth century than contemporary life, but there are also trad moms whose central mission seems to be valorizing traditional femininity and masculinity rather than growing their own beets or stitching their own calico aprons. As Darby writes, "The only requirement is that it derive from a mythical, unspoiled version of history and celebrate clearly defined masculine and feminine archetypes."[55]

Bernadine (@bernadine.bluntly) lacks the nostalgic aesthetic appeal of Kelly Havens Stickle, but she makes up for that in more aggressive messaging. She hawks fertility-tracking devices ("swipe to learn more!"), and, like many traditionally monetized momfluencers, she sells her own merch (such as pink hoodies featuring a picture of two presumably female cherubs that read: "And the truth shall set you free. RIP feminism"[56]). But, as is probably clear from the sweatshirt example, she does not assume an apolitical stance. Most of her account is devoted to infographics and memes promoting the traditional nuclear family unit, including a post that shows a split screen of a young white bride and groom tagged "2009" alongside a family photo featuring that same couple with five children tagged "2019." The central text reads: "How to start your own nation from scratch." Alongside the meme, Bernadine includes the text "Unfiltered truths about the culture and how to break free from the lies and embrace traditional values. This community is the best community. #trad."[57]

Many trad momfluencers are not quite as overt in their messaging as Bernadine, but her suggestion that one might build their own mini nation (with or without a militia?) by way of a patriarchal family is very much tied to whiteness and power. Much has been written about how traditional family structures inform the organization of our social structures. In her paper "It's All in the Family: Intersections of Gender, Race, and Nation," social theorist Patricia Hill Collins writes about how the idealization of the traditional heteronormative white family structure disempowers and empowers people according to identity:

> The "family values" that underlie the traditional family ideal work to naturalize U.S. hierarchies of gender, age, and sexuality. For example, the traditional family ideal assumes a male headship that privileges and naturalizes masculinity as a source of authority. Similarly, parental control over dependent children reproduces age and seniority as fundamental principles of social organization. Moreover, gender and age mutually construct one another; mothers comply with fathers, sisters defer to brothers, all with the understanding that boys submit to maternal authority until they become men. Working in tandem with these mutually constructing age and gender hierarchies are comparable ideas concerning sexuality. Predicated on assumptions of heterosexism, the invisibility of gay, lesbian, and bisexual sexualities in the traditional family ideal obscures these sexualities and keeps them hidden.[58]

White momfluencers who continuously celebrate the heteronormative family structure might not always be deliberately working to render other family structures invisible, but it's worth considering how the proliferation of large white families dominated by traditional gender roles (Dad working outside the home and Mom working inside the home) have an impact on how we consider a good family, or a good mother. Hill goes on to explain how patriarchal white power within family structures bleeds into the logic of broader social organization, like, oh, I don't know, walls that physically separate one country from another. "In this logic that everything has its place," she writes, "maintaining borders of all sorts becomes vitally important. Preserving the logic of segregated home spaces requires strict rules that distinguish insiders from outsiders. Unfortunately, far too often, these boundaries continue to be drawn along the color line."[59] There is absolutely nothing inherently harmful about growing one's own vegetables or creating a self-sustaining home. But when momfluencers idealize lives predicated on insularity combined with the glorification of a family structure empowered by gender, class, and race, their accounts can have a numbing effect that protects the status quo, which assumes that white, heteronormative family structures are the best family structures, that they are the "norm," something American culture has long valorized (ahem—MAGA hats).

Bernadine's suggestion that we might create our "own nation[s]" through procreation is certainly more explicitly white nationalist than some trad momfluencer accounts, but why should a white momfluencer's love of "simple life" raise red flags if she's merely extolling the virtues of home-cooked meals and feminine arts? Why should Michelle Clair's account (@rememberingthe oldway), which features her and her daughters in full *Little Women* cosplay, cause us to do anything more than roll our eyes or maybe smile, depending on one's mood? In one photo, Michelle is pictured in front of a Christmas tree wearing the "Marmee skirt" made by a company called Little Women Atelier. She's holding a vintage teacup and looking fondly at her daughter, who is at her knee, dressed in similarly vintage garb and reading a vintage book. A cat sits atop her lap. I can almost hear it purring through my screen.[60]

I emailed Koritha Mitchell, associate professor of English at Ohio State University and author of *From Slave Cabins to the White House: Homemade Citizenship of African American Culture*, to ask her why nostalgia for the good old days and the romanticization of traditional values is inherently tied to whiteness. She told me that accounts like Michelle's "reflect the pleasure to be found in a particular kind of escape: insularity. They maximize the sheen of respectability and implicit justification that come with traditional homemaking. By default, the heteronormative nuclear family configuration is viewed as ideal and beneficial, even as those assumptions are constantly contradicted."[61] Remember Kate Lindsay and her enjoyment of the escapism she derived from following trad-wife accounts? Remember how she pointed out the attractiveness of a worldview that assumed homemaking and motherhood are inherently worthwhile pursuits? It makes sense that photos featuring women supposedly blissed out on domesticity and maternity feel like an escape, because—whether we're mothers or not—we are constantly faced with headlines descrying the opposite: that motherhood in this country is a mess, and that mothers are burnt out.

However, Koritha points out that the "aggressive prioritizing" of motherhood enacted by white trad momfluencers is a smoke screen, often proclaiming apoliticism when in fact the romanticization of a time and place in which only white, cis-het, nondisabled women of a certain class could access privileges by their proximity to white patriarchy is inherently political. "How can anyone say their priorities are in the wrong place if they're elevating motherhood?" Koritha asks. "But it's a particular motherhood, one whose politics are rooted in keeping things as they are rather than working to make the world less hostile for more people. In other words, a motherhood that pretends to be apolitical is cherished. Whenever politics revolve around maintaining the status quo, everyone is taught to see that as devoid of politics and somehow pure." Koritha draws attention to how white trad-wife momfluencer accounts encourage white people to continue to see themselves as "good and decent just because they exist, not because they do anything even closely related to the public good."[62]

A close cousin of the trad momfluencer is the wellness mama momfluencer. The wellness mama can be characterized by her distrust of Big Pharma, Big Tech, Big Medicine, Big Detergent, Big Mold, and, obviously, Big Plastic. She believes good intentions "have been known" to cure cancer, and that healing maternal energy is more powerful than any sort of treatment Western medicine has to offer. She is anti-vax (full of toxins), anti-mask (destroying our children's social skills), and pro–homeschooling, pro–essential oils, and definitely pro-dirt (good for the microbiome). She thinks giving birth to babies in hospitals is sacrilege and espouses "free birth" as the indisputably right, "natural" way.[63] This particular momfluencer often overlaps with the other white identities we've covered. Rose, one of our QAnon momfluencers, is vehemently anti-sunscreen (full of toxins), and a proud homeschooler. She is anti-vax and anti-mask. When faced with a mask mandate on an airplane once, she shared a photo of her "mask," which seemed to be made out of filmy gauze, to her Instagram stories with not a little glee.[64]

There are plenty of wellness-oriented momfluencers who provide really useful, evidence-based information for their followers, and plenty of them are recognized experts in their particular fields. In this chapter's critique, I am not referring to these momfluencers. I'm referring to ones like Yolande Norris-Clark (@bauhauswife), who claims with stunning authority that "every woman can choose to experience birth as euphoric and even orgasmic. . . . Pain and fear during childbirth is entirely optional. It's a simple choice; a shift in perspective."[65] Or Kendra (@the.holistic.mother), who claims that "every person's health and longevity could benefit" from, among other things, "a better mindset."[66]

Hayla Wong (@haylawong) is not one of these momfluencers, but, if you're not paying attention, you might think she is. Her Instagram bio reads "Disrupting, writing about, + parodying BS in Spiritual Wellness," and she's created a series of parody reels based on wellness influencers that she calls "A Day in the Life of a WooAnon Goddess." The text alongside each of these reels features a disclaimer that the videos are satire along with a brief definition of how she understands WooAnon goddesses: "WooAnon is my term for the spiritualization of disinformation, alt-right ideology and conspiracy theories that are rooted in racism, ableism, bypassing, and general cruelty."[67] One of her reels depicts Hayla looking blissed out next to a caption informing us about a "womb awakening" in Texas. The next slide juxtaposes her musings about this "divine place where divine feminine destiny and bodily autonomy are thriving" with a news headline about Texas governor Greg Abbott signing a law against abortions after six weeks. The next slide shows her baby playing with her cat (who plays a chiropractor in all of Hayla's WooAnon videos). She writes that the chiropractor is training her baby in "holotropic breathwork." Hayla offers followers legitimate (not satirical) critiques of wellness culture alongside her reels, and she explains that her inspiration for this particular one stems from her observation of "selectively apolitical gender essentializing wellness influencers":[68]

> 1. Why is it that when I peruse the accounts I draw *inspiration* from, they all seem to be moving to Austin? It is becoming a hub for new age barely masking (in both senses of the word) alt-right peeps. 2. The double standards of bodily autonomy when it comes to vaccine mandates while also enacting an oppressively strict abortion law that other states will now model theirs on. 3. I've seen some say that pregnancy is a person's divine destiny and see no issue with the heartbeat bill. Those are the same folks who also express TERFy ideas about what is "natural" of a person and their gender. Note here that people of all genders can become pregnant. And it should always be a choice.

I cannot stress enough how funny Haya's account is (her cat plays a chiropractor!), but, in addition to being hilarious, Hayla brilliantly explicates why wellness mama accounts are so confounding, enraging, and contradictory. More often than not, these mamas are white and have enough disposable income to worry more about which farmers' market they'll be patronizing than, for instance, whether or not their children will get enough to eat. They routinely co-opt feminist language about bodily autonomy while also demonizing mothers who, for example, either cannot or choose not to breastfeed (for any number of constraints or preferences), or mothers who choose to use Tide laundry detergent or to vaccinate their children. There is nothing feminist about claiming there is only one right way to mother, and certainly nothing feminist in invalidating the experiences of mothers who can't or don't want to ascribe to wellness mamas' particular worldviews.

I reached out to Hayla to get more context about her own experience with wellness mama culture, and to ask about the inspiration for her (very very very funny—have I mentioned they're funny?) videos. So began a long text exchange in which Hayla told me she got "sucked into the new age movement in 2019" and says the movement "did more damage than it helped heal me." She, much like Ayla before she found white nationalism, was interested in "goddess spirituality, sacred spirituality, and virtual women's circles," and she said that many of the leaders she followed in such spaces started "embracing conspiracy theories about COVID and the election while gaslighting about and bypassing racial justice and trans rights. . . . And so I wanted to capture the absurdity of some of the conspiritual [a term coined in 2011 to describe the convergence of New Age spirituality and far-right conspiracy theories] ideas, rolled up with the sparkly vanity aesthetic, and couched in spiritual supremacy.[69] I didn't think it would land the way it has but now that's kinda how people know me and they send me the crap they see and I'll use it as inspiration for the next installment because it really feels endless."[70]

She thinks that wellness mama ideology is attractive because there are very real structural problems with maternal healthcare, and Big Government is legitimately scary in that it continues to police women's bodily autonomy and reproductive rights. But to assume all mothers are privy to the same combination of race, class, cultural, and socioeconomic privilege, and so all mothers are able to simply "free think" their way out of whatever problems arise, is to ignore and erase the experiences of many, many mothers. In Hayla's words:

> The free birth movement is life-saving for birthing people of color but has been co-opted by white women to almost be this symbolic flex of feminine supremacy rather than an act of protective agency. This may be an offshoot, but one mechanism of white supremacy is the narrative of what is natural versus what is inhuman (read: primitive, animalistic—all

terms used to dehumanize persons of color). Some of that
is very present in the language of free birth. Plus a lot of
TERFy ideas which is also a spin-off of white supremacy
and gate keeping gender.[71]

If women are "naturally" meant to give birth by sheer dint of
the sex they were assigned at birth, where do trans women fit into
this logic? How can they lay claim to their own maternal goddess
cards? And if white women with layers of privilege co-opt the free-
birth movement, how do the very real life-or-death problems of
Black and Indigenous birthing people become prioritized? Hayla
said that, in the wellness space, "motherhood gets weaponized." She
went on: "It is simultaneously a privilege and also is oppressive. In
our society, mothers are devalued and held in binding double standards. At the same time, probably due to those double standards,
maternal care can get mistaken for moral superiority and moms
are largely still responsible for shaping their kids' values. So the
'mama goddesses' use all that—co-opted anti-oppression language,
mothering solidarity, wolf mom ferocity, Girlboss feminism." She
points to Chloe Angeline (@selfhealingmama) as embodying many
of these co-opted ideologies: "She kept appealing to this sense of
sisterhood between 'mamas,' care for our children, oppression
within women's healthcare, and women's intuition to peddle disinformation about the vaccine causing infertility." Conveniently for
the purposes of my chapter organization, Hayla said that Chloe
Angeline also co-opted tenets of #bossbabe momfluencer culture
by turning her apparently altruistic messaging into profit by selling a "womb healing webinar" series to any one of her thiry-two
thousand followers.[72]

There's more to say about white nationalist momfluencers,
QAnon momfluencers, trad-wife momfluencers, and wellness mamas; frankly, this chapter could easily have become its own book.
But before we leave this focused exploration of whiteness and
motherhood, I would be remiss if I forgot about the #bossbabes
of white feminism who have built their brands on telling moms

we can do it all and have it all if we only buy this one book or this brand of kombucha or just wake up earlier or manifest our dreams or banish self-limiting beliefs or accept this amazing opportunity or, in the words of Rachel Hollis, just wash our faces. *Girl!*

We met Rachel Hollis briefly in the previous chapter, where she graced us with her tiger stripes. I want to explore her here as an example of how white feminism has functioned—and continues to function—in momfluencer culture. Hollis is a mother of four and the author of best-selling self-help books like *Girl, Wash Your Face*. She has also made a lucrative living as a blogger and podcaster, and, in years past, she has run the self-help empowerment conference Rise, tickets to which run anywhere from a few hundred dollars to $1,800 per ticket.[73] She's come under widespread scrutiny in the past couple of years for plagiarizing Maya Angelou (and subsequently blaming her "team" for the mistake), and, in a completely misguided TikTok video, for referring to her housekeeper as a "woman who cleans my toilets."[74] This particular TikTok was created in response to critiques that Hollis was no longer "relatable" to her followers, whom she had gained and made money from *precisely* because of her carefully honed self-presentation of being a #relatable everywoman. In the video, Hollis compared herself to other unrelatable women from history, like Harriet Tubman, Frida Kahlo, and Malala Yousafzai ("all unrelatable AF").[75] Much has been written about the spectacular fallout, and I highly recommend Kate Kennedy's three-part deep dive on all things Rachel Hollis on her podcast *Be There in Five*, as well as the two-part series Aubrey Gordon and Michael Hobbes did on their podcast *Maintenance Phase*. Kennedy does a wonderful job tracing Rachel's connection to MLMs and professional horrible person Tony Robbins, while the *Maintenance Phase* team eviscerates Hollis's contribution to toxic diet culture and toxic positivity.

For my purposes, I'm interested in Hollis as a representative of a certain type of white momfluencer who relies on the rich history of white feminism to present her version of motherhood as not only ideal but also attainable for all moms, regardless of race, class, and myriad life circumstances. The message of moms like Hollis is simple: Get up and grind (no excuses!) every day and you can be a badass at work and a fun mom at home, and you can do both (career and parenting) well. As long as you believe in yourself. As long as you "choose joy" (no excuses!).

In 2020, Hollis posted the following on Instagram alongside a photo of her wearing a T-shirt, cream-colored leather jacket, and, as is typical, a big, open-mouthed grin. "CHOOSE JOY. Every. Freaking. Day. Choose a positive outlook. Choose to ground yourself in gratitude. If you can't find the positive energy, BE the positive energy. Choose laughter and happiness and dancing and smiles; not because you believe life is always easy and fun but because you know that even amongst darkness, YOU can create our [sic] own light."[76]

This passage is illustrative of the bulk and breadth of Hollis's advice meant to apply to *all* women, despite the fact that she is not a trained and certified mental health professional or even, like Brené Brown, an accredited and widely published academic with years of research experience. The central problem is the implication that such advice is universal and that all experiences of motherhood and womanhood are universal. At the time of this writing, the United States currently holds the world record for the most COVID-19 cases per capita (we're number one!). On January 5, 2021, reportedly 1 million people contracted COVID-19 in the United States.[77] Parents across the country are experiencing PTSD from last year's long winter of childcare disruptions, illness, and school closures. There aren't enough SAD lamps in the world to help most of us right now.

But, according to Hollis's logic (from which she has forged a career profiting), depression caused by the state of the world or one's individual circumstances is a mere *choice*. I'm unsure how being "the positive energy" is helpful to a mom trying to work from home while also quarantining from her sick kid while also attempting to help her other kid with remote learning. I'm unsure how recommendations to choose "dancing and smiles" can eradicate that mother's very real mental and emotional anguish or help her get dinner on the table when every cell in her body feels like giving up. Most of all, Hollis's mandate that women manifest their own joy negates the structural problems many women are living with, problems that have nothing to do with individual choices or individuals failings to create their "own light."

In another post from 2020, Hollis implored her followers to "use the resources you have no excuses! 🙃"[78] Again, this ignores the reality that many women's and mothers' most central problems *are a direct result of a lack of resources.* For the mom who is forced to return to her minimum-wage job a week after childbirth because she needs the paycheck to feed her family, which resources are available to her? Even in circumstances where resources *do* exist—say, for a mother struggling with postpartum depression (*if* she has the means to pay for mental health counseling)—if her condition renders her incapable of accessing those resources for herself, are we to believe it's her fault? That she has "no excuses" to lean upon when she feels hopeless, exhausted, and defeated?

In another post (I promise, last one), promoting her Rise conference, Hollis claims, "It takes about 5 seconds to change your mood from something negative to something positive. The amount of time it takes you to clap your hands is as long as it takes you to make the decision to change your mood. Dance it out, jump up and down, say a prayer—do whatever you need to do but don't let a circumstance change how you show up."[79]

It is JUST. NOT. THAT. SIMPLE. Or easy. Or, often, possible. But white feminists like Rachel Hollis have been making claims predicated on an all-embracing essentialist understanding of womanhood and motherhood for a long time. Hollis and others are just the latest iteration of white women espousing individualist, self-optimizing rhetoric as an ideal worldview and as a way to make money.

And what is white feminism? It's not intersectional feminism, which is concerned with access to pleasure, ease, accessibility, and equity for all people. The idea of intersectionality, which considers

how various forms of marginalization and oppression interact
with each other, was developed by theorist and scholar Kimberlé
Crenshaw.[80] Cultural critic Flavia Dzodan famously wrote: "My
feminism will be intersectional or it will be bullshit."[81]

In the book *White Feminism*, which is necessary reading for all
white women, especially if they want to understand what kind of
feminism they've been taught to espouse, and how that feminism
might be actively harming marginalized people, Koa Beck writes
that white feminism is "a specific way of viewing gender equality
that is anchored in the accumulation of individual power rather
than the redistribution of it. It can be practiced by anyone, of
any race, background, allegiance, identity, or affiliation. White
feminism is a state of mind."[82] Beck notes the allure of this type
of feminism, since (like Rachel Hollis) "it positions the singular
you as the agent of change, making your individual needs the
touchpoint for all revolutionary disruption. All you need is a better morning routine, this email hack, that woman's pencil skirt,
this confidence, that newsletter. The relentless optimization of
the self often means that systemic and institutionalized barriers,
to parental leave, to equal pay, to healthcare, to citizenship, to
affordable childcare, to fair labor practices, are reframed as personal problems rather than collective disenfranchisement."[83] Beck
traces white feminism to the first wave of the American suffrage
movement, when white feminists deliberately chose to prioritize
the voting rights of white women over a slew of other issues impacting women with intersectional identities, including access to
the right of Black men to vote. Beck explains how the women's
movement of the 1960s and 1970s was again dominated by the
concerns of white women, noting how Betty Friedan's prioriti-
zation of women pursuing jobs outside of the home completely
negated the experience of the Black and brown women who were
left to do domestic work and childcare once white, class-privileged
women found roles in the marketplace. See bell hooks's pivotal
book *Feminist Theory: From Margin to Center*, which speaks to and
against Friedan's message in *The Feminine Mystique*.

Again and again, white feminists have prioritized the optimization of self, and their lack of collective consciousness has proven harmful to marginalized activists who have long recognized the imperative of community and collective change. Beck writes that these grassroots feminist groups understood—and continue to understand—that "communities having access to clean water, to education, to public spaces, to institutions, to food are valued over a single person's ascent, success, or acceptance. This is a completely different way of envisioning and demanding equality."[84]

According to Beck, #bossbabes are simply new models of an already existent archetype, an archetype of white feminism that can be bought, sold, and worn. White suffragists from the early 1900s had to consider "consumer culture" as a means of disseminating their message, and "Macy's was declared the 'headquarters for suffrage supplies' in 1912, offering an official parade marching outfit that included hat pins, lanterns, a sash, and a war bonnet, among other need-to-have accessories . . . you could, and in fact should, buy your feminism."[85]

I am nothing if not guilty of buying my feminism. Numb with despair following the 2016 election, I bought myself a "The Future Is Female" T-shirt, my son a T-shirt emblazoned with the word "Feminist," and my daughter a onesie that read: "Future President." What I didn't do? Find a group already invested in intersectional feminist work and figure out how best to support them. What I didn't know? That "The Future Is Female" shirt is widely considered problematic, exclusionary of trans people, and inherently anti-intersectional feminist. According to Sam Miller in a piece for *Left Voice*, "'The Future Is Female' is a corporate feminist slogan. It erases queer, trans, and other non-binary people entirely, and it implies erasing men, which is not feminist."[86] At the time, though, I wasn't thinking much about anyone except myself and how I might clearly delineate myself from Trump's racist and misogynist politics.

Beck writes about the problem of commodifying feminism as something one can simply wear or buy: "Sanitizing 'empowerment' away from radical, deeply historic activism was pivotal for fourth-wave white feminism because it had to become transactional—something you could buy, obtain, and experience as a product rather than an amorphous feeling that rushed in from challenging power."[87] My postelection purchases did nothing to help the people more immediately impacted by Trump's election; they only served my own self-mythology as being "a good person," and they only contributed to some random Etsy seller making a few extra dollars. Apparently, I wasn't the only person who obeyed the siren song of commodified white feminism after 2016. Beck writes that, "post-Trump, we are knee-deep in #Resistance-wear, which puts phrases like 'Nasty Women Unite' and 'Nevertheless, She Persisted,' on everything from cell phone covers to mugs to tote bags. #Feminism is abundant, particularly for marketers who would like me to purchase my politics on T-shirts, buttons, stickers, and even makeup."[88]

Rachel Hollis sells a medley of feminist-friendly merch: planners telling you "yes you can" and notebooks urging you to "start your own path" and stickers that read: "You grow girl." But wearing your feminism to signal your own virtue or commitment to self-optimization is not the same thing as the work radical feminists of color have been doing for centuries and continue to do—work that is focused on making differences in the lives of real people, not simply adding a little feminist flare to one's bedside table.

In the following passage, Beck beautifully illustrates the limitations of white feminism's #bossbabes who commodify feminism for profit (and their "empowerment" conferences like Rise) in an analysis of Cosmo's 2014 Fun Fearless Life conference, tickets to which ranged from $99 to $399:

> But while fevered attendees were whooping up thin blond
> speakers and scribbling down their "style spirit animal" for
> their name tag (I found the entire exercise puzzling and put
> down "Rose Byrne"), many women of color couldn't even
> have afforded to walk in the door. Around the time of this

initial conference, the median wealth for single Black women and Latinas was $200 and $100, respectively. This means that even the cheapest ticket for attendance would cost all if not half the money they don't otherwise put toward living expenses. You know what the median wealth for white woman was? $15,640. This is how the business of feminism stays middle class and white in practice. How conversations about optimizing your "career, health, and love life" are reserved for certain women and decidedly not for others. The very basic framework of their lives [is] not considered for entry.[89]

Rachel Hollis's message is not for everyone. It is for women who can afford to attend empowerment conferences, who can secure childcare to enable them to attend empowerment conferences, and who have jobs that allow them to take time off to attend empowerment conferences. It's for women with disposable income to spend on "start today" journals, with the privilege of time to write in those journals, and with enough mental and emotional headspace to ponder the notion of "style spirit animals."

This chapter was hard to write. When I first conceived of this book, it seemed plausible to confine the specter of whiteness and its role in the buying and selling of motherhood online to a single chapter. I now realize the naivete in ever imagining whiteness could be so neatly contained. I was lucky enough to speak to Louiza "Weeze" Doran about how thoroughly whiteness and white supremacy inform cultural understandings of "good" motherhood, and when I told her I was hoping to use some of our interview for a "chapter" on whiteness, she raised her eyebrows and said, "How much time do you have? We could write a dissertation." By that point in my research, I knew she was right.

I initially reached out to Louiza after seeing her quoted in a *New York Times* piece about Rachel Hollis's "toilet cleaning video" fiasco, which Louiza called "the most disgusting capitalistic, privileged flex that was so quick, but it said so much about how she as a human being views the power dynamic and the social hierarchy."[90]

Louiza is an anti-racism and anti-oppression educator, and her Instagram Live rundown of Hollis's infamous TikTok is an excellent resource if you want to know exactly why and how Hollis's words were so egregious.[91]

Louiza told me that in order to approach the performance of motherhood from any angle (aesthetics, psychology, marketability), an understanding of how the construct of whiteness has been critical to the way we view the ideal family—and ideal mom—is paramount. Louiza explained that the concept of the nuclear family was deliberately constructed to separate white "civilized" people (BIG scare quotes) from different types of family structures that were deliberately othered and labeled as "savage" (BIGGER scare quotes). "I don't see how we can separate that conversation from whiteness," she said, "because it was literally created to separate whiteness as we know it today, right? From all other forms of racial and social identities and social subcultures."[92]

According to Louiza, even our individual mixed-up feelings about why we love and hate momfluencer culture are related to whiteness:

> That's why so many people end up either rejecting these notions of motherhood, or they get on the internet, and they're like, *Wow, this makes me hate everything about myself about my kids about my partner.* And it's like, *Why do I even hate this?* Well, you hate it because you're constantly consuming very subtle, nuanced narratives of white supremacist oppression. This narrative has convinced you that the only way to feel better about yourself is if you perform the heteronormative tropes of white supremacist momming.[93]

As we've seen, this type of "momming" requires we look the right way, buy the right things, marry the right people, own the right homes, paint our walls the right colors. The imperative to "do motherhood right" is intrinsically connected to a construct of white motherhood that was created by white men as a way of subjugating and controlling nonwhite, nonmale bodies. Depending on our intersectional layers of oppression and privilege, it's going to make some of us feel shittier than others. But it's going to make us *all* feel like shit at one point or another. Until we start to unpack how white motherhood has impacted not only our own mothering journeys but also those of the women who mother alongside us—our partners, our babysitters, our teachers, our domestic workers, our friends, our neighbors who are more concerned with teaching their kids how to survive a routine traffic stop than what kind of macrobiotic powder to add to their kids' oatmeal—we all stay stuck.

7

Disrupting the Feed

Erica Nolan is a trans mom. But before Instagram, that wasn't an identity she would've felt comfortable expressing. I found Erica through the hashtag #transmom, which has been used nearly ten thousand times, and had the opportunity to talk to her over Zoom about her relationship to Instagram and motherhood on a chilly January afternoon.

"Without Instagram I wouldn't have transitioned," she told me, taking a little pause to let the stark reality of that statement hover between us. Erica grew up in a conservative, rural part of the country, and, for most of her life, representation of trans people was limited to toxic "snippets of Jerry Springer." She didn't see any "positive representation whatsoever" until she started "questioning and looking" for representation online.[1] Once she started finding and following trans women on Instagram, she began to slowly gain a sense of what might be possible for her own transition, and gained the confidence that she could emerge on the other side, not just intact but thriving.

"The reality is that one of the ways I came to terms with my trans identity," Erica explained, "was following other trans women on Instagram and seeing that not only was transition possible but also that it could lead to such positive outcomes." Now with nearly twelve thousand followers on Instagram, she started her account (@erica_evolution) as a way to chart her particular journey as a trans woman and, as she writes in her bio, create "visibility one selfie at a time." The decision to contribute to furthering trans representation by sharing her own story was not an easy one for Erica, who describes herself as "pretty introverted," but she felt a certain responsibility to give back to the trans community.[2]

"I started realizing that there seems to be a cycle with trans women who choose to be visible," she told me. "The ones who choose to share their transitions are highly visible at first, but, as time passes, being transgender becomes less of a focal point and therefore they begin being less and less visible online. Those who are new to transition or who have made a commitment to maintaining visibility are left shouldering the burden." Erica cited a conversation she had about this cycle with a friend of hers—whom she met through Instagram—that inspired her to make her own account public, start using hashtags, and "give back to anyone else out there struggling."[3]

While Erica does not make her daughter the focus of her account, she makes a point to post photos of her every now and then, with a sticker over her daughter's face, just to normalize her own identity as a trans mom. She also thinks that a lot of trans moms probably choose not to share similar posts because of the amount of "baggage" that attends trans motherhood, including custody issues impacted by biological understandings of the roles of "mother" and "father" and negative feedback from both strangers and friends and family.[4]

And, Erica assures me, there's definitely negative feedback. But she credits her Instagram community with identifying trolls and flagging hateful comments and reporting them to Instagram, which relieves her burden of labor. "It feels really good when you see someone doing that for you," she shared. And despite the "hateful comments and horrible messages," Erica always comes back to the fact of how critical representation was for her when she was struggling with her own transition. "It's why I choose to be visibly transgender online," she said. "Without that visibility back when I was questioning my gender, I don't know if I would have sought professional help and chosen to transition."[5]

I found myself in tears when Erica told me a beautiful story about when her toddler daughter started calling her "Ma" instead of "Daddy," as many of the adults in her life still directed her to do. Erica's daughter came up with "Ma" all on her own, which underscores the capacity of children to understand the gender spectrum with an ease and openness that so many adults have been trained to unlearn. I'm still floored by the indisputable fact that, in Erica's case, the representation she found on social media directly led her to embrace and live her own truth. Her story highlights the ability of social media, despite its many, many flaws, to literally change lives—or, at least, provide platforms for people to effect change, in their own lives and in the lives of others.

That's what this chapter is all about. How Instagram, while shitty and toxic in a lot of ways, can also provide moms from a variety of marginalized identities, from a vast breadth of life circumstances, the space to find community, support, and, sometimes, as in Erica's example, themselves.

It's easy to find a mass of data, articles, op-eds, essays, and documentaries about how social media is killing our attention spans, wasting our time, surveilling our identities, and sucking our souls. There's evidence in this very book to support the idea that social media, when consumed uncritically, can have a negative impact on our mental health, our senses of selfhood, and our bank accounts. But to label Instagram and momfluencer culture as all bad is to erase a vast community of mothers who are using Instagram on their own terms, not just to showcase their clean countertops or handcrafted German wooden hedgehog toys (listen, I have a handcrafted German wooden hedgehog, and she's great but she's not making me a happier, better mom), but to advocate for themselves and others.

Louiza "Weeze" Doran—the extremely wise thinker from the previous chapter who pointed out that the relationship between whiteness and motherhood could fill the Grand Canyon—says that the too-simple fallacy that social media is objectively damaging and rotting our brains can actually be used by oppressors to prevent disruption to dominant narratives. She notes that, while most institutions have been created as tools to uphold white supremacy, social media provides dissenting voices a relatively accessible way to spread their messages to audiences they might not otherwise reach.

"All of our institutions are privatized," Louiza explained to me, "so social media is actually the first time that we have seen effectively free press for collectives of people whose voices and experiences are historically very intentionally marginalized and erased."[6] On our Zoom, Louiza illustrated the power of media to change hearts and minds by citing the Black Panthers' newspaper (while pointing out that the way we've been taught to view the Black Panthers is proof of who controls the historical narrative).

"It was news for the community that impacted the community that was told by the community," she told me. "And that newspaper is a primary reason the FBI and the American government made sure to destroy the Black Panther Party." Because media, whether used for good or evil, is powerful. Louiza also pointed out how costly traditional media is to produce, both in terms of actual money and of time. "So, what social media did is a couple things. It removed that barrier to access, and there was no one to control the narrative, there's nobody to say, *This isn't going to press*; *this can't be published*." Louiza views social media as revolutionary because it allows opposing narratives to thrive. "People can connect, they can also share real life experiences, they can share what's happening on the ground locally in their grassroots movements. We started to see folks talking about decolonization, we started seeing Indigenous and melanated folks talk about liberation, to a point where now white folks are like, *Tell me more about liberation*."[7] And *this*, Louiza points out, is how social media can shake the most privileged free from their echo chambers. Marginalized people can find connection, community, and resources where otherwise they might be hard to access, and their stories, which have been deliberately obscured so much of history, can start to take up more space in mainstream, traditionally white, patriarchally mandated spaces. Momfluencers who don't uphold a white, cis-het ideal of motherhood *are* taking up space on Instagram. And, while I have no way to prove it, I believe that these moms, who are disrupting the stories of motherhood we've been taught to view as normative, are at least partially responsible for an influx of white moms signing up for Louiza's liberation courses on whiteness and colonization. Of these white moms specifically, Louiza says they come to her with similar requests. "They say to me, *There has to be a better way. I'm seeing all this stuff on Instagram that makes me hate everything about my life, and it gives me imposter syndrome* and all the other things. *But, like, there's clearly another way where happiness and joy and messiness and imperfection is actually celebrated. Like, I want that.*"[8]

And there is another way. There are lots of other ways. Ways that don't prioritize linen jumpsuits or artful lunchbox composition as the apex of maternal achievement. Some of the disruptor moms discussed in this chapter celebrate "happiness and joy and messiness and imperfection," some of them educate, some of them draw attention to critical issues impacting their communities, and some of them do all of the above.

Mia O'Malley (@miaomalley) does all of the above. She shares wreath-making pictures, lots of outfit inspo, plenty of reels excoriating anti-fat bias in healthcare, and vibrant beach portraits taken by her three-year-old. On her other account (@plussizebabywearing), Mia utilizes her training in baby-wearing to help moms in larger bodies and also, according to her bio, to celebrate "Fat Parenthood" and "Fat Joy." Her posts feature lots of cute kiddos snuggled up to their moms. Lots of smiles.

I hope Mia writes a book someday because in only forty-five minutes, I came away from our Zoom conversation feeling as though I had learned at least a few books' worth of information.

Mia's Instagram journey began in 2015, when she started photographing herself to "reconnect" with her body, at first just for herself, and eventually to post on Instagram. "It was a way of facing my fear and my fear was my body," she told me. Mia said the simple act of photographing herself *for* herself created a "big shift" and made her feel "really different" about herself and her body. "Every time I photographed myself," she said, "I felt like I like meeting the boogeyman, you know? And staring him down in the face and being like, *Oh, you're not so scary, actually.* Like, *I'm not actually afraid of you. I don't actually hate you.*" A few years later, she got pregnant and found herself "so craving seeing people who had pregnant bodies like [hers]." As a fashion lover, she spent hours "scouring and scouring and scouring Pinterest," trying to find sartorial inspiration for her changing body, but that inspiration—or even simple representation—"was just so hard to find."[9]

Mia, who gradually realized her "isolating" experience of pregnancy was not happening "in a vacuum," clarified that her initially disorienting experience of pregnancy didn't have anything to do with not liking her body:

It's because I didn't see anybody around me who looked like me. If you search pregnancy photos on Pinterest, nothing. If you're looking at motherhood Instagram accounts, nothing. I mean, let's not even talk about plus-size maternity clothes or plus-size nursing bras. There's a lack of access to actual products. There's lack of representation in media and there's a lack of support. And unfortunately, almost everything about pregnancy and postpartum is centered around weight so even straight-sized pregnant people feel bad about themselves because it's so wrapped up in weight and diet culture.[10]

Mia felt pretty "yuck" during her pregnancy (#relatable) but decided to take some pregnancy photos to "lay claim to her identity."[11] She said that posting those photos, alongside the essay she wrote to accompany them for the blog *Plus Size Birth*—run by Jen McLellan [see https://plussizebirth.com/about/] (@plusmommy), one of the digital foremothers of fat-positive maternal advocacy—

changed her life. The photos went viral on the blog and on Mia's various social media accounts. Her essay "My Invisible Plus Size Pregnancy" beautifully elucidates the uniquely painful experience of navigating pregnancy without the attendant consideration and care that often is granted to thin pregnant people sporting "cute baby bumps." In the piece, Mia writes, "You may try to put your hand on your belly in public, to touching it softly, maternally, in hopes of finally communicating to society that there is something special. Your pregnancy is still a secret artfully hidden by your plus size body."[12]

Motherly (@mother.ly), a blog with one million Instagram followers, reached out to Mia, asking to feature her photos and essay on their website. She was initially OK with this, until they came back saying that the editorial team had "had a discussion" and felt that the term "plus-size" had "negative connotations," and asked would Mia mind revising the piece to be about "curvy pregnancy"? Mia's response? "No. And I completely shut down conversations after that. . . . Nobody is googling 'curvy pregnancy.' That is not a thing." I guess I shouldn't have been as shocked as I was when Mia told me this, but I was. And I'm still so mad on her behalf. I think what I find most confounding and infuriating is the possibility that the "editorial team" maybe didn't even read Mia's essay. Or at least didn't read it carefully. Because, if they had, surely they would've understood that that their request for her to render her expression of her own pregnancy less "negative" was exactly what Mia was writing against! By suggesting she make her pregnancy more editorially palatable, they were attempting to render her pregnancy—and her artistic expression of it—invisible. Mia pointed out that this incident occurred in 2018 and said she doesn't think such a thing would happen now, because, although conditions for fat pregnant people are still *bad*, she thinks they have gotten "just a little bit better."[13]

Mia posted her pregnancy photos on all of her social media accounts, and she still gets feedback from plus-size mothers who feel seen by her words and images. The photos are stunning. In some of them Mia wears a diaphanous scarlet gown, in others fawn-colored sequins and tulle, and her expression manages to convey that other-worldly coalescence of mystery and reverence that pregnancy often evokes. Mia recalls messages from people who never took their own pregnancy photos because they "hated" how they looked and who ended up regretting it, as well as messages from people inspired to take their own pregnancy photos because of Mia's example. Part of the reason Mia thinks her photos still resonate nearly four years after she initially shared them is because "there are still a tremendous amount of people who struggle with pregnancy simply because they don't see themselves represented anywhere."[14]

I asked Mia if she thought representation alone was powerful in and of itself, regardless of whether that representation is accompanied by much-needed structural change, and her answer was definitively yes: "The psychology of it, the way we internalize the images around us has a serious impact." She went on to say that when there's a lack of representation in media *as well as* inequity in healthcare settings, plus-size pregnant people can suffer both physical and psychological harm. "Pregnancy is the most fat-phobic experience you will have to navigate as a plus-sized person," she said. "And so, compounded with the fact that you don't see yourself represented, you are made to feel completely abnormal. You feel completely invisible."[15]

Mia said that both fat activism and the body positivity movement have helped move the needle toward positive change, and she thinks Instagram allowed for both movements to spread in meaningful ways. She also thinks Instagram is a useful platform for sharing resources and networks. Mia launched the @plussizebabywearing account not only to provide representation for plus-size parents who want to baby-wear but also to show how to do it. Anyone who's ever looked at a blobby newborn and then looked at a baby wrap that appears to be a mile long and tried to figure out how to combine those ingredients to make a blissful baby-wearing situation knows that baby-wearing can be super intimidating. Imagine how much more intimidating that might be if the tutorials never featured bodies that looked like yours. Mia said that when she first considered baby-wearing, she figured it "wasn't an option," adding, "I didn't know if brands even carried something that would fit me. There's actually a lot of brands that have carriers that will fit plus-size bodies, but they don't advertise it, so people assume it won't work for them. And baby-wearing is an incredibly useful postpartum tool. It can also be incredibly healing for those of us who've had traumatic births due to anti-fat bias."[16]

When Mia first started using the #plussizebabywearing hashtag, there were only a handful of posts. Now, she says, there are thousands. Mia has found true community from her advocacy work on Instagram, and she thinks that, especially for marginalized communities, the mere act of sharing one's story has the potential for creating community:

> If you share a story when you're fat, you can't help but bring people in because so many people have that shared experience. And so I just kept sharing my story. And through sharing, I created a community. I'm so glad I did because I needed it myself. And I've made so many friends doing this that I wouldn't have been able to make if I hadn't told my story. I don't know where I would be honestly, because at the time, I didn't really have any fat friends. Or really any friends with kids. So I just felt so validated.[17]

While Mia speaks of the many friendships she's made through her advocacy work on Instagram, she also details how she and other moms fighting for better treatment of mothers in larger bodies have created more awareness, and she thinks the importance of that can't be overstated. Only after awareness that a problem exists, and that potential solutions to that problem exist, does change follow.

> So, you have the awareness of the person who is trying to conceive or has conceived that they deserve respectful care,

that they deserve a care provider who is not gatekeeping
fertility treatment, that is not suggesting they freeze their
eggs and go have weight loss surgery and lose one hundred
pounds before they will give them any kind of support in
terms of fertility. You have awareness of what they should
expect when they meet with a healthcare provider and that
another option does exist if they want it or if they can find it.
Then you have the increased pressure on healthcare providers understanding that we're aware of their anti-fat bias.[18]

Mia has created her own directory of motherhood-centric
providers largely through crowdsourcing, and she mentioned Jen
McLellan's network of weight-inclusive providers (which includes
OB-GYNs, midwives, and doulas) as another important resource.
She told me that Nicola Salmon (@fatpositivefertility) trains people
to navigate the "very scary" experience of being a fat mother in a
largely anti-fat culture. Too often, Mia says, plus-size moms simply
don't know there are better options available to them, because so
many of them have been mistreated by the healthcare system.[19]

There are women who spend a decade with a doctor who
will not prescribe them Clomid, who will not prescribe them
progesterone until they lose X amount of weight. And they
waste a decade of their life with this provider. They change
a provider, they're pregnant in a month. There are people
who have who have terrible, terrible traumatic births because
they've been labeled high risk when they have no other health
risks aside from an elevated BMI.* And that is a practice-
to-practice decision and not actually based on science or
evidence. And the high-risk label not only usually costs you
more with insurance because you have additional testing,

---

*Check out the *Maintenance Phase* podcast for a thorough, fascinating break-
down of the racist, sexist, classist roots of the BMI and why using it as a
health marker is complicated and problematic.

but it limits your access to where you can birth, who you can have at your birth, how you birth, all these different things that really impact us.[20]

Infertility, pregnancy, childbirth, and the postpartum experience can all be fraught experiences in the best of circumstances. But plus-size moms are routinely disrespected, dehumanized, and mistreated because of anti-fat bias in healthcare. People like Mia are changing that. And social media is helping her to do so.

Aaronica Cole (@aaronicabcole) is a sustainable lifestyle and parenting blogger. She told me that her experience as a fat mom and a Black mom exposes her to both racist *and* anti-fat treatment during pregnancy and childbirth. After trying for a year to spontaneously conceive, she was told by a doctor that she'd have to lose weight or undergo fertility treatments. The doctor offered no clear diagnostic reasoning for Aaronica's supposed infertility. "No tests were run," she told me. And when she did become pregnant, her doctors explicitly told her not to gain weight. Aaronica recalls throwing up *four times a day* for almost the entirety of her pregnancy. Her intense, life-altering nausea was never treated; in fact, her doctors considered her relentless vomiting to be a positive. "They were like, *Oh, excellent. This is great, because now you don't have to worry about losing weight after you have the child*," she recounted. "And I just remember that if it wasn't for my doula, I would have had a really traumatic pregnancy."[21]

When Aaronica had her second child, she felt the urge to push during labor but was told by "dismissive" nurses that it "wasn't time yet." She recalled, "My husband was above my shoulder. And he looked down, and was like, *I can see the baby's head.* And the nurse was like, *Oh, my God, that baby's coming out!* And I was like, *Yes, this is what I said. I said that it's time.* Nobody heard. Nobody listened to me."[22] For anyone who has felt what it feels like to *have to push* an actual human being out of your actual human body, this is beyond enraging. It's not a feeling one imagines! Or a feeling one can easily control! It's not a feeling that can be corralled by "timing."

Aaronica believes stories like hers need to be told to combat both anti-fat and racist bias in healthcare settings. "Doctors and nurses are taught that Black women do not feel pain the same way that white women do," she said, "that we have a higher pain tolerance, and that we can endure much more. So we're coming in talking about our pain and then told to *just let it go*. And to deal with it. But then there's also the added layer of being plus size and, of course, fat-phobia within medicine is very widespread."[23]

Mia O'Malley says she spends a significant amount of time devoted to her advocacy work despite not making any money from it. Why? "Because it's literally life-changing for people to connect with care providers that will treat them without anti-fat bias, *especially* in pregnancy. And, yeah, I think that has changed a lot from Instagram."[24]

Among the pregnancy and maternity companies doing a good job with both representation and inclusive sizing, Mia cites Wild-Bird, which makes baby wraps; Hope and Plum, which makes ring slings; and Storq, which makes beautiful (at least I think they're beautiful! I lived in their leggings and tank tops during and after my pregnancy with my third kid) basics for pregnancy that easily transition into the postpartum period. Mia wishes Kindred Bravely would do better; she says their nursing bra is incredible but only goes up to size XXL. She's also quick to point out that we still have way, way, way further to go. A few brands doing a good job is not enough. Mia notes:

> I want to see more diverse bodies on accounts like *BabyCenter*, like *Motherly*, like *Parents*. I want to see more diversity on Pinterest. Because it's just gonna be better for everyone. Because most people who are pregnant are afraid of being fat. And then people who are pregnant and fat are just *alone*, and don't feel like there's a place for them. And so, if we're all less afraid, it'd be better. I mean, these big motherhood accounts all talk about postpartum mental health. How about they also mention that the average size of the American woman

is between sixteen and twenty? How many people pictured on their accounts do you see that fit that scope? How are you going to talk about postpartum mental health without talking about anti-fat bias?[25]

Frankly, because of my thin privilege, it had never occurred to me to draw the clear line between a lack of fat-positive representation in motherhood media and negative mental health outcomes for people trained to view their bodies as less than, as undeserving of care, respect, or celebration. But now that Mia has pointed it out to me, I can never unsee it, never unknow it. And this is the gift momfluencers like Mia and Aaronica give all of us. Education. Awareness. Understanding. So we can help make things better.

As we learned in the previous chapter, mothers have always been involved in activism rooted in hatred, exclusion, and white supremacy. Mothers have also been involved in activism founded on inclusion, liberation, and collectivity for just as long. In *White Feminism*, Koa Beck writes about how, in 1935, a Polish American mother, Mary Zuk, armed with little more than fierce determination, fought against inequitable food prices. During the Great Depression, the cost of meat skyrocketed due to prohibitively expensive taxes: "With two children and an unemployed husband, Zuk found herself trying to economize feeding a household and struggling with meat prices. She came to social justice because she had to—there was no other way to ensure that her children could eat regularly."[26] Zuk didn't set out to be a social justice warrior—she became an activist out of necessity and ended up getting elected head of the Committee for Action Against the High Cost of Living. Zuk's work ultimately led the Supreme Court to rule against the high meat taxes, calling them unconstitutional.

In her book, Beck covers another meat boycott organized by mothers in 1948, illustrating how technology changed the way their message was disseminated. Mothers were able to gain support for their boycott through elaborate phone trees. Beck underscores that this type of grassroots recruitment would later become widespread on social media, pointing out that hashtags like "#YesAllWomen, #SolidarityIsForWhiteWomen, and #MeToo can go national and sometimes even international in a matter of hours."[27]

In *Reclaiming Our Space: How Black Feminists Are Changing the World from the Tweets to the Streets*, Feminista Jones focuses on how Black feminists have utilized social media as a powerful megaphone. She thinks that the lack of gatekeepers on social media specifically contributes to more people being able to gain power and influence when otherwise they might have been prohibited from contributing to mainstream dialogues in meaningful ways. While this is important for feminists sharing their work online, Jones explains, it's just as important for people who might otherwise not have been able to access those feminists' ideas if they were confined to traditional academic or media outlets. "Go to almost any social media platform today," she writes, "and you will see a gathering of some of the most important feminist thinkers of modern generations. . . . Who could have imagined that the pound sign, once valuable primarily for its use on touch-tone landline phones, would become one of the most powerful weapons for Black feminists?"[28]

Jones argues that many of the most effective social justice movements of our time have been initiated online by women of color. She evokes Tarana Burke's #MeToo movement as an example of how a simple hashtag can lead to consequential public conversations that ultimately lead to perpetrators being held responsible for harmful actions. And, after the 2014 murder of unarmed teenager Michael Brown by a police officer in Ferguson, Missouri, Jones herself was "able to coordinate over 119 vigils that took place five days after Brown was killed, in forty-two states and five countries. This is the power of hashtag feminism."[29]

In *White Feminism*, Beck focuses on the intersectional feminist activism historically enacted by women of color and contrasts their work with the type of white feminist activism which too often dominates Instagram. "The white feminist practice of Instagram framing of activism as 'brunch,'" she writes, "stands in stark contrast to Black Lives Matter protestors being shot and Black civil rights protestors losing their lives in the 1960s. Enduring here is that for white feminism (as well as white and white-passing women), protest is a safe endeavor."[30] If we conflate activism with hearting a few posts and then moving on with our day, or donning pink pussy hats and crafting Insta-worthy protest signs, we are undertaking activism for our own cultural capital gain, signaling that we are good without stopping to consider how our "activism" is helping. Or hurting.

And, as Lyz Lenz notes in a *Washington Post* article about the "Wall of Moms" protests during the unrest following the murder of George Floyd in the summer of 2020, only a certain type of maternity serves as a shield against violence, only a certain type of maternity can be weaponized, for good or bad. Of the white mom protestors who rallied in Portland, Oregon, Lenz writes: "They knew their presence, their maternal bodies, would make a difference. But it wasn't just their motherhood, after all. . . . Black mothers had been out there protesting injustice for more than 50 days. They had been tear gassed. But the collective cultural horror over tear gassing mothers only happened when white moms showed up."[31]

Beck's notion of the relatively risk-free "brunch activism" practiced by moms with layers of privilege cannot be confused with the type of work being done by Mia and others, work that is meaningfully impacting peoples' lives, regardless of whether or not it looks good on someone's feed. It's critical to recognize the powerful role Instagram and other social media platforms play in activist work while remaining wary of how activism can so easily be bought and sold for the benefit of identity surveillance or capitalistic profit. Beck writes:

> Facebook, Twitter, and Instagram, all legitimate spaces for organizing and protesting, have also allowed political allegiance and identity politics to become performative—with audiences, followers, and endorsements. . . . And with the intersection of social justice and capitalism, white feminism is right there to sell you everything from co-working spaces to

lingerie with activist imagery from the past and present. . . .
You can craft a post that supports Equal Pay Day and then
do another that shills a "feminist" sweatshirt made by women
who were definitely not paid well. The same people who liked
the first post will probably like the second.[32]

Beck says that one way to distinguish between performative
social justice and activism intended to eradicate systemic inequality
is to assess whether the activism is predicated on cache or clout:

> What's decidedly different, though, about a Jewish housewife
> from 1902 refusing to buy meat with her neighbors and an
> actor doing an Instagram post for #WomensMarch is those
> Jewish housewives weren't trying to then parlay #NOMEAT
> into cultural relevance. There was no social currency in them
> walking out of synagogue when men told then they were an
> embarrassment to the community. There was no professional
> gain to be had in pulling meat from customers' hands—but
> there was a lot to lose.[33]

Many of the moms I spoke to for this chapter routinely field
hateful messages from trolls. They render themselves vulnerable in
a very public way, not to seem cool by way of caring, but because
they want conditions to change for the better, even when they have
a lot to lose personally. This is activism, not #activism.

Andrea Landry doesn't think about whether a post will get
good engagement, or whether it will lead to more followers. She
doesn't particularly care if her posts will be meme-able or aesthetically catchy enough to be printed on a T-shirt. On her Instagram
account, @indigenousmotherhood, she simply posts about what
she cares about, what matters most to her.

Andrea lives on the Poundmaker Cree Nation reservation
in Canada and started writing about Indigenous motherhood in
2015, when she was four months pregnant, as a way to process the
sudden loss of her mother. Grieving her and all that Andrea might

have learned from her about motherhood, she took to Instagram to find community. There and on her blog—also called *Indigenous Motherhood*—she wrote about "what it means to be a mother," and tackled themes like mourning, loss, trauma, and issues specific to the experience of Indigenous mothers.

On the phone, Andrea and I spoke about her work as a writer and life-skills coach, and the way she's utilized her training on social media. Her mission has always been rooted in community and collectivity, she told me, and that community, which grew from the seed of her own need, has become "huge."

> I wanted to build a community of mothers who are striving to reclaim our original ways of how we used to relate to our children before colonization, and how to reclaim who we are and where we come from as Indigenous mothers. And for me, it created a space of not feeling so alone amidst my grief. There are so many Indigenous mothers out there who are experiencing all kinds of traumas. And we're still mothering, we're still raising our kids day in day out, regardless of what we're experiencing.[34]

Her Instagram page @indigenousmotherhood has nearly forty-six thousand followers, and Andrea says she "loves" reading the messages she receives, and that connecting with people she might otherwise never have come into contact with has been an "awesome experience." People write to Andrea "every other day" saying they've gone through "something similar," or "my parents went through something similar," or "I relate to the trauma you highlight in the last post."[35] She says she's made lifelong friends from her work.

At the same time, Andrea echoes Koa Beck in recognizing that authentic activism can all too easily be co-opted on social media. She said, "I think there's the danger of cultural appropriation to occur when someone who's not Indigenous can be launching some hippy program in the middle of the States somewhere and basing it all on Instagram content from an Indigenous account."[36] Remember satirical mastermind Hayla Wong of the "WooAnon Goddess" reels? These white-women-run "hippy programs in the middle of the States somewhere" are exactly the type of thing she does such a brilliant job parodying. But these programs are not coming from out of nowhere. They exist to serve and profit (usually) white women, and, more often than not, they've been culturally appropriated from people of color.

The images on @indigenousmotherhood are often beautiful. Andrea features photos from a variety of artists and creators celebrating their own experiences of Indigenous motherhood, including work from artists Yacunã Tuxá, Wakeah, and Brooke Betsuie. But the activism undergirding the account often highlights very ugly realities. Andrea told me that Indigenous children represent the largest percentage of children in Canadian foster care, often as a direct result of ongoing colonization. "And so they're being raised in non-Indigenous communities, in non-Indigenous homes, far from their culture, far from their language, where maybe they had a healthy *kokum* [grandmother] or *moshum* [grandfather] who spoke the language fluently in their own community. But now they're living in town an hour away, and they no longer have access to that."[37] Other issues specific to Indigenous mothers are generational trauma, poverty, reservation schooling, geographic hurdles (Andrea lives an hour away from the nearest grocery store), and dental trauma. Andrea explained that there's a dark history of Indigenous people being harmed by dentists, in circumstances when teeth were pulled without any pain reduction.

For Andrea personally, her biggest challenge as an Indigenous mother has been processing her instinctual fear that her child will be taken away from her for the slightest perceived parenting infraction:

> For me, the biggest thing I had to work through was making sure my daughter was always clean, always had her hair done, had her nicest clothes on when we went to town be-

cause I always had this fear that, *Oh, someone's gonna look at her and think her clothes are too dirty and call CPS on us.* And, speaking to a lot of Indigenous mothers, it was the same experience. It was like, *Yeah, we have to make sure our kids have their town clothes on. Make sure their hair is done and make sure they look great, right?* I know I'm a great mom. But there's always that fear.[38]

Andrea is clear that she no longer operates from that same place of fear, that she has worked through much of her inherited trauma, but the fact that she had to work through such trauma at all speaks to how far we have to go. Her story also clearly demarcates which mothers are culturally granted the allowance to opt out of a hair-brushing battle, and which are not. My daughter is seven, and I have spent almost every morning of the last three? four? years engaged in a power struggle about tangles. I often cede victory to her. Because it's 8:13 and we need to leave for the bus stop at 8:15 or because she's crying or because I feel like crying or because I don't think snarls particularly matter in the moment. I've never once worried that my fitness as a parent would be called into question over a crooked part. All parents should be given such grace.

Another problem plaguing many Indigenous moms is lack of access to anti-racist maternal healthcare. Andrea told me that, up until the late 1990s, even the early 2000s (!), there were cases in Saskatchewan of Indigenous women being sterilized without their consent, waking up from C-sections to discover that their doctors had performed hysterectomies.[39] Like Mia and other activists advocating for equitable healthcare for plus-size mothers, and Erica sharing her transition experience to support other trans people, Andrea and other Indigenous moms have long held each other up by trading stories about which hospitals and practices offered the best chances of a non-racist experience.

I was told, like, *Don't go to this hospital, here in town. Drive the extra two hours and give birth at that hospital, because this one, there's a lot of racism, you're not going to be treated properly, and your baby's not going to be treated properly.* . . . We pick and choose the hospitals that we hear the best stories from. And it's all based on looking out for one another and our concept of a community of mothers.[40]

While Andrea says that these social networks between Indigenous mothers have always existed, Instagram and other social media platforms have enabled them to reach far more people than they have in the past. And, like Mia, Andrea values the IRL friends she's made through her advocacy work at @indigenousmotherhood. She's grateful to be part of a "collectivity" of "like-minded" moms united by a shared "purpose": "To undo what colonialism has done to our families and create a thriving space for our families. The collectivity definitely helps. And it could happen in real life, that collectivity, but I think the reach is far greater, obviously, on social media."[41]

Both Mia and Andrea speak generally positively about their experiences sharing their particular motherhood stories online. But for Rebekah Taussig, writing about motherhood for her Instagram audience has been, at times, "excruciating." Rebekah, the author of *Sitting Pretty: The View from My Ordinary Resilient Disabled Body*, which she wrote prior to having her son, started her Instagram account (@sitting_pretty) in 2015 as a graduate student trying to make sense of what she was learning in school. At the time, her focus was disability studies, and she refers to her grad school experience as "earth-shifting."[42]

When I Zoomed with her, Rebekah—who was surrounded by a veritable greenhouse of flourishing plants—explained how she used her Instagram account as a sort of de facto diary to process her quickly evolving thoughts. "I usually go to writing as a place for me to understand or navigate all the questions I'm trying to work through," she said. "I just created the account as a way of processing personally what I was reading about academically. . . .

And I was very, very surprised that anyone cared to read it, and I still am!"[43]

Rebekah discovered she was pregnant twenty-four hours after submitting the final manuscript of her book to her editor, and at first, she thought pregnancy and motherhood would provide rich fodder for her future writing. "I was like, *Well, I'm gonna say so much about this. There will be so many new experiences and there will be so much to understand,* and the need to understand is what drives me anyways. And it's been excruciating to write about motherhood. Like, way more painful, way more vulnerable than anything I've ever written before, and I've written about some pretty vulnerable stuff."[44]

While I haven't written much about my motherhood for Instagram, I fell into professional writing largely because motherhood consumed me with a need to better understand both my new sense of self and also the structures that made my new motherhood feel so disorienting. I deeply relate to Rebekah's inner drive to write as a way to understand. And I get why it's excruciating, too. I once wrote an entire essay about my toddler's pediatrician offhandedly referring to him as "quirky," and how the word unearthed an avalanche of my own insecurities as a human and as a parent. So, yeah. Both parenting *and* writing about parenting can be excruciating! But I'm so glad Rebekah is doing it anyway. Because her writing is beautiful, poetic, expansive, and unflinching. On January 13, 2021, Rebekah posted a blurry close-up of her face pressed against her son's, both of them caught mid-grin. Part of her caption, which is framed as a letter to her son, reads:

> I can't think of anything more fantastical than hearing you string words into sentences, then paragraphs, then pages. Surely this is tantamount to man landing on the moon, this feat of biology—this miraculous, most mundane spark of cognitive development—hollering on about DUCKS while I try to talk to my accountant in my serious phone voice about my taxes. And also. I'm trying to figure out how—no really,

how?—to hold onto myself enough to be A Me when we meet again, somewhere down the line, when you're 8, then 14, then 20. In those days I hope we know each other—when we look into each other's faces—you and me.[45]

See? Beautiful. And while I think we can all understand (to an extent) why writing about one's motherhood is an unavoidably vulnerable act, Rebekah's particular experience—and the whys behind the excruciation—are important to understand. She maintains her Instagram largely, she says, because she wants to contribute to representation of disability and motherhood, which she says is "hardly anywhere." She told me, "If there is someone like me in the world, I want them to have that representation and I want them to have an honest depiction of the things that are possible and the things that are hard. But it's excruciating. I have not enjoyed it. I mean, there's parts of it that feel good. I think anytime I'm interacting with other disabled parents in the online space, it feels really good."[46]

Sometimes, though, her interactions on Instagram feel less good. Rebekah says she has "wobbly feelings" when it comes to even well-meaning nondisabled mothers engaging with her content in ways that seem to erase the particularity of her own experience—as if the mere fact of motherhood is a universalizing force that blurs the many real differences between the experience of a disabled mom navigating the world and that of a nondisabled mom. "I think sometimes people think, *Oh, we've all been there*, you know?" While Rebekah acknowledges that, sure, we can all empathize about toddler tantrums or sleepless newborn nights, "the actual experiences can be planets away from each other." Rebekah cites as an example the concept of maternal self-doubt that almost every mother grapples with at one point or another. "I want to say, *Is it written into the law that you can lose your child just because of this part of your identity? It is for me.* So that's different. Our concepts of self-doubt are different."[47] Here Rebekah is referencing a set of laws in thirty American states that differ in specifics but are similar in their mandate that children can be removed from disabled parents because of the sheer fact of their disability, without any need to prove abuse, mistreatment, or neglect.

While Rebekah doesn't fear that any of her specific Instagram posts will lead to her child being taken away, the existence of such laws certainly impacts her concept of maternal security. Despite this, though, she shares her story, because learning from other disabled mothers on Instagram has been "like a lifeline" for her.

> Being able to connect to other disabled moms in California, or the UK, or in Virginia, is really helpful to be able to feel close in an experience that is really rare. There are fewer disabled people, fewer disabled people with the support and resources to, like, choose to have children, and even fewer disabled people in wheelchairs. So being able to connect with other disabled moms in a way that I just couldn't in real life feels invaluable to me. The real understanding to the unique specificity of this situation, and resources, tools, and, like, figuring out how to logistically do parenthood from this position is really difficult. It's not represented. There are no pictures of it anywhere, or hardly anywhere. The tools aren't made for people like me, and so being able to have the resources to connect with people who can strategize is really helpful.[48]

Tools, resources, and community have all been huge factors in why Rebekah continues to publicize her experience of motherhood on Instagram. Rebekah said, most significantly, "Honestly, I don't know if I would be a mom if I hadn't seen [other disabled women] become moms first."[49] Like Erica, who says she might not have transitioned were it not for the representation of other trans women she accessed online, Rebekah's life has been incontrovertibly impacted by representation.

Two of the disabled moms who make up Rebekah's "lifeline" of support and understanding are Alex Wegman (@alexwegman) and Dani Izzie (@daniizzie). Of Alex, Rebekah says she thinks about two of her posts "like, every other week." In one of them, Rebekah says, Alex wrote "about being able to not just, like, forgive the ways that I am not matching the idealized mother, but like, lean into and *embrace* the particularities of who I am as a mom, and viewing them as assets, or as a defining part of our dynamic as a family." Dani has twins, and Rebekah says that she writes "really honestly and practically" about that experience.[50] She is also the focus of a forthcoming documentary called *Dani's Twins.*

I had been a fan of Rebekah long before this book was even a shitty first draft in proposal form, and I've been a fan of writer Ashley Simpo (@ashleysimpo) for just as long. She's written some searing, gorgeous essays about single motherhood, Black motherhood, and the way the idealization of a certain kind of mom constrains us all. I want to reference two of my favorite of Ashley's Instagram posts to illustrate what kind of momfluencer she is. Overlaid on a photo of a field of yellow wildflowers is this caption: "Buy play kitchens for boys, buy baby dolls for boys. Introduce them to things that teach them how to nurture themselves and others. The world has its fill of grown men who have no idea how to care for things."[51]

Another post I love is a screenshot of one of Ashley's tweets about normalizing divorce. The caption alongside it reads: "A marriage that ends in divorce can produce financial and career gain, beautiful children, nurture creative accomplishments, etc. The idea that it absolutely must last forever, even when abusive or otherwise harmful is an incredibly dangerous notion. To insist that anyone who has a divorce has failed at something is also an incredibly dangerous notion."[52] I appreciate Ashley's Instagram because she provides concise statements that quickly illuminate the heart of a complicated issue. She invites readers to examine what many of us view as cultural norms from new angles, which might be my favorite genre of motherhood-writing.

Ashley and I started our Zoom by comparing and contrasting pandemic childcare/education messes. I'm writing this a few months after our interview, so, truly, I can't even remember what our particular messes were, but I'm sure either one or both of us were in lack-of-childcare hell. Just as Rebekah acknowledged that *some* aspects of motherhood are universal, Ashley says she "so loves" connecting in a grocery store checkout line with a fellow mom of a fourth grader, for example, but that to assume all aspects of each mom's experience are identical is problematic. Rebekah's concept of maternal self-doubt is different from mine and yours, and Ashley's notion of "unapologetic" motherhood is not identical to anyone else's. "We do all have very different experiences in terms of how we have to show up in the world," she told me.[53]

Ashley named her now-defunct blog *Mine's Broken* because she "felt like she was doing everything wrong" as a mom, and she's "always noticed" that mothers with marginalized identities are held to a different standard from mothers with more privileged identities. "The white version of motherhood can be a lot more unapologetic, I think, than the Black and brown version," she said. "There's not as much space for Black mothers to make mistakes or to be frustrated or overwhelmed." Because of Ashley's awareness that this disparity exists both in the culture at large and in motherhood spaces on social media, she has prioritized using her platform as "a voice that represents not just parents and mothers, but specifically Black mothers in a way where we don't necessarily have to fit into a box."[54]

So, while Ashley self-identifies as "just a normal person trying to figure it out," she understands that her experience as a Black mother is informed by racism, and that issues which might affect her as a parent—housing, access to mental health support, family structure—will be impacted by racism as well. She thinks that white momfluencers don't have to shoulder as much of a burden to incorporate social justice into their motherhood narratives online, mostly because white privilege insulates so many white mothers from having to educate themselves or fight against so many issues, and that that privilege allows some momfluencers to be a "little bit more lighthearted and fun" at times.[55]

Ashley has every reason to feel weary of how her experience as a Black mom is not always "lighthearted and fun."[56] White supremacy has, historically, brutally ripped the right to parental joy from Black mothers, and continues to do so in varying contexts and degrees. Black moms have been historically held to different, racist standards, stemming from enslavement, when their own babies were stolen and they were forced to serve as wet-nurses for white children. Feminista Jones notes that this violent history, post-slavery, also contributed to preventing some Black mothers from participating in social justice movements. She writes, "Black women were often kept out of engaging in empowering activities that would allow them to advocate for themselves as women, such as the suffrage movement, because they were relegated to serving as wet nurses for White women who were marching in streets and attending important organization meetings."[57]

Black mothers' fraught historical relationship with breastfeeding is one example of why representation can be so immensely powerful on social media. Jones details the story of Karlesha Thurman, who went viral for posting a photo of herself breastfeeding at her college graduation in 2014. "It was a bold move," Jones writes. "Both to do it and share it online, but she inspired so many others to follow suit and show their photos. I recall some of the discussions being about how we do not often see pregnant or breastfeeding Black women in major parenting or motherhood advertisements and magazines, which has long been a form of erasure of the Black motherhood experience."[58] Lack of representation of Black motherhood reaches beyond mainstream media and even impacts the types of images pregnant people see in medical environments. In December 2021, Chidiebere Ibe went viral when he posted a medical illustration of a Black fetus on Twitter. One user wrote in response: "This is beautiful! I have my master's in the states and not a single Anatomy textbook had a Black illustration in it! Netter is the only text used! I'd love to see your book distributed in the future!"[59] The fact that a single anatomical illustration caused such public support indicates how much more work needs to be done to advocate for representation of all kinds of parents, on social media and off.

Feminista Jones believes that many online communities have been created explicitly to provide safe spaces for Black mothers who often feel left out of mainstream discourses on motherhood. "With every topic, from managing the work-life balance discussions to breastfeeding," she writes, "Black mothers have struggled to fit into many of the major motherhood communities and discussions online. So, as we often do, we created our own."[60] Jones explains that, because of structural, systemic racism, Black mothers face unique challenges, and "race-specific" online communities allow Black moms the room to work through these challenges without interference from external voices that don't understand specific racialized contexts. Of these communities, Jones writes, "New moms could ask each other about the best formula for a colicky baby without having a barrage of White mothers berate them about not breastfeeding instead."[61]

One such community was created by Tanya Hayles, who launched Black Moms Connection, which has at least ten thousand members worldwide. For *Reclaiming Our Space*, Hayles told Jones that most negativity found in Black Moms Connection stems from white mothers of Black children not comprehending the different contexts from which they mother: "There is almost a demanding and resentful energy hurled toward BMC when the Black mothers do not feel inclined to engage the White mothers, and whenever BMC garners mainstream media attention, a new wave of attacks and insults come its way."[62]

Breastfeeding is only one way in which Black mothers might approach parenting from a different perspective than mothers from different backgrounds. During our Zoom, Ashley Simpo evoked the racist idea of the "welfare mom," which can be connected to the Moynihan Report, published by then assistant secretary of labor Daniel Patrick Moynihan in 1965. The "report" basically blamed Black poverty on the so-called dissolution of the Black family structure, which Moynihan characterized as inferior because of "absent Black fathers" and matriarchal Black mothers.[63]

Ashley clarified, "There is this idea that a Black mother on welfare is a problem. And a white mother on welfare is just doing what she has to do." With this example, Ashley explains that the cultural allowance for the struggles of white mothers (or even for their humanity) is not granted to all mothers. She cited another image with which many of us are familiar: a mom yelling at her kid in public. "A lot of people will see a Black mother yelling at a child and think, *Oh, my god, she's abusive, and she's, like, horrible.* Why aren't they thinking instead of what kind of support that mom has, about her mental health? Is she experiencing postpartum depression? Is she supported by her family or by her partner? Is she traumatized? This is not to say it's OK to yell at a toddler, but we need to understand that people show up with their entire experiences."[64] When we idealize a mother as someone who never screws up, whose emotions can always be contained, who can compartmentalize and ignore past traumas, we're erasing mothers' humanity in the process. (See Jessamine Chan's *The School for Good Mothers* for a harrowing fictional accounting of what happens as a result.) And when we stigmatize mothers for their failure to adhere to ideals, we're simultaneously strengthening the power of those ideals while rendering the human behind the lost temper or late-pickup-at-school or whatever invisible.

In *Reclaiming Our Space*, Feminista Jones argues that the revolutionary power of Black feminists on social media can benefit all of us, including white women whose understanding of feminism has been shallow at best and harmful at worst (see me and my "The Future Is Female" T-shirt; see Rachel Hollis and her toxic white positivity). "Social media has played a huge role in the increased awareness of intersectionality among White feminist women," Jones writes. "Many have been, for the first time, exposed to intersectionality as feminist praxis by way of women like me, Trudy

@Thetrudz, Mikki Kendall, Imani Gandy, and Kimberlé Crenshaw herself, who introduced the term."[65]

Sometimes, Jones says, Black women online can be viewed as superhuman, immune to exhaustion or burnout, as ever-renewable fonts of wisdom from which people can relentlessly extract. She calls this harmful phenomenon "Mammy 2.0." According to Jones, "Mammy is a Black woman who takes care of White people's needs. From household domestic work to child rearing and family nurturing. She is always there, willing to cater to the needs of White households, often sacrificing her own health and well-being to be present for struggling White people."[66] Jones argues that audiences, however well-intentioned, "have begun to see us as Mammy 2.0, the perpetual supplier of digital comfort and salvation. They regarded us as wise (we are), they acknowledged us as strong (we can be), and they tried to position us as wells from which they could drink and be filled with refreshingly new points of view that made them feel better about being White (you cannot)."[67] Jones credits the particularly difficult and confounding state of the world as well as the historical entitlement of white people to take whatever they want or need from Black people to contributing to the Mammy 2.0 problem: "Everyone feels entitled to us in one way or another, and social media platforms merely facilitate this abusive relationship in ways we probably did not imagine would happen."[68]

I asked Ashley Simpo if she's ever encountered this type of intrusion or boundary-crossing pertaining to her work online, and she said that she has: "A lot." She said it mostly crops up in the comment sections rather than in DMs ("and it's almost always a white woman") who will ask for further explanation, challenge a particular point, or request more commentary from Ashley. "An explainer" by nature, Ashley admitted that it's "tempting" for her to do the additional labor of responding, but she acknowledges that she doesn't have the time or bandwidth to address each and every comment. "Also, there's a specific reason why I don't go into much depth in Instagram posts," she told me. "I'm a writer and I'm paid to write longer pieces. . . . I also feel like it's triggering for me as a Black woman when the content has to do with the safety of Black children or issues that impact the Black community. I'll speak from my own experience and I'll be completely emotionally wiped out for a day. Because now I'm thinking about my uncle or I'm thinking about my son."[69] She totally understands that many people are simply curious and that their questions might be well intended, but, in spite of this, the requests for *more* can still deplete her. And sometimes the questions feel like they're coming from a place of entitlement, which is something else entirely.

To illustrate how we can all check ourselves before making unnecessary and potentially harmful demands of social media creators, Ashley told me about an occasion when she and another Black friend watched the episode of *And Just Like That...* when Carrie goes to a Diwali celebration and wears a traditional Indian lehenga:

> And an Indian woman on social media said, *this is so tiring*, and that was kind of it. That was her caption. Both my friend and I really wanted to know what she thought. If you invite a white person to a Nigerian wedding, for example, you might ask them to show up in Nigerian clothing, because that's what you do in that ceremony. Does that mean they're appropriating? Should they say no? I would love to know what the Indian woman thought about it all, but I asked myself if I might be burdening her with the task of explaining something that will further frustrate her, you know?[70]

Ashley says curiosity is totally natural, as is a desire to gain a more comprehensive understanding of a particular issue. But Google exists. We can talk to our friends. Or we can do our own reading and research before reflexively demanding time, energy, and unpaid labor from creators.

Regarding the shifts in representation of Black motherhood, Feminista Jones believes that social media is helping to dissolve harmful stereotypes. "We're seeing an increase in positive representation of Black motherhood that directly counters a generation of vilification," she writes.[71] Ashley is also hopeful about increased representation on social media of different types of mothers, but she thinks single mothers are still very much stigmatized, and that the issues unique to their experiences are "swept under the rug." She told me, "I think that it's just something that people don't want to think about. It's so attached to a negative stereotype that keeps it locked up in this space that nobody really wants to open up. And I feel like people think, *Oh, it's just this one particular type of person who ends up a single parent*, or *I'm going to choose my partner really well*." She believes that this avoidance and silence prevents single parents from being honest about their experiences and partnered people from understanding the reality of single parenthood. She also rightly points out that "single parenthood can exist within marriage," which, YES. But if a married mother does all the childcare, domestic work, and emotional labor and carries the entirety of a household's mental load, culture generally views her as a "success" solely by virtue of her partnered status. Whereas single moms—who are single for any number of completely valid reasons—still get relegated to a lower echelon of motherhood. This has real consequences beyond social stigmatization (which is bad!) that extend to a lack of resources and safety nets. Ashley hopes the representation of single parenthood "gets louder," and intends to use her own platform to make some of that noise.[72]

I would argue that Ashley's Instagram feed is visually dynamic. Her use of color catches the eye, and her sense of graphic design makes her account feel cohesive. But she cares less about aesthetics than she does about the message accompanying the pretty picture. While cute kids will always provide pleasure by dint of their cuteness, Ashley "doesn't care" if you heart a photo of her adorable kid: "I care more about whether or not you are voting in your local elections in a way that supports the families in your community, right? I'm much more concerned with whether or not you make space for parents on the subway, or whether or not you consider the children in your vicinity when you're cursing on the phone or whatever. Those types of things matter more. But I think that as a society, we're so obsessed with *what it looks like* and how cute it is."[73]

Pleasure in aesthetics is completely valid, but it gets complicated when paired with social justice or activism for the sake of cultural capital. And, again, Ashley argues, #activism removed from action isn't helping anyone aside from the person whose ego is bolstered by sharing an aesthetically pleasing infographic about Black Lives to her stories. Ashley speaks about her experience living in Brooklyn as a way to illustrate how to be an active community member who cares not only about her insular family but also about everyone else. She advises, "Find out, like, what is the concern and how am I impacting it? How can I contribute? Can I donate to it? Can I offer a resource?" She's not sure how that type of IRL community involvement "translates to influencer culture": "Because it is kind of like *just click here* and let me amplify something. And there's a place for that."[74] But, according to Ashley, that type of social media amplification has its limits if it never translates to real-life change.

Among the moms Ashley follows online who nourish her are Qimmah Saafir (@qimmah.saafir), who created *HANNAH* magazine—which, according to the @hannah.magazine Instagram bio, is a "Thoughtful, Intentional, Loving Ode to Black Women in Print, Digital + Real-Life Community"—and organizer Zola Ellen (@zola.ellen), who does abolitionist work in Minneapolis. Ashley applauds all of Zola's accomplishments since the murder of George Floyd, and she admires Qimmah's centering of "her own self-evolution through the process of motherhood."[75]

When she was pregnant, Imani Payne (@realgrowingpaynes) started her Instagram account with the express intent of speaking up about the "cracked nipple" side of motherhood. Because she's into photography, she enjoys creating visually pleasing imagery, but in her captions she emphasizes honesty and openness. As for her stories, she says, that's where you'll find her "everyday hot mess."[76] When she first created her account, she told me via Zoom, she had to be "super intentional about finding other Black mothers or mothers of color to follow." She was hard-pressed to find them on her Discover page, where she was bombarded with "super manicured" momfluencer accounts showcasing their "picture-perfect" lives. "And I gravitated toward other moms online who were being honest," she said, "or, like, at least talking about the hard parts as well."[77]

Some of the "hard parts" Imani has written about on Instagram include pregnancy loss, the difficulty of egalitarian partnerships, and infertility. When she experienced a traumatizing ectopic pregnancy, she found Sara Brawner (@sarakbrawner), who has written about maternal grief, and says that Sara's writing just felt "so familiar": "I'd never had a conversation with anyone about the fact that a lot of pregnancies don't end with a healthy baby. . . . I was just so confused and I felt so isolated and I found Sara's account and I just connected with her. And it was really helpful. And I don't, I can't really describe *how* it was helpful or exactly *why* it was helpful but it just . . . It just *was*."[78]

Part of what Imani attributes to the power of sharing our motherhood experiences online is simply the knowledge that we're not alone—that no matter what we experience, no matter how challenging or how rare it is, chances are, there's someone else out there who can relate, who can empathize, the awareness of whose very existence provides comfort. Referring to her ectopic pregnancy, Imani says, "I was able to think, *OK, this is not a super uncommon thing. There are other people out there that have gone through this experience.*"[79] Feminista Jones echoes this understanding in *Reclaiming Our Space*, in which she writes: "For some, just simply being able to say what happened 'out loud' helps them begin their journey of healing. For others, finding solidarity with others who have experienced something similar serves to alleviate a lot of their stress and internalization of blame."[80]

One of Imani's posts I often think about has to do with a lost pregnancy of her own and her belief in the importance of online community. In June 2021, she posted a photo of herself in bed looking at the camera with an expression that seems to say, "Something awful happened to me, and I'm gonna share."

> I wasn't sure if I was going to share this. I've been thinking a lot about privacy and boundaries lately, where/when/how to draw lines. I still don't have it figured out. I do know, that after my first miscarriage, I turned to the internet for community. I searched for women who could understand my grief and found them. Their stories, honesty, and vulnerability helped me. So here I am paying it forward. Last month I had another miscarriage. That's three now. Three unexplained, devastating, traumatic losses. Today I went in for genetic screening and made an appt with a high risk fertility specialist. It's hard to explain how I'm feeling, some complicated mix of fear, hope, guilt, gratitude, jealousy, envy and rage. 1:4 women experience pregnancy loss. One in four. I absolutely understand why people don't talk about it and yet it's so incredibly important to share our stories. Let's normalize our grief. I'll start, I'm really fucking sad. #1in4 #ihadamiscarriage #ttc #ectopicpregnancy #pregnancyloss #rainbowbaby[81]

Imani received *so* many comments in response to her vulnerable post. Some commenters expressed their condolences, their love, their empathy. Sara Brawner wrote: "I wish I could hug you right now."[82] Many people expressed their gratitude, saying they felt less alone because of Imani's decision to share. One comment especially stands out: "Thank you for sharing your story. Your vulnerability is helping us who've experienced this unbearable type of loss feel less alone in their grief."[83]

Imani and I discussed her ambivalence about Instagram as a platform, influencer culture at large, and the constant weirdness of performing one's identity for an audience, but ultimately, she says, "what's really keeping me on Instagram and keeping me posting is my miscarriage experience." She fully realizes that her openness is "super helpful" for people, and she wants to "be there" for others going through experiences that might align with her own.[84]

Laura Danger (@thatdarnchat) is similarly bolstered by her ability to not only provide representation for people but also to use her skills as an educator to spread awareness of gendered inequities in the home. I was first introduced to Laura's work when one of her TikToks about "weaponized incompetence" went viral; I wrote about the term and Laura's TikTok for *InStyle*, and since then, I've been following—and loving—Laura's approachable, empathetic, funny, and impassioned work on both TikTok, where she has 370,000 followers, and her recently created Instagram account, which is less than a year old but already has 104,000 followers.

While we Zoomed over iced coffee (her) and watered-down kombucha (me), Laura told me she grew up "chronically online," but didn't start experimenting on TikTok until 2020, when she was stuck at home, like many of us, trying to make sense of the world and her place in it. A K–8 educator, Laura has taught for the past decade in both private and public schools in Chicago. She also invests in abolition and mutual aid work. In the summer of 2020, she had been confining her "unhinged rants to the abyss" about the state of the world to her personal Instagram account (she hadn't yet set up her @thatdarnchat Instagram), but when protests about the murder of George Floyd started to erupt, she began focusing her Instagram on "research and statistics and sharing and amplifying information."[85]

When some of Laura's advocacy work on Instagram gained traction, a friend suggested she check out TikTok. She did, and, in her basement while her kid was napping, she learned a TikTok dance and laughed at herself as she recorded her first video. "I think the fifth video I ever did was about how the American education system is built on white supremacist values," she told me. "And I did this, like, silly dance and then did an overlay of text." She played around for "months and months" with it being very "hit or miss" until one of the strands of virtual spaghetti she had been throwing against the wall stuck and one of her videos went viral.[86]

This particular video was what I'd call classic @thatdarnchat: Laura took a seemingly mundane moment many women experience on a regular basis, and tore it apart to expose the sexism and gendered inequity at its root. The video's inspiration was an Instagram post shared by an acquaintance about the acquaintance's husband watching their baby for thirty minutes so she could exercise. The post was tagged "best husband ever" and featured the cranky-looking husband holding the baby and staring at his phone. Laura said, "And I made a fifteen-second video where I'm like, *If I see one more Instagram post congratulating a dad for doing the bare minimum, I am going to flip a table. And it got, like, hundreds of thousands of views."

Laura's work is so good. Her videos are the ones you text to friends, followed by lots of profanity and maybe the head-exploding emoji. Laura skillfully marries relatable problems with smart, informed reflections about how gender inequities creep into domestic life (and what you can do in response!). She says she's gotten lots of feedback from fans who praise her directness, frankness, and disarming delivery.

Laura says that it's harder to grow on Instagram, and that she feels confined by some of the platform's more formulaic, algorithmically informed trends, whereas on TikTok, she feels like she's "just in someone's living room."[87]

Laura confided that she's never been as passionate about something as she is about fighting gendered domestic inequities and elevating unpaid labor. These issues recently became viscerally personal for her. After ten years as the primary earner in her family, her leave of absence from teaching has recently expired, and aside from her caregiving work and activism, she's newly unemployed. Laura's trying to figure out how to use her unique skillset as an educator and social justice organizer to create change, and says she has "seen huge, huge ripples" from her work online, and that the experience has been "so empowering." She's found "lifelong connections" through both Instagram and TikTok, and remembers cluster-feeding her infant in the middle of the night and feeling comforted that she could access community online, likening that community to "a big group chat."

> I think the power of social media is incredibly profound specifically for the work I want to do, which is showing people what they're worth. When women feel undervalued, they start to believe it. And if they can see other women owning their value and their voices, they can start advocating for themselves, they can leave their deadbeat husbands and start getting the time they need. Or their husbands can step up to the plate! So I'm, like, the whisper in their ear right now. I don't take it lightly. And I want to keep doing it.[88]

When I asked Laura about the power of social media activism in particular, she said unequivocally that it plays a significant role in making issues "public" and encouraging open conversations that might be difficult to facilitate IRL or in more traditional settings. "When it's an ongoing public conversation," she told me, "you feel strengthened to call it out when you see it offline." She also thinks it's reductive to assume that social change can only be initiated by one particular approach: "It's not an either/or. We still need traditional advocates and traditional activism." For the record, Laura says she's also happy to give a speech at the White House, the thesis of which would be "What the fuck are you doing not giving us paid leave? Give it to us. Like, NOW!"[89]

While I really want Laura to give that White House speech, there are already plenty of people giving White House speeches, albeit maybe not quite as direct or succinct as Laura's would be. And that's a good thing! We can't all be giving speeches, or making reels, or canvassing neighborhoods. But, as Kristin Rowe-Finkbeiner, the CEO and cofounder of MomsRising, told me via a phone call, we all can do *something* to make motherhood less shitty. For everyone.

According to their website, MomsRising is an "on-the-ground and online grassroots organization of more than a million people who are working to achieve economic security for all moms, women, and families in the United States."[90] One of the many things to love about MomsRising is how easy they make activism: they do all the work of research and organization so that people like me, overwhelmed and often dispirited by the state of maternity, can quickly and easily find a way to use their voice in a way that will contribute to change.

Kristin and I only spent an hour on the phone together, but her passion and energy for creating better conditions for caregivers was absolutely infectious. I started the call feeling the way I do most days: depressed about how little our country seems to care about people who mother. But, when I got off the phone, I felt reassured that there are very smart people working tirelessly both online and off to make things better. And they've been at it for a long time.

MomsRising has only about twenty thousand followers on Instagram, but their work goes far beyond social media. Kristin first became interested in maternal activism when her son's primary immune deficiency forced her to leave the workforce due to a lack of paid family medical leave. Kristin was raised by a single mom, and while her family was OK thanks to her husband's salary, she felt suddenly overwhelmed by her awareness of how others could be so easily negatively impacted. "I thought, *Wow, this unexpected medical emergency is pushing me out of the labor force and if this had happened to my mom it would have been an outright disaster,*" she recalled. "Because we don't have an actual care infrastructure. We have a freefall."[91]

Kristin's frustration with her situation made her want to learn more about mothers and labor. So she contacted the US Census Bureau (might as well go straight to the source, right?), who told her that they don't track mothers who aren't in the workforce because "they don't track unpaid labor"—the implicit message here being, of course, that unpaid labor doesn't matter, that unpaid labor doesn't "count." Kristin was furious when she realized how many people's labor was "rendered invisible." While the census does track married moms (whose husbands are in the workforce), Kristin points out that this still leaves out a huge swathe of the population. "Johns Hopkins recently reported that over 60 percent of millennials are unmarried," she told me. "This is not a small group of humans."[92]

Kristin discovered that "being a mom is a greater predictor of wage and hiring discrimination than being a woman, and moms of color experience compounded wage and hiring discrimination due to structural racism." To illustrate just one facet of racialized maternal discrimination, she told me that, right now, in 2022, "Latina moms are earning just forty-six cents to a white dad's dollar."[93] Women also make up the overwhelming majority of domestic workers (91.5 percent), and 52.4 percent of these women are Black, Hispanic, or Asian American/Pacific Islander women.[94]

Kristin's research led her to more research, which led her to writing a book, *The F-Word: Feminism in Jeopardy*, and then another book, with Joan Blades, *The Motherhood Manifesto: What America's Moms Want—and What to Do About It*. And in 2006, she and Joan got together with forty-eight other groups with the shared goal of moving maternal rights issues forward politically—and MomsRising was born.

When I mentioned my crummy attitude about conditions ever meaningfully changing for the better, Kristin told me a story about a bingo card. She says that when MomsRising was first created, many of the people involved made bingo cards with boxes like "family medical leave" and "affordable childcare" and "pay inequality," and they would track political speeches to see how often such issues were mentioned.[95] Back in 2006, she says, most of the bingo boxes were empty. But, especially after the passage of the Affordable Care Act, Kristin noticed more and more bingo boxes began to fill up as more and more politicians started paying attention to issues related to maternal caregiving and well-being.

In addition to invoking the bingo card as evidence of change—despite that change being slow-moving—Kristin recounted a recent incident when she overheard a woman in a grocery store checkout line telling a friend that, because Washington State had finally passed paid family medical leave, she could now start the family she had put off for so long. "This woman didn't know about how many years of work it had taken to get there," Kristin explained. "They didn't know about the long fight."[96]

Kristin is certain things will get better because, she says, they must. The status quo has to change because the situation for mothers in this country is "untenable." She asserted, "This is an emergency. Moms are in emergency. And in that state of emergency, you can access hope by understanding you're not alone in the emergency. Like, there are a lot of fricking people in the emergency! But when you're in an emergency, it's easy to feel isolated."[97] And social media, according to Kristin, plays a huge role in lessening that sense of hopelessness and isolation.

The bingo card really helped me understand the incremental nature of progress, as Kristin's layer-cake metaphor noted below, neatly illustrates the importance of multilayered approaches when it comes to advocacy and activism. We can demand change in all sorts of ways; we can make phone calls, we can write letters, sign petitions, or, as MomsRising has recently done, set up a marching band outside the US Capitol or place an ad in the *New York Times* (both of which were advocating in favor of the Build Back Better bill). Social media, Kristin says, is one layer of a very "delicious cake"; it is "amplifying and allowing people to connect and share, and to actually get involved." Kristin says most of the growth at MomsRising has occurred through moms telling other moms about the organization. "Often they do this by sharing action links on social media, people saying, *Hey, this is ridiculous, right? Here's a link to take action* or *here's a link to make a phone call.*"[98]

Even the act of sharing one's individual story online can contribute to creating larger waves, Kristin believes. By the time of our call, MomsRising had received over eleven thousand stories from its members throughout the pandemic, and they've shared these stories on both social and traditional media. The cumulative effect of these stories, Kristin said, not only proves that a *lot* of people are facing similar struggles but also that, given the vast quantity of stories and the similarity of these stories, it's clear that the failures are not individual but structural. This point is particularly potent when applied to motherhood, an endeavor many have been encouraged to tackle as a solitary venture, a job at which individuals can either succeed or fail by sheer dint of their "goodness" as moms, regardless of whether or not they're receiving external support. According to Kristin, it's critical to recognize the "national structural situation that we can and must solve together."[99]

Kristin has been "humbled" by the immense power of mothers coming together. To further convince me that all is not hopeless, she told me that, during 2021 alone, "even though people were busy, even though everything was on fire, the members of MomsRising reached out to Congress *over a million times* to say, basically, *What the hell.*"

I could sense throughout our call that Kristin genuinely wanted me to believe that change is coming, that it's inevitable, not solely because, like, it has to be or we'll all crack up, but because more and more data is becoming available to prove that giving mothers and caregivers an infrastructural safety net isn't just good for individuals—it's good for business. "Studies show that when you build a care infrastructure, people of all genders have access to it," she explained. "When you have paid family medical leave, affordable childcare, and healthcare for all, you actually lower the wage gap between moms and non-moms. And this helps get rid of pay-parity issues or pay inequality, and lifts not only families but business and the GDP."[100] I don't necessarily love that capitalism might be the reason conditions ultimately improve for mothers, but I also don't care what finally moves the needle as long as something does!

Author of *The Fifth Trimester: The Working Mom's Guide to Style, Sanity, and Success After Baby*, Lauren Smith Brody (@thefifth trimester) cites cold, hard facts, too, as a reason to hope. We talked about how she went from a position as an executive editor at *Glamour* to becoming one of the loudest, smartest voices advocating for moms both on Instagram and off. She agrees with Kristin that change is inevitable, not least in part because of the pandemic. "It's been so well spelled out in the media," she said, "and articulated in studies that show, for example, the positive impact that giving mothers a little bit of money every month has on a baby's brain development." Lauren explained that when studies like this can prove causality, activists are better armed to fight for things like the Child Tax Credit. She said the increase in media coverage during the pandemic has armed all of us with language to finally discuss the things that might have felt very wrong for a very long time. "You can't ignore what's happened to parents, caregivers, children during the pandemic, even if you have a heart of stone," she told me. "And if you want an economy, you need childcare. And so people who are advocating for these things and have been for years have language and statistics to create more widespread buy-in than ever before."[101]

After she left *Glamour*, Lauren's journalistic background made Instagram seem like a logical place to center her advocacy efforts, and the platform allows her to utilize the bits of magazine work she "really, really loved." She told me, "It's the word 'play.' It's the love of storytelling, and quality images, and then, you know, it's *not* the pieces of magazine work I didn't necessarily love, like staying up until 2 a.m. editing a page of mascara wands while my babies were home sleeping."[102]

On Instagram, Lauren shares tips for talking to relatives about the importance of paid family leave; she's spread the word about a #Mothersstrike organized by advocacy groups like Save Paid

Leave; she advocates for the importance of rendering invisible work visible. She's like the cool big sister you always wanted who also happens to be a maternal activist powerhouse. And she loves what she does. She finds her work "genuine" and "fulfilling," and being able to devote herself fully to what she truly cares about has been like "a breath of fresh air."

One of the unique benefits of social media advocacy in particular, Lauren told me, is the ease with which you can assess people's specific needs. Through Instagram, she has spoken to "brand new moms" or moms who worked in fields totally different from her own. "You know, it's almost like an interactive focus group," she said. When Laura was invited to a White House briefing on paid leave, she was able to poll her Instagram followers about what kinds of questions they wanted her to ask in advance. "That's just a really natural moment to share directly with an audience." And while she used to primarily use her social media platform to help people understand the concept of the "fifth trimester," which, for the purposes of her work, she initially defined as "the return to paid work after maternity leave," her mission has "totally expanded because of the pandemic."

> As more people began working from home and having to navigate their personal lives alongside their working lives, and also to do so with more transparency, and as more people started to ask for adaptability in work, I realized the fifth trimester goes way beyond maternity leave. The pandemic just exposed inequities that had always been there, but that we didn't all have language for. We can now see that these issues go beyond our own lives and needs, and we can see that the structural problems are universal. Suddenly it dawned on me, like, *Oh, holy shit, everyone's in their fifth trimester now.*[103]

As in the case of Laura Danger, the pandemic made Lauren's advocacy work personal. At one point, her husband was working fifteen-hour days, her two children were Zoom-schooling at home, and, Lauren says, "It was all me . . . I was cooking every meal and doing every bit of laundry. And I had this big reckoning of, like, viscerally understanding what I'd been saying for years, which is that *unpaid labor absolutely counts and it has value, and I'm doing a whole shit ton of it right now!*" This experience inspired her to create @chamberofmothers with several other activists in November 2021, the goal being to act as a "megaphone" for already existing maternal advocacy organizations. Lauren explained that the folks at @chamberofmothers get in touch with advocacy groups, ask how they can help, and then just "*go.*" She said @chamberofmothers can communicate things "more fiercely" online than other organizations might be able to do, for a variety of reasons. "We can use language and images that, you know, perhaps are not becoming of an organization that has, you know, a daily war-room meeting with the White House."[104]

Both Lauren and I think the visual medium of Instagram influences how @chamberofmothers can spread awareness as well as which kinds of audiences it attracts. Their logo itself immediately communicates that this organization is not, like, your grandmother's nice, mannerly women's group. Against a shell-pink background are pictured two women's hands folded together in such a way as to look like, well, a vulva. Or a heart! The hands are deep burgundy, and a drop of what looks like blood drips from two index fingers pointed downward. The image is direct and galvanizing, and importantly, it communicates a real sense of rage, of powerful fed-up-ness. The Instagram account @chamberofmothers has thirty-seven thousand followers, and their grid is aesthetically cohesive and attention grabbing. It's advocacy and it looks good, and whether it's fair or not, the cool aesthetic is maybe just one of the tools in their toolkit that helps to elicit engagement.

But @chamberofmothers's good looks are not to be confused with "brunch activism." Even within the organization itself, Lauren told me, the "founding mothers" operate the way they want the rest of the world to operate. If someone has a sick kid, for example, another member will pick up the slack. It's not a big deal;

it's just a part of life. Lauren explains it far more evocatively by saying, "We're like this flock of birds. The ones at the front are kind of doing the hardest work right now. And then you're allowed to kind of, like, sit back and glide. And we all take turns being out front. And we all take turns gliding." I love this. It's a practice that mimics what Lauren and her peers want to see in the wider world, which is a collective concern for all types of caregivers (and all types of people). She believes that every time one of us speaks up on our own behalf for more maternity leave, or better childcare or more flexible work-from-home options, our individual actions will lead to collective change. "You're not just doing it for your own little family," she said. "You're actually doing it for everyone around you who for some reason or another has less privilege or less agency than you do. It's important that we all stretch a little bit for the greater good."[105]

There are so many more moms I want to rave about in this chapter. There's Shisi Rose (@shishi.rose), who advocates for Black maternal care and provides actionable tips for allies who want to help. There's Cia (@theenbymama), who wrote a beautiful, thoughtful post about the unique gender dysphoria they sometimes feel nursing their child as a gender-nonbinary person. There's KC Davis (@strugglecare), who brilliantly calls the design and maintenance of a pretty laundry room "a hobby," whereas the necessary labor of providing a family with clean clothes is a morally neutral care task. There's Nicole Lynn Lewis (@nicolelynn lewis), who wrote a book about her experience as a young single mother and who works tirelessly to advocate for other young, disenfranchised moms. There's Danielle Aceino (@missverse), who has documented her gender-nonconforming kid's experience with grace and empathy while also offering support and resources for parents who want to do the same. There are countless brilliant, passionate moms on Instagram that are doing radical, important work on their platforms.

And yes, Instagram sucks. Of course. But it also is an invaluable resource for advocacy and activism, and to deny the impact these mothers and many others have had because of how they've utilized their Instagram accounts is both short-sighted and also mistaken about what is actually most pernicious about "mommy content." Momfluencer accounts that celebrate and uphold a harmful, outdated version of ideal motherhood are certainly not great. Algorithms deliberately designed to keep us glued to screens are pretty objectively bad. But the education and calls to action you can find on those same screens is anything but. If nothing else, the web of disruptor momfluencers on Instagram is like a modern-day phone tree: a giant text thread of moms whom you will feel good about connecting with, moms who want to create a world in which we care less about buying our kid the trendiest neutral sweater of the month and more about each other.

8

Cruel Optimism and Dreams of Motherhood "Destined to Be Dashed"

It's been twenty-one weeks since Naomi Davis (@taza) posted on Instagram. Her last post was a carousel of three photos featuring herself; her toddler, Beatrice; and her husband, Josh (@tiesand fries). It's classic Naomi—all jubilance and light. She's wearing cherry-colored cat-eye sunglasses and a pink-and-red-checkered top. Beatrice, in a pale pink dress with red polka dots, is sandwiched between Naomi and Josh, who is wearing a tie because he's always wearing a tie. The tie is green. Everyone is smiling. Rays of sunshine halo the trio.

Because this is a book about—among other things—my consumption of momfluencer culture, I take a minute to do a pulse check on what this photo evokes in me. Per usual, I admire Naomi's freckles, I notice the way the hair on either side of her middle part smooths down against her cheekbones. No fuzzies. I look closer and think I detect a nearly imperceptible bobby pin. The elbow-length sleeves of her top are blousy without being frumpy. I think of my own arms, which I'm sort of self-conscious about because they're not as "willowy" as I'd like them to be (shout-out to diet culture *and* Lucy Maud Montgomery). I think Naomi's sleeves would make me feel good about my arms. I wonder where her shirt is from; Naomi didn't tag the photo with the brand, so I'd have to spend some time googling it. I muse about Josh and Naomi's relationship. What is it like to be with someone who, like you, has a penchant for posing in cutesy photos? Is it annoying? Is it fun? Naomi's teeth are very white.

What was I doing again? Why am I doing this again?

At the time of this writing, it's March 2, 2022. Two days ago, @layvoos commented under Naomi's last post: "Where are you? miss you 😞." Five days ago, @ispyabrownbair commented: "Missing your posts! Hope everything is ok! Praying for your family 💜." Five weeks ago, @better.better.better.better commented: "Anybody else coming here daily to see what the next comment is?" Six weeks ago, @skyqu33n commented: "So bizarre, I feel like I lost a friend."[1]

Yesterday I tweeted my own musings about Naomi, speculating whether or not she would ultimately emerge from the ashes of her Instagram past with a podcast, a newsletter, or a TV show. Momfluencer expert-extraordinaire Kathryn Jezer-Morton replied: "Product line . . . furniture etc. I don't think she wants to be a personality anymore (just a guess)." @Oliviamdh replied: "A lot of those OGs aren't posting anymore." She went on to cite @ramshackleglam (Jordan Reid) and @whatiwore.[2]

Prior to my tweet, I had actually spoken to Jordan Reid (@ramshackleglam) about her experience as a blogger and a momfluencer. We talked about the pressure to assume a particular aesthetic, the way the industry has changed over the years, and the particular "sadness" of having to perform motherhood for an audience. When I asked Jordan to speak to this sadness, she told me a story about her managers urging her to embrace a more minimalist, modern, "all white" aesthetic. She had a new baby at the time, whom she remembers laying on a gingham blanket and attempting to take a photograph emphasizing negative space (her managers had told her negative space was aesthetically on trend). During the photo shoot her daughter was bubbly and smiley, but in retrospect, Jordan told me, the memory was "depressing." She said, "Just that very first moment of trying to figure out how to create this aesthetic that my managers were asking me explicitly to create. Yeah, the fact that it was tied to my child is striking to me."[3]

I wonder if Naomi thought about taking a photo for Instagram the morning of her last post. I wonder if she chose her toddler's outfit strategically to match her own. I wonder why she didn't address any of the things momfluencer consumers wonder about momfluencers in her 2021 essay collection, *A Coat of Yellow Paint*.

Halfway through our conversation, Jordan casually asked if I had heard of *GOMI* (*Get Off My Internets*), an infamous blog devoted to gossip about influencers. *Yes*, I said, *of course*. *GOMI* has been the home of so much salient momfluencer discourse, the breadth of which ranges from stunningly hateful to mildly curious. One of *GOMI*'s bigger moments in the mainstream was during a rumored spat between Naomi Davis and Natalie Lovin (@heynataliejean)— something to do with a white wall? In 2018, Lydia Kiesling wrote about Natalie (who, Kiesling writes, was the subject of 2,500 pages on *GOMI*) and rightly calls the blog "a site of internecine warfare so complex and intense that it could support a doctoral thesis."[4]

Naomi Davis's book was roundly mocked on *GOMI*. One user wrote the following assessment of *A Coat of Yellow Paint*:

> She had absolutely no business writing a book other than to satisfy her vanity. She is and always has been an abysmal writer, though that can sometimes be overlooked if the story is terrific. But her story is not terrific. She's just a mid-30s Mormon stay at home breeder who lived in New York City for a few years and took a few nice vacations. What gripping, unique story could she possibly have to share about her life that is worthy of a book deal? That she can make babies? Congrats, the feral alley cat at the bodega can do that four times a year, where's her book deal?[5]

I disagree with this particular commenter because I, for one, would kill to read an honest accounting of what it's been like for Naomi Davis to perform motherhood online for thousands of people who love her and who love to hate her for over a decade. I'd love to know what she thinks about how momfluencing has changed throughout the years. I'd love to ask her what she might've done differently. I'd love to know what her career as a momfluencer has given her. I'd love to know what it's taken away.

I'd love to know if she thinks it's been worth it.

Remember Amanda Montell's notion of "cringe-following?" There's some of this on *GOMI*, sure, but you're also likely to see plenty of more straightforward hate-following. In response to one of Jordan Reid's Instagram stories in 2017, which featured her children, one *GOMI* user commented: "What the f**k is wrong with you. Fame w***e."[6] On *GOMI* things go from mildly gossipy to dark pretty quickly. (For more intel, definitely check out Jo Piazza's interview with *GOMI* founder Alice Wright on Jo's podcast *Under the Influence.*)

Anyway, according to Jordan Reid, *GOMI* was not always *GOMI*. First, she said, it was *Reblogging Ramshackle Glam*. The name referenced a popular snark site of the time (around 2009/10), called *Reblogging NonSociety*, which targeted one of the first internet celebrities, Julia Allison. Jordan told me that *GOMI*'s first iteration, *Reblogging Ramshackle Glam*, probably ultimately became *GOMI* because there's only so much material one can glean from a single blogger: "There are limits to how much fun you can make of someone's cooking or big teeth or whatever things about me that *GOMI* found worthy of mockery." Jordan laughs sardonically about all of this now, but back then, being the subject of so much ire and angst ("People were writing about me every day") was "terrifying." She was a new parent at the time, and, like most of us, experiencing the specific hells of new parenthood: sleep deprivation, mood swings, identity shifts. "It was beyond anxiety-inducing," Jordan told me. "They would tear down my parenting, even mock my children. And whatever I did, whether I did a thing one way today and the opposite way the next day, was worthy of the most vicious, personal, targeted criticism."[7]

I was recently a guest on Virginia Sole-Smith's podcast *Burnt Toast*, and we interrogated the phenomenon of gentle parenting on social media. To illustrate the type of gentle parenting content that irks me specifically, I told Virginia about @milkgiver (real name Rachel), who cited her "crunchy" lifestyle choices as evidence of her maternal prowess in a post about liver shots and wellness: "This crunchy mama road isn't always an easy one, and high five to anyone else desperately trying to keep their kids away from the junk being thrown at them right and left, I see you! It's not always an easy path, but it is one I enjoy and ultimately follow because I like feeling good, I like keeping my kids healthy, and I like having energy, because that helps me to be a better mom. That's my top goal in life currently, and being mostly healthy helps *a lot* with it."[8]

Since Virginia's podcast is concerned with diet culture, Virginia and I critiqued the notion that abstaining from all processed foods (or whatever) somehow makes one a better mom than someone who packs Cheez-Its for their kids' school snacks. But we also snarked. The day after recording the ep, Virginia and I texted, wondering about the line between cathartic snark and unproductive personal criticism. I try very hard to stick to cultural critiques of the structures underpinning individuals' behavior versus critiques of the individuals themselves, but I'm also a person. And as a person who has made the deliberate decision to not "desperately" try to protect my kids from junk food, it's hard not to take @milkgiver's post personally—hard not to second-guess my choices when I read her words and view her reel, which features her looking into a mirror bedecked with a dried orange-slice garland. She looks happy and relaxed, and if there's one state I wish I could inhabit more often in my maternal life, it's happy relaxation. Would I have chosen this particular post to critique if @milkgiver didn't look so chill? If she didn't implicitly attack my own maternal choices by espousing her own? If her account didn't make it so easy for me to project, project, project my own shit onto? Snark may be cathartic, but I've been reflecting more and more on the slippery slide from snark to hatred. The line between *GOMI* posts attacking Jordan Reid for being a "fame whore" and me allowing my personal parenting insecurities to bleed into my criticism of gentle parenting tropes isn't as distinct as I'd like it to be.

Jordan started experiencing some uncomfortable feelings about other momfluencer accounts herself when she got divorced in 2018. "I had never felt any animosity toward anyone I follow," she told me. "I was like, whatever. I mean, like, *I'll just not follow you if I don't enjoy your feed.* And then, after the divorce, I noticed myself getting judgmental and angry when I saw, like, the perfect, perfect family feeds. And it was the first time I sort of understood where the people who had trolled me were coming from." She said she has always felt a certain amount of empathy for people targeting her on *GOMI* or elsewhere, "because it's always coming from a place of jealousy or anger about something in your own life. Always." But when she was dealing with the dissolution of her marriage, she became aware of "ugly" feelings. "So I just unfollowed those accounts because it just . . ." She paused for a second. "I didn't like the *words* that were popping up in my mind. You know what I mean?"[9] Yes, yes.

Jordan is one of the many moms I interviewed for this book who said she won't allow her kids to touch social media until they're eighteen ("Absolutely not. Under no circumstances"), and she's still trying to tease out the impact Instagram, specifically, has had on her sense of self as a person and as a mother. "I have definitely given this twelve years of intensive thought," she said, "and have questioned my choices in the past and continue to question them. I still cannot resist posting, like, the idyllic childhood shot. And I definitely wrestle with *why*, especially since, now, my children are older. And so they're participating in the conversation. They're like, *Why did you post that to Instagram?* And I'm like, *That is an excellent question.* At this point, it doesn't really have any material impact on my career." Jordan noted that posting cute kid pics to Instagram is similar to how we used to print photos and put them in albums, and that she likes recording moments in her kids' lives. But she thinks if her income was not at least tangentially related to her Instagram content, she'd make her account private. "That'd be the obvious answer," she said.[10] Jordan also sees a difference between placing photos in a family album that only a handful of people ever see and posting those same photos online for possibly thousands of strangers to consume, as entertainment. Or something else.

Recently, Katy Rose Prichard (@katyroseprichard) has been forced to reevaluate her own Instagram platform and usage thanks to a stranger stealing photos of her and her children to use for "role play." In this case, "role play" means taking someone else's photos and using them to start new accounts and create fictional identities and story lines to accompany the photos. When interviewed for *Good Morning America* about Katy and her experience, Jo Piazza said that role play can attract sexual predators, "because they're playing with fictional identities of very, very real children."[11] And, even if sexual predators aren't involved, stealing someone else's family memories and creating new narratives about someone else's children is objectively creepy.

Katy and I spoke about both the incident and her ever-changing perception of Instagram as a platform. After discovering her children's faces plastered all over a stranger's account (an experience she called "terrifying"), she spent weeks painstakingly removing all photos of her kids from her own Instagram feed as well as from posts in which she'd been tagged. Katy had been toying with scaling back from kid-centric content for a while but says the role-play nightmare was the "nudge" she needed. "As much as I hate what happened," she told me, "I am so thankful it did. Because I wouldn't be where I'm at right now with all of it if that didn't happen."[12]

Katy says she loves being a mom but has been trying to "edge away from the mommy sphere" on Instagram for a while now, simply because "mom" is only one part of her identity, and she's eager to express other sides of herself. She has also been thinking about how the performative aspect informs her self-identity and how the urge to perform impacts her kids. She says her four-year-old is really becoming aware of herself and the world around her, and it's been unsettling for Katy when her daughter calls out, "Take a picture, take a picture!" She told me, "And in the back of my mind, I'm like, *It's in her head that, for everything we do, we need a picture.*"[13]

Observing her teenage daughter's relationship with Instagram has made Katy question her own "addiction," noting that her daughter now has opinions about how she looks in photos, how she's presented, what she wants to be shared. "A lot of [popular momfluencers] just have younger kids. And it's easy to be, like, *This is fun!*" (Katy frankly admits to "bribing" her kids when they were little with "suckers" or whatever, "to make it fun.") "But now, having an older kid, it just kind of made me realize that these kids will have their own voices someday. Why wait until they can voice their permission?"[14]

Katy's grappling with whether or not she wants to keep her account just to promote her writing, podcast, and other creative endeavors, or if she wants to delete it altogether. She believes that the things she initially loved about Instagram—the potential for connection and artistic expression—can be found elsewhere, with fewer strings attached, less damage to one's psyche.

For Katy, the fraught nature of performing her motherhood online has made her "so reliant on others' insights and likes." Katy told me she has generalized anxiety, and that Instagram has impacted her self-esteem and her "need to always be perfect." She said, "I don't think it's healthy. It's just that I'm programmed to do it. I just think we're set up for failure on Instagram. You're always comparing yourself and you're always having to re-innovate your life, a.k.a. your brand. I *hate* that. Like, we just need to live life! Life is so short. It's precious. And it's hard enough as it is." Katy hopes she can keep "sharing, writing, and creating art" on other platforms, while simultaneously "eliminating all the noise of social media and the distractions and the comparison game and all of that."[15]

Hitha Palepu (@hithapalepu)—remember Hitha's hatred of the term "momfluencer" and her toddler's disinterest in *CoCom-*

elon from chapter 1?—made the decision to stop incorporating her kids in her content (for which they were paid) once her oldest son told her that, for him, it "was no longer fun." She wishes companies like LTK and ShopStyle, which exist solely to support and financially benefit from the influencer economy, would start offering momfluencers benefits, health insurance, and options to set up trusts for their kids.

When I asked Hitha what she thought the future of her involvement with Instagram would be, she laughed. Like, a *lot*. "From day one," she replied, "I've always said that you never ever build a business completely on a platform you have no control over. Instagram is making a lot of decisions that feel very, very immediate and short term and not at all focused on the future. That is their choice."[16] Even after Instagram became a huge platform for creators, Hitha always maintained her blog. Now, she's taken her written content to Substack, which she's "very impressed with. . . It's the best-in-class written communication platform. It gives me the control I need over my community and is also working to give me the tools I need to grow on that platform. When I bring back a podcast, it will be hosted on Substack." Ultimately, though, momfluencers need to put their own needs first, Hitha says, and ask themselves, "Am I getting what I need from this particular platform? Am I getting value?" Stephanie McNeal, senior culture writer at *BuzzFeed*, told me via email that after surveying several influencers for her book, "almost every one said they planned on diversifying . . . I think the trend now is to build a sustainable business that you own fully, so your income isn't determined solely by Instagram."[17]

Sometimes, regardless of the platform, and whether or not the platform makes it easier or harder for a momfluencer to find and create community or earn a living, the simple act of being a mom online is dangerous enough on its own. Virginia Duan (@the mandarinmama) wrote a supremely relatable essay for *ScaryMommy* about how her parenting style of "benign neglect" not only gives her space to be an autonomous human but also contributes to her kids being "happy, useful" people. Here's one of my favorite passages: "And if necessity is the mother of invention, then me refusing to do the myriad of shitty things a parent is supposed to do for their kids is actually me teaching them important life skills. You cannot convince me otherwise."[18] The essay is so, so, so innocuous. It's hard for me to imagine any actual parent reading it and taking issue. But some did. Because of course.

When Virginia and I talked over the phone about the essay and her experience on social media, she told me this essay (and others) led to her being doxed by white nationalists. "I got death threats," she said. "I got rape threats." After conservative columnist Matt Walsh tweeted about Virginia's work, "then a bunch of mad white dudes made YouTube videos about me, and I had to file police reports. That was fun to call the police, you know, mostly white men." While Virginia's presence on Instagram wasn't the inciting incident for this wave of racist, sexist hatred, she thinks all women—especially women of color—risk something by using their voices online. And she thinks consuming motherhood on social media "is warping our brains."[19]

Virginia doesn't necessarily think the current generation has it better or worse than our parents did in terms of external judgment. To her, social media is only "reflecting what society is already telling you." But, she said, these societal messages are so much more pervasive than they used to be. So omnipresent. "Now we just have more places to see them, to be reminded of what society wants us to be. . . . And the more you see it, the more you'll feel bad about yourself, and I don't like to feel bad about myself as a general rule, because I feel bad about myself enough." Virginia doesn't offer any neat solutions, but she did tell me she is deliberate about how she curates her feed, because "what we see every day affects us."[20]

What we see every day affects us. I often wonder how much brain space is occupied by the momfluencers I follow. I wonder how much my perception of my own reality is impacted. Would my love of Shaker cabinets have been instilled by another external force if @mamawatters hadn't gotten there first? Would I view clean countertops as something illustrative of ideal motherhood if momfluencer culture didn't exist? Would I wake up at 1 a.m. to pee and stay awake brooding over having impatiently snapped at my toddler for demanding to balance his large, rotund panda stuffie on *top* of his diminutive sippy cup and making us late for preschool in the long, drawn-out, doomed-to-fail-by-virtue-of-gravity process? Do all the smiling, graceful moms and all their voiceless, beautiful children contribute to me feeling sporadically dissatisfied with my own life? Surely, yes. But it feels impossible to quantify the heft of its impact. How would the hours of my day feel if I wasn't consciously and subconsciously defining my motherhood against the motherhoods of so many strangers on social media? I can boast about having as much critical awareness about harmful gender norms as I want, but in the end, *what we see every day affects us.*

Lynzy Coughlin of the blog *Lynzy and Co.* quit Instagram in December 2021—when she had roughly five hundred thousand followers—and posted about her decision on her blog, the heading of which reads: "You can never get enough of what you don't need." Chief among her many reasons for deleting Instagram from her life was the sheer amount of mental and emotional energy required to respond to the thousands of comments and DMs that flooded her on a daily basis. The unending nature of the work of influencing, she said, became a "nightmare."

> I have never been one to want someone to answer my emails or DMs as this is MY brand and I feel that it needs to be ME who answers people. This has all taken its toll over the years to the point where I feel suffocated. The truth is the work of an "influencer" is never finished. There is no "end" to the day. There is always more you can do and a never ending inbox of messages on the gram and email. For a personality like mine, this is a nightmare combination and it's hard for me to disconnect.[21]

According to Emily Hund and Lee McGuigan, the blurring between self and brand is intrinsic to the influencer industry: "In the social media economy, there is no separation between one's work and oneself. Professional ideas and skills must be enmeshed with a 'personality' that is both perceived to be authentic and able to be leveraged within the confines of commercial structures of social media platforms—where likes and followers are metrics of success, and images should be able to merge seamlessly with monetization tools."[22] It's no wonder that more and more momfluencers are finding the uncanny valley of performing one's "authentic" identity for profit (personal, monetary, whatever) stifling and ultimately opting out.

Especially when only the top, top, top percent of momfluencers make significant money. Katy Rose Prichard, who has nearly one hundred thousand followers, told me she could "*maybe* earn 20 or 30K a year if I gave it my all, if I devoted every second to it."[23] Professional, monetized momfluencing is hard, time-consuming work, requiring a unique combination of identity performance and marketplace savvy. And the fact that there are so few safety nets in place, so few guarantees of financial viability, makes momfluencing not only personally tenuous but arguably not worth the significant psychological toll.

For momfluencers of color, the task of performing motherhood "right," and getting paid enough to make it worthwhile, is even more Sisyphean, since white momfluencers still, for the most part, make more money than their Black and brown counterparts. Writer Amil Niazi told me via email that she feels alienated by white momfluencer culture because it simply reflects the institution of motherhood itself as being "completely whitewashed":

> The entire narrative of who can be a mother, who can be a good mother, is centered around whiteness and an idea of purity that is rooted in racial stereotypes. White momfluencers still make the most money and have the most followers. Moms outside that ideal are still very much on the edges of

this world and have to push for the kind of brand deals and sponsorships and campaigns that come much more easily to their white counterparts. Advertisers push the narrative of the domesticated woman as much as anything on social media.[24]

And, of course, the impossible performance of authenticity is amorphous and trend dependent. While a photo of a mother snuggling her freshly bathed baby in the evening sunlight streaming through a window might have once been deemed "authentic," now "vulnerability" is hot. Tears get likes, which means human despair and sorrow are financially lucrative. In *No Filter*, Sarah Frier explains how Instagram execs are "privately advising its stars to stop trying so hard to be perfect, and start posting more raw and vulnerable content. They explain that perfection is no longer novel. Vulnerability now gets better engagement, because it's more relatable."[25] Of course, "engagement" is just code for something that can be bought and sold for profit. To call the situation dystopian feels like an understatement. And, at the risk of beating a dead horse, selling one's "vulnerability" is particularly bleak when applied to motherhood, an undeniably vulnerable experience. The idea of a momfluencer whose economic stability depends on her influencer work performing "sad mom" drag when she might actually be really fucking sad leaves me speechless with rage.

While Barrett Prendergast (@barrettprendergast) dabbles in monetized momfluencing, it's not her bread and butter. She owns a boutique gift-box service, Valleybrink Road, so momfluencing jobs make up only a fraction of her income. When we spoke on the phone, she told me influencer managers are fully aware that vulnerability sells, and they tell their clients as much. "Managers are literally telling people to cry, or talk about, like, the hardest thing in your life, or the most vulnerable moment," she said. "Like, you need to capture that, you need to talk to the camera, you need to be crying."[26] Moms have a lot to cry about. And I guess the fact that our tears can be useful to build more "relatable" brands is just another thing to add to the list.

In her Instagram breakup blog post, Lynzy Coughlin cited information overload (particularly as it relates to mothering), the lack of "blank space" in her days, and a longing for "stillness" as additional reasons for leaving Instagram. "There is no healthy way to use social media, anymore," Lynzy wrote. "That is my opinion and I know that may make some people upset to read. When something is designed to be addictive, it doesn't *exclude* anyone from its wrath."[27]

And, of course, Instagram *was* designed to be addictive. All social media apps are designed to be addictive. In an interview for *Insider* with Hannah Schwär, app developer Peter Mezyk explained that there are two kinds of apps: "supplement apps" that fulfill a specific need quickly (like navigation apps), and "painkiller apps" (menacing!), which aren't designed to fix an already established problem (like needing to find one's way around twisty city streets without a physical map), but simply to be "attractive" to their users. "'They typically generate a stimulus,'" Mezyk explained to Schwär, "'which usually revolves around negative emotions such as loneliness or boredom,' he said, citing Instagram and Facebook as examples."[28]

Mothers are often lonely and bored.

I could go on and on about the corrosive nature of social media addiction, but I think most of us are pretty well versed in the fact that Instagram is not a company that aims to make the world a better, more just place. It's a company that operates by making as much money as possible. And so of course it's in their best interest to keep us glued to our screens for as many hours of the day as possible.

Instagram is also apparently anti–real motherhood. The company loves aesthetically pleasing motherhood, idealized motherhood, but they're less enthused about images of motherhood that prioritize the lived experiences of real moms. In 2019, Grace Kapin and Courtney Klein, founders of the maternity and postpartum clothing brand Storq, wrote an essay on *Medium* entitled "You Should Definitely Breastfeed. But I Would Rather Not Have to See It." The title alone beautifully elucidates how mothers can never win in our culture. The contradictory nature of culturally mandated expectations of motherhood ensures that we will always fail in one way or another. When Kapin and Klein swapped out professional models for real women who were actually pregnant or postpartum or breastfeeding, Instagram and Facebook almost immediately began censoring their ads, claiming them to be "sexually suggestive or provocative" or "overly focusing on one body part," and, thus, in violation of their community guidelines.[29]

In their *Medium* piece, Kapin and Klein write that they typically get "mixed results" from appealing the bans, noting that once, during a call, a Facebook employee suggested they photograph the clothing flat on a white background instead of featuring the clothes on models. To anyone who has ever shopped for maternity clothes, this is patently absurd. You need to see the garment on a pregnant body (or, at the very least, a body wearing a fake bump). Kapin and Klein recognize that the censorship of real motherhood cannot be blamed on algorithms alone, since algorithms reflect already sanctioned cultural norms. But in America, and in many other Western cultures, we live in a world that assigns value to women based on the perceived attractiveness of their various body parts. Instagram is awash in tits and ass. Kapin and Klein write: "The real problem is not that our ads feature boobs, bellies, and butts. We see this stuff everywhere to sell anything from beer to car insurance. It is how they are featured, because the context is that our company makes products for pregnancy and postpartum. These images are not ok because the women in them are mothers."[30]

I emailed Grace in 2021 to get an update on whether or not Instagram has relaxed their restrictions against Storq's "obscene" ads, and she flatly replied, "Nope," sending me a screenshot of a recently flagged ad.[31] Guys. The ad does not feature a nursing bra. It does not feature maternity underwear. It fucking features a woman and a newborn baby, who is held tightly against the woman's body by a baby wrap. The woman is wearing a long gray cardigan, which is partially draped against her wrapped baby.

She's wearing jeans. Her face is exposed. Her hands are exposed. *That is it.* Nary a belly button. Not a clavicle in sight! The "policy violation" for this ad reads: "Listings may not position products or services in a sexually suggestive manner."

Because I understand Instagram to be motivated primarily by profit potential, I asked Grace why it wouldn't be in Instagram's best interest to make money from Storq ads. Why dredge up completely ludicrous policy violations when Instagram could let the ads make money for them? Grace thinks an argument could be made that, in the end, some old white dude just might not want to see mothers in a certain light.

> In a nutshell we think the data that feeds the algorithm is inherently flawed because it's been crafted through a cultural lens that is fundamentally patriarchal. . . . Rarely is the ad rejection an actual nursing mom with a baby on the boob, but perhaps because it was a few times now the system knows we may post that type of content so it flags everything we submit even when it's completely innocuous (e.g., a lady in a sweater with a baby in a wrap). We have tons of screen grabs of ads we get served all the time featuring nearly naked sexy ladies modeling lingerie in sexually suggestive ways. It does seem to have something to do with the actual products we're selling.[32]

Storq sells products designed to conform to real mothers' lifestyles and needs, and this fact seems important to unpacking the brand's censorship problem. In the case of the gray cardigan, if nipples are not the problem (said nipples in this case were covered by a bra, a shirt, a baby, a baby wrap, *and* a voluminous knit cardigan), the fact that moms are granted access to products that will make their lives better or freer *does* seem to be the problem. Storq's nursing bras and camisoles and fucking cardigans (!) are not created to please the male gaze—and therein lies the objection (for white patriarchy).

Karni Arieli, founder of @eyemamaproject, has experienced the algorithmic distaste for representations of real motherhood more than once. The posts she shares have frequently been flagged for "obscenity" (at least eight were removed altogether), and, once, the account itself was deleted for four days. At that time, Instagram gave Karni no reason for the deletion, and it was only after Karni enlisted hundreds of moms to complain that the account was reinstated. Remember, @eyemamaproject features images that show motherhood in full technicolor. Quiet, mundane moments. Otherworldly moments. Raw moments. A baby drooling. A kid picking his nose. A mother's IV-ed arm draped around a swaddled newborn.

Karni believes that, in addition to straightforward patriarchal bullshit, an inherent fear of mothers is twisted up in the censorship issue as well. "You can't just say *nipples are wrong*," she said, "because, if you're breastfeeding, nipples are part of it. If society tells us that nipples are wrong, we feel dirty when we breastfeed outside. And if you feel dirty breastfeeding outside, how can you be empowered, right?"[33] Right! Because if mothers live in a culture that makes them feel ashamed for feeding their children outside the home—while also plastering OB-GYN exam rooms with signs that read "Breast Is Best"—that same culture is implicitly encouraging those mothers to not leave the home.

"On Instagram," Karni said, "you get removed when you show yourself breastfeeding your child, which is, like, a wholly impressive activity that's really hard to do! And anyone who's ever done it can tell you it's impossible and really hard and you get cracked nipples and it's crazy and it demands a lot of energy and it's exhausting. And that's *if* you manage to do it, right?" Karni's point is that breastfeeding, one small act of mothering, is a metaphor for the labor of motherhood in general: "It's crazy and it demands a lot of energy and it's exhausting."[34] And many people don't want to see images that reflect those realities. They want to see close-ups of babies' downy heads. They want to see mothers smiling. They want to consume a static, one-dimensional version of motherhood, not the loud, pulsating, sticky-apple-juice reality. Because, who knows? Imagistic representation of the act of mothering, rather than the idealization of motherhood, might make the casual viewer think to themselves, "This looks complicated, this looks hard, this looks interesting. Perhaps the people doing the work of mothering should be supported in ways that don't involve pink cards on Mother's Day."

Karni also speaks to the personal toll it takes to be told by a big power—Instagram—that something she is doing is "bad," is "wrong." When she sees that an image on @eyemamaproject has been flagged, she immediately feels a visceral response. "Like, *oh, god, society says I did something bad*," she told me. "*Did I do something bad?* I immediately take that feeling on because, as women, we do that, right? We're trained to feel bad or to feel like it's our fault."[35]

It's not just Instagram policing maternal representation online. It's the brands, companies, and advertising agencies working with momfluencers, too. In our interview, Bethanie Garcia and her manager, Tami Nealy, both relayed to me a story of being told by an agency representing a brand that Bethanie's profile photo, in which she's wearing a bodysuit sans pants, was potentially problematic for that particular brand. Tami explained that the agency owner called to tell her the brand in question is "conservative," to which Tami responded, "*Well, then, why did you choose Bethanie? I tried to walk away from this job two times. You needed her.* And he's like, *The bodysuit she's wearing looks too much like her flesh. Can she put on a red, yellow, or purple shirt?* And I'm like, *Have you even looked at her feed? I don't think she owns that color clothing! She wears neutral, muted colors.*" The most maddeningly ironic part of this whole exchange, according to Bethanie, was that this campaign was meant to celebrate women's empowerment.[36]

And here's the thing. So much of the quagmire that is performing and consuming motherhood online is blamed on individuals. It's my fault I feel bad about my inability to enjoy motherhood because I made the choice to start scrolling. It's my fault I'm bored by motherhood because I don't try hard enough to be delighted.

It's my fault for making another mom feel shitty about her motherhood because something captured in a photo meant to represent my motherhood is triggering for her. But all of these individual feelings would not be so easily evoked if larger systems did not loom so large, did not wield so much direct power over the lives of moms—if the people controlling the systems were not so often influenced by white, patriarchal, capitalistic incentives.

■   ■   ■

As part of a "Taza Talks" Instagram series to promote Naomi Davis's book in the spring of 2021, Naomi interviewed Hannah Neeleman.[37] In the video, Hannah's perched outside somewhere near Ballerina Farm (presumably), interrupted occasionally by a young child (or two). Her hair is swept back in a ponytail, and she's wearing a nondescript blue T-shirt. Naomi looks more polished and is likely lit by a ring light. Her hair is in long pigtails, she has just the right amount of no-makeup makeup on, and she's wearing a blousy white lace top. Her freckles are adorable, as ever.

I've watched this interview at least four times and have different feelings every time. The general thesis, which Naomi seems to have determined before starting the conversation, is that none of us are "just moms," that our work as mothers is important and worth celebrating. Great. Both women talk about getting married while studying dance at Juilliard, and how their decisions to prioritize family so young were viewed as a bit . . . different. "I struggled with feeling judged," admits Naomi. Hannah nods and says, "When I found out I was pregnant with Henry, we were surprised, and I was just . . . crying. I had just gotten back to New York about to start my senior year. We were talking about going to Europe and auditioning for touring companies." In the video, as Hannah speaks about this surprise pregnancy during her senior year at *Juilliard*, a school most performing artists would kill to get into, I can't tear my eyes from her face as she struggles to speak through her tears. Is she grieving her lost opportunity to dance professionally? Is she mourning herself before she became a mother? Is she crying because of joy for her son? Is she allowing herself to imagine what might have been, had motherhood not been her primary ambition as a Mormon girl-woman? Is it all of these things at once?

Hannah continues, still tearful: "I remember finding out I was pregnant and going on my knees and being like, *God, you know I have big dreams and I have my senior year ahead of me*, and I was a little bit frustrated, honestly. I went to ballet class, and I was doing barre with tears coming down my face." The first time I watched this video, I felt the urge to cheer Hannah on. Yes! Be frustrated! Yes! Your dreams!

And then Hannah goes on to explain that, during barre exercises, the pianist started playing one of her church's most well-known songs, and she "knew it was right." She said, "And when we think the timing isn't right, it is. And God has a plan. So, it was hard but looking back there were so many moments that were beautiful." She sobs the word "beautiful." This is the part of the video that is the hardest for me. Because, sure. Signs are beautiful. Embrace them! But the almost immediate skimming over of her very legitimate grief is just tough to watch. And I guess it's only tough for me to watch because of my own history and the way I'm projecting that history onto a stranger's social media post. Which is entirely on me.

Hannah explains that "you sacrifice a lot" as a mother, but she "knew [she] wanted a family unit that was strong." Naomi smiles and nods and appears moved by Hannah's retelling of this first pregnancy before responding: "I love that . . . You really set the stage for showing that prioritizing family or having kids young doesn't mean that everything else is over. You know? I think you can absolutely can still live this very fulfilling life and pursue dreams with little ones by your side, which I think is really powerful to see."

I have no interest in speculating about what might have happened for Hannah—or Naomi—had she not grown up in a culture that prioritized motherhood and wifehood above all else, nor do I have any right to judge their choices. I guess what strikes me about the video, though, is the almost palpable desire both women seem to feel to be recognized as people who have done something important. Both women are natural performers. And they're geniuses at what they've chosen to pour their performative skills into (momfluencing). But their insistence in this video that it's motherhood alone that fills them up, that makes them whole—it strikes me as disingenuous, or at least, as only a partial truth.

I want motherhood to be respected as a worthy and noble pursuit. I also want it to not be the only identity girls and women are taught to lust after. And the fact that these two artists have found ways to use their motherhood as vehicles for self-expression *while also* contributing to the valorization of idealized motherhood—it's a lot to process.

Hannah recalls counseling a new mom struggling with adjusting to her new identity, and telling her, "And you can have yourself, and have joy in whatever you find joy in, but the time and investment you put into your family, those little ones and your husband you will never forget." Naomi concurs, saying, "It's so great" that women can find their identities outside of motherhood (she calls these women "warrior women"). "*But*," she continues, "as you're saying, Hannah, I really feel that motherhood is probably, actually not even probably, but the *most* important, valuable title you might ever hold . . . We need to remind ourselves that *I'm a mother* and there's nothing greater."

In this video, I see two women who have capitalized on our culture's love affair with the beautiful, happy mother who loves motherhood above all else. And that's great for them! But the fact that these women espouse the joys of motherhood *for motherhood's sake* without acknowledging that, maybe—for them, at least— their satisfaction as artists might not be bound up in mothering as labor so much as in motherhood as performance. And this lack of awareness that satisfaction in mothering is not the same thing as satisfaction in artistic expression feels dangerous. For any one of the 2,319 people who hearted this video, yes. But maybe also for Naomi and Hannah? Referring back to Emily Hund and Lee McGuigan's "A Shoppable Life": "The work combines the outer-directed labor of performing a branded self that commands recognition, prestige, and economic value, with the existential work of creating personal and professional identities that meet one's own standards of integrity and self-actualization. This carries profound emotional freight since it involves the very constitution of meaningful personhood for participants."[38]

I worry for the twenty-four-year-old new mom watching this video and feeling like something might be wrong with her for failing to access Naomi's and Hannah's ironclad joy and unshakable sense of purpose. I worry for women like Naomi and Hannah, whose sense of "meaningful personhood" can never be wholly removed from the "outer-directed labor of performing a branded self."

■ ■ ■

When I first attempted to make sense of momfluencer culture on the page, it was for a piece I wrote for *Harper's Bazaar* entitled "Momfluencer Culture Enrages Me. Why Can't I Look Away?" I didn't write the headline, but it felt apt enough at the time. I interviewed media studies expert Jorie Lagerwey for the piece, and she immediately sliced through my momfluencer ambivalence by evoking literary critic Lauren Berlant's notion of "cruel optimism" to explain why I gobbled up pretty moms in pretty homes despite feeling simultaneously revolted and desirous.

Via email, I had explained to Jorie that I follow a number of momfluencers, many of whom are white, cis-het, thin, religious, nondisabled, and marketably attractive. I told her about @mama watters's home goods shop and @ballerinafarm's pork chop biz; I told her about many others who simply take beautiful photos of their beautiful homes and beautiful children and accompany those photos with captions about cherishing the little things, living in the moment, and feeling exalted by motherhood.

It was November 2020 when I first emailed Jorie, and at the time, few of my hours could be described as beautiful. My older kids were spending their days "virtually learning," and my baby was happy but feral. My husband and I were drowning. I felt an almost constant urge to escape my moments, which piled atop each other with blurry ruthlessness. I asked Jorie (begged her?) to explain my perverse attraction to an idealized version of performative motherhood on Instagram when I felt as though I should "know better." Why did I consume pretty mommy perfection when, more than ever before, it was making me mad?

Jorie obliged my outsized request for clarity. I consumed maternal fantasies that made me mad, jealous, disgusted, and curious, she theorized, because of cruel optimism:

> I'm mixing two of her books together here, but Berlant says that when you see a pattern (like these unbelievably perfect moms) over and over again, even when it's a genre (Berlant's writing about literature, but this type of account is an Instagram genre) repeating its pattern, you expect that pattern. You expect to see it unfold in your own life, and you aspire to it, even if you know it's bad for you. So, it's optimistic in that it's an aspiration, but it's cruel in that what you want either doesn't actually exist, or does exist but is actively harmful to you. Fantasy is attractive even when it sparks envy and rage. They make it look easy, and wouldn't it be a great life if that much beauty was easy?[39]

I don't think I've ever consciously expected my children to become static background figures that exist mostly to uphold my subjectivity as a beatific maternal goddess (as some accounts might have you believe), nor do I think consumption of those accounts made me consciously expect that my own motherhood would become an endeavor guaranteed to delight and fulfill me at every turn. I'm an angry feminist, after all. I don't consciously want to be a domestic angel of the house devoted wholly to serving others at the expense of my own selfhood. But I'm not so sure about my subconscious expectations. I can't speak to those.

And as for the desire of ease, yes. Yes, I want motherhood to feel and look easier. I want Hannah Neeleman's easy smile as she traipses through Disney World heavily pregnant, with six children in tow. I want assuredness. I want Amanda Watters's unfaltering belief that homemaking is not only noble but also fulfilling and energizing. I want the stuff of everyday life to look a certain way. I want my messes to be Rudy Jude messes. Balls of hand-dyed yarns, tiny jam jars, an open sketchbook, a single slim taper alit in its pewter candlestick holder. A toddler with bedhead peering through the fibers of a half-woven rug. I wanna be wearing Rudy Jude jeans and looking hot while still somehow being comfortable. I know this is impossible. For me.

Because away from the scroll, I am always me. Relentlessly me. My mouth tight from whisper-screaming *shhhh!* at the big kids when their little brother is napping. A person who'd rather lock herself in her room and listen to the *Poog* podcast than be fulfilled by a clean countertop. My mess is Nutella smears, a child's sock, a herd of plastic triceratops. A tiny piece of plastic that goes to something (we'll never remember what). A tiny piece of plastic that must not be thrown away.

Apologies to any real literary theorists who might be reading this, because I'm surely about to completely oversimplify Lauren Berlant's extremely rich, complex work, but I'll do my best! In *The Female Complaint*, Berlant writes, "Everyone knows what the female complaint is: women live for love, and love is the gift that keeps on taking."[40] In this case, "love" can be interpreted as romantic love, as idealistic love, as maternal love. The point is, Berlant argues, that women's desire to locate love is a motivating force in their lives, and this desire is intrinsically connected to their consumption of "women's culture," which can be interpreted broadly. Maybe it's rom-coms; maybe it's chick lit. Maybe it's a pretty mom on

Instagram living her best life. "My claim," Berlant writes, "is that gender-marked texts of women's popular culture cultivate fantasies of vague belonging as an alleviation of what is hard to manage in the lived real—social antagonisms, exploitation, compromised intimacies, the attrition of life."[41]

There's so much happening here. A momfluencer account that features a cis-het, marketably attractive white woman is certainly a "gender-marked" text, since a main part of its appeal, its profitability, is wrapped up in a performance of gender. And this type of momfluencer account certainly works to "cultivate fantasies of vague belonging." When I engage with this type of content, the longing I feel has to do with living a life in which I feel like my existence makes sense, in which I "belong" (even if that belonging is "vaguely" defined). And that longing for belonging exists because my actual life, my "lived real," is not as simple or as apparently fulfilling as a daisy-field rendition of motherhood must be, if we're to buy into the imagery of it all. The awkward playdate-arranging text exchange with slightly Trump-y parents of your kid's friend ("social antagonism"). The harsh facts of mothers' unpaid and undervalued labor ("exploitation"). The gaslit experience of being a mom in America, of being worshipped and told to stay invisible, to do the "hardest job in the world" simply because you love it, and if you don't love it, if you want renumeration for the hardest job in the world, then you're a bad mom for turning something that's supposed to be selfless into something transactional. The "attrition of life." These ingredients, the mess of our lives, lead us to seek comfort in "women's culture." Of course they do.

And "women's culture," according to Berlant, is an "intimate public"—an evocative phrase if ever there was one. Lydialyle Gibson, in a piece for the *University of Chicago Magazine*, quotes Berlant as defining an "intimate public" as a social structure that involves "a scene where people feel emotionally attached to people they don't know and maybe wouldn't like or couldn't identify with in any other way."[42] I can't think of a more clarifying illustration of

Berlant's intimate public than influencer culture at large—momfluencer culture specifically. By now, hundreds (maybe thousands) of people have publicly mused about Naomi Davis's whereabouts. Is she OK? Are she and Josh getting a divorce? Is she leaving the Mormon church? Is she suffering from mental illness? Is she just a bitch who doesn't care about her followers? We are emotionally attached to momfluencers even (or maybe especially) if we can't "identify with them in any other way" other than through our shared identities as mothers.

When we participate in "intimate public" spaces, Berlant says, aspiration is certainly part of the equation. Intimate public spheres often make us aspire to be better, look better, live better. And some momfluencers often encourage that aspiration (for good reason). But it goes beyond aspiration, Berlant argues: "One of the main utopias is normativity itself, here a felt condition of general belonging and an aspirational site of rest and recognition in and by a social world."[43] We are compelled to consume utopian momfluencer content for aspirational reasons (sometimes), but the power of these accounts lies not so much in making us want something nebulously better, but in their upholding of cultural norms. Consuming accounts that depend on our understandings of "normativity" can elicit a sense of "general belonging." Such idealized momfluencer content provides a sense of "rest" in a very busy, very noisy world. *Here is a mother. She is a good mother because I have been culturally conditioned to see signposts of good motherhood in the way this mother looks, the way she dresses, the way she decorates her house. If a mother is good, all is right with the world. The home is healthy. The mother is healthy. The children are healthy. The state is healthy.*

The supposedly objective truth of the momfluencer's good motherhood as represented on Instagram also allows us to recognize markers of "good motherhood" in our own lives. And these false binaries (good versus bad motherhood) provide a calming influence in turbulent contemporary life. It can feel good to find respite from the messiness of gray, even if shades of gray make up most people's lived experiences.

Aimée Morrison, an associate professor at Waterloo University, is the author of a paper called "Suffused by Feeling and Affect: The Intimate Public of Personal Mommy Blogging," which I loved. Via Zoom, Aimée kindly helped me parse the complexities of Lauren Berlant's work. Aimée defines an intimate public as a "community of feeling." She explained that intimate publics can "exceed the bounds of our personal acquaintances and homes so it becomes a larger sort of affiliation with even like-minded strangers." And Aimée thinks that, while most influencer communities can be intimate public spaces, momfluencer culture in particular is an ideal model, since "the category of mother is so culturally loaded; it's an all-consuming identity category."

This role is both essential to the maintenance of an inequitable nuclear family and our like, national self-construction, right? None of it happens without a mom's work. But she's not supposed to complain about that work, because it's un-American, right? Or it's not feminine. So, I think it is because the category of motherhood is so paradoxical, conflicted, extractive, exploitive, ideological, because it is all of those things simultaneously, we're going to have nothing but images about it, because like, we're not going to pay for universal childcare, right? We're not going to pay for universal birth control, we're not going to insist on sort of more gender equity from childhood forward so that men do parenting instead of babysitting, right? We're not going to do any of those things. So we just will keep talking about how important motherhood is and how rewarding it is and how beautiful mothers are and how much we love them, and we have a whole day for them![44]

Fuck Mother's Day.

The role of mother, Aimée explains, is forced to "do a lot of work in terms of distinguishing what is private from what is public." Throughout this book, we've explicated the thorny nature of performing an inherently private experience—mothering—for public consumption. It's different from fashion influencing, for example, in that personal style and fashion sort of *depend on* an external audience, whereas the labor of mothering, the acts of mothering, mostly take place in private, intimate spaces. No one needs to witness me kissing my kid's boo-boo for that act of care to matter. But momfluencer culture isn't about the kissing of boo-boos; not really. It's about how we can package ourselves as moms, how we can turn our bodies and Instagram accounts into texts for others to peruse. Online motherhood abides by its own set of rules that only sometimes overlap with the mandates of mothering.

But, Aimée rightly points out, most of us have become mothers having already inherited scripts about how to be, based on our personal histories and life experiences. "The role of mother already seems to have all of its lines written for it, right?" Aimée asked. "And so, it is the adult woman's job to transform herself into someone who recognizably occupies the role of mother or she will be policed for it."[45] In a sense, all moms take on the job of transforming ourselves into a being that most people would recognize as "mom" whether we're on social media or not. And it's weird! I still feel like all the moms at preschool pickup are "real" moms while I'm just an imposter who struggles to recognize the maternal authority I supposedly hold sheerly by dint of my having had children. And my discomfort with inhabiting an identity that seems simultaneously too big and too small to contain me is a relatively innocuous example of how the loaded meaning of motherhood can chafe against individuals. For mothers who cannot or will not stick to the script, the consequences are far greater, including (but not limited to) the forced removal of parental rights, public censure, and private and public shaming, as well as the availability of resources, cultural capital, soft power, housing, and education. The script must be incinerated.

In *The Female Complaint*, Berlant writes about "affect labor." Motherhood requires specific types of affect labor—labor, that when done well, communicates what type of role you play in a particular society. During our Zoom, Aimée evoked the idea of the "bake sale mom" as a way to illustrate one form of affect labor particular to motherhood.

> Having spent twenty-five dollars on ingredients to sell cookies for five cents each? I could just write you a check for two hundred dollars. But I can't write that check, because that's sort of turning something that was meant to demonstrate what a good mother I am into something transactional. By doing a fundraising activity that is in no way going to raise real funds, but *is* going to prove my devotion, right? Through the giving of my time and the giving of my smiles and the preparation of foodstuffs, the cost to whatever my evening was going to be.[46]

In many ways, momfluencer culture on Instagram is a culture that exists and thrives based on affect labor. We follow momfluencers depending on whether or not their affect labor is having the intended effect of reflecting specific maternal qualities (devotion, naturalness, gentleness, patience, sweetness, warmth, energy, selflessness, sensitivity). If a momfluencer spends time writing a thoughtful, vulnerable post about the wonder of motherhood, or snapping and editing photos until the photo that ends up on our feeds is a perfectly lit and composed representation of the type of mother we (should) aspire to be, she is performing affect labor. And her labor communicates—to her audience, yes, but maybe even to herself—that she is a good mom because she gave her time, her energy, to display the beauty of her motherhood, just as the bake sale mom is a good mom because she has completed the maternal, domestic task of cookie baking to theoretically support the welfare of children. The public performance in both cases is critical. Not many people will know about your two-hundred-dollar check to support the chess club or whatever. Not many people will know that you cherish the beauty of motherhood if you take a picture and write a passage and simply stick it on your fridge. And if people don't know you are a good mother, how do you yourself know?

As I hope is clear by now, neither Aimée nor I take issue with the profession of momfluencing. To blame individuals for participating in a system that values hyperfeminine maternal ideals and the values of the nuclear white family over pretty much all else is akin to facile arguments that real feminists should never wear makeup or care about how they look to the male gaze. It's like blaming a fish for swimming in water. Aimée wonders, though, if or *how* some spheres of momfluencer culture can "ultimately help individual women's relations within their family or relations to one another? Is that an intimate public that is supported? Or is it more one like Berlant is describing women's culture generally as being a way of commodifying anxiety forever?"[47] Momfluencer culture commodifies picture-perfect motherhood, and the resultant product is so addictive, so traffic-accident-compelling, because the idealization of motherhood speaks to so many cultural anxieties—about women's rights, feminism, gender, class, race, family structure. About plastic. About placentas. About macrame wall hangings.

Until the ghost of the perfect white mom no longer dominates how we think about motherhood, women's cultural texts like Instagram momfluencer culture—which both perpetuates that ghost and also speaks directly to and against everything that ghost represents—will continue to take up space in our imaginations. None of this is any one person's fault.

But we can't ignore the ghost of the perfect white mom because she doesn't merely contribute to other white moms feeling inadequate. She also contributes to Black moms not receiving quality healthcare because of implicit racist bias. She ensures that a mom of color who snaps at her kid in a grocery store will likely be subject to harsher scrutiny than a white mom who does the same. She makes it harder for queer moms to create families. She makes it financially and geographically impossible for low-income moms to access safe abortions because "good moms" never want or need abortions. Her thin body contributes to fat moms having a harder time accessing fertility treatments. When the default imagery of a good mom is something that can be accessed and performed by so few people, the vast majority of moms must do extra work to ensure that our worthiness as mothers is seen—by healthcare providers, by teachers, by other moms scheduling playdates, by mortgage lenders. Our culture believes in good moms, but it vilifies and denies services and support to moms who don't adhere to a hyper-specific version of "good."

In a piece for the *New Yorker*, Hua Hsu wrote about Lauren Berlant's work and its impact on modern life. He defines "cruel optimism" as "our attachment to dreams that we know are destined to be dashed." Hsu also quotes Berlant as explaining that "a relation of cruel optimism exists when something you desire is actually an obstacle to your flourishing."[48]

When something you desire is actually an obstacle to your flourishing.

Here's my truth. I grew up unthinkingly attached to a particular dream of motherhood: a motherhood that would help me be my best self, that would light me up and lift me up. A motherhood that would be beautiful by way of tiny porcelain cocoa mugs and a pregnancy glow. A motherhood that would make me self-actualized so I didn't have to carve out my identity on my own. It was only after having kids that I could see the heartbreaking cracks in my dream, which doesn't require the particularities of an individual's personhood but instead seeks to erase the sharp edges of individuality altogether. A dream that exists only in service of whiteness and gender essentialism and capitalism. A dream that *should* be "destined to be dashed." Because this dream of maternal bliss is just a dream of maternal objectivity that communicates certain things about whiteness and femininity and the buying and selling of stuff. A good white mom made whole by motherhood communicates the message that no mom should want anything more from motherhood than personal fulfillment. A good white mom in her good white home ensures that there is such a thing as a good mom and a good home, which means that anyone that doesn't look like the good white mom or live in the type of home a good white mom lives in is unworthy—of resources, of respect, of notice.

And the good white mom needs things to put in her good white home and on her good white body. Her goodness is bolstered by her good capitalist consumerism. She buys makeup to make her look younger for as long as she can and once the makeup stops working, she graciously cedes into the background and accepts her invisibility. She spends as many hours as possible hating her body and buying the right food, exercise equipment, and diet books because, while is a mom, she is also a woman, so she must never forget to "glow" for the male gaze. She is vacuuming and dusting and flower arranging and cooking and googling her one wild and precious life away in search of the best countertop spray. She should not worry her pretty little head about agency because she is cleaning her countertops instead.

And she must be white because white supremacy depends on her being white. How else would racist policies that disproportionately target moms of color exist? How would our moral panics about "crack babies," "welfare queens," "Black matriarchs," and "teen moms" stay afloat?

Despite my intellectual awareness that my old dream of motherhood is both no longer serving me and arguably harming others, I keep scrolling. Because, as Aimée put it, my real-life motherhood is a "series of tasks." Aimée sometimes views motherhood this way, too: "And I just want to see that if I go through all of the work of mothering, maybe I'll get that beautiful backlit photo. You know the kind of photo where the arm hair is kind of lit and you look like an angel? And my child is smiling and running through the wildflowers and is grateful for the experience of nature without an iPhone in their hand? I would like to think that all of my efforts will someday result in this beautiful picture that makes it look like I fucking won for a change."[49]

While I'm so heartened by the work the moms discussed in the previous chapter are doing to advance maternal rights and advocate for social justice reform, I also agree with Aimée that holding onto hope for meaningful change is work in and of itself. Sometimes I feel inspired and hopeful, *especially* when I talk to brilliant women who are on the front lines of change. But sometimes I look at the minutes and hours in my day and I just don't have much room for big-picture hope because respect and support for my mothering is still mostly theoretical. And those moments—when I don't want to toast a third slice of bread because the first one was the nutty kind and the second one was a little burnt, or when I'm pressing my fingernails into my upper thigh to tamp the impatience I feel when my kid wants to ask me "just one more question" at bedtime and I just want to watch *Cheer*—are the moments that propel me to shop a momfluencer's feed. For a bathing suit cover-up. Or fucking bone broth. I wonder if I'd be so willing, so *quick*, to scroll in search of a better way to experience motherhood, if I got a check at the end of the month that put the goddamn burnt toast in perspective. Or if I lived in a country that didn't view a woman's bodily autonomy as a point of debate. Or if all moms had access to quality, affordable childcare. I don't know. And, most of the time, I simply can't inhabit that place of rage and despair, so I scroll instead. Aimée thinks the unique power of momfluencer culture, and maybe Berlant's notion of women's culture in general, is its ability to "help reconcile ourselves to a reality that's too big for us to change."[50]

I can control the type of bone broth I buy and maybe even my willingness to believe in its magical attributes. I have immediate control over diaper balm. And, as Aimée wryly joked, I'm "too busy changing diapers to organize a revolution anyway . . . And so, do we collude in our own oppression? Yeah, because we gotta get through 'til tomorrow."[51]

In his *New Yorker* piece about Berlant, Hua Hsu writes: "We like to imagine that our life follows some kind of trajectory, like the plot of a novel, and that by recognizing its arc we might, in turn, become its author. But often what we feel instead is a sense of precariousness—a gut-level suspicion that hard work, thrift, and following the rules won't give us control over the story, much less guarantee a happy ending. For all that, we keep on hoping, and that persuades us to keep on living."[52] It might seem silly to view the act of scroll scroll scrolling through a stranger's nursery tour as a way to keep living or the purchase of an eyelet bathing suit cover-up as a way to keep living. But I do believe we do these things as small acts not so much out of defiance, but because we need to hope in small ways just as much as we need to hope in big ways. Because we're human. And mothering *and* motherhood are hard. It feels good, if only for a second, to suspend disbelief and choose little "h" hope. Hope that the bone broth will make it better. That the bathing suit cover-up will imbue me with fun mom energy instead of tired mom energy. That Rudy Jude's hair-volumizing tea recipe might give me Rudy Jude hair. We can control little "h" hope in ways that elude us with big "h" hope.

Mothers know that, for most of us, "hard work, thrift, and following the rules" won't make motherhood in a culture that doesn't value motherhood any less exhausting, infuriating, or soul-crushing; only systemic change will do that. And until then, why torture ourselves about searching for cute toddler backpacks or family-friendly weeknight meal ideas or a DIY yogurt face mask? Why hate ourselves for the sin of wanting? We can be mad about capitalism and motherhood and do our best to contribute to positive change. We can also take pleasure in consuming and shopping for maternal fantasies. Both things can be true at once.

I think my dashed dream of motherhood is probably too interwoven with my psyche to ever be fully exorcised, but I'm working to create a new dream, one that doesn't actively contribute to my oppression and the oppression of moms far more vulnerable than I. "Maybe relinquishing or recalibrating our fantasies of the good life doesn't lead to absolute darkness," writes Hsu. "It can simply be a matter of coming to grips with different possibilities of communion, figuring out who benefits from our collective weariness."[53]

Angela Garbes lays out her dream of motherhood in her new book, *Essential Labor*, which examines how mothering can be an act of resistance, how mothering can contribute to social change. I read the book in one propulsive fell swoop on a pearly gray winter day, and Garbes's chapters about mothering as a way to honor appetites, pleasure, and carework took my breath away with their inherent belief both in the importance of community mothering, and in the value of caregivers' labor, whether or not something bigger than us sees or applauds it.

Garbes in no way sugarcoats the sometimes boring, sometimes frustrating, never-ending work of mothering, but she encourages mothers to adopt a different narrative about our daily grinds, if only to change the way we see ourselves as people, and as care workers. Maybe, she surmises, if we can see ourselves in all our maternal power, that alone can contribute to a wider cultural shift. She writes, "The repetitive tasks of mothering—wiping butts, cleaning food off the floor, reading books over and over, keeping track of clothes that are on the verge of being outgrown—constitute everyday life. This is essential work that makes all other work possible. It is vital to the economy, yet it is underpaid, if compensated at all."[54] Garbes points out that even the supposed "truth" that reproductive and domestic labor is unskilled labor is "a myth used to perpetuate a class system that designates some people as less worthy than others."[55]

According to Garbes, there is real power in recognizing the mythologies and dreams that keep us bound up in a maelstrom of wanting and discontent. There is power in viewing mothering as hard, yes, but worthy. Even if, especially if, external validation for the value of our work might be years away. There is power in looking in the mirror and claiming one's own worth. "Day in and day out," Garbes writes, "This work can be our most consistent, embodied resistance to patriarchy, white supremacy, ableism, and the exploitation that underlies American capitalism."[56] She asserts: "Change is happening. How much further we go is up to us. This is an inflection point: a once in a lifetime moment to invest in the people who mother children, whether bound by blood or affection."[57]

Consciously or not, I sometimes grieve the impossibility of my original maternal dream—mostly the fact that I chased a fantasy for so long. But alongside the grief that the motherhood I was taught to want never existed in the first place lives a little seedling of something else planted by women like Angela Garbes. A seed of possibility that a new dream of motherhood might nourish and inspire me and others in ways that I don't even have the capacity to understand. Yet.

■ ■ ■

My family and I went to Florida during the kids' February break to visit my dad. Fleeing the cold, drab whiteness of February in New Hampshire for the talcum-powder sands of Florida in February was heaven, and I took the opportunity to iron the sunshine into my soul by deleting Instagram from my phone. As I was waiting for a pot of water to boil for mac 'n' cheese, I stared at the gray tile backsplash. Or at *Masha and the Bear* playing from a nearby TV. When I went to the bathroom, I stared at the wall. My mind skipped along or it didn't.

In the mornings, sometimes my phone was dead because I had lost track of it the night before. When it wasn't, I texted with my friends while sipping my PG Tips. At night, my sister and I ducked into a bedroom away from the kids to gossip or bitch or both. On the beach, I didn't take many photos of the kids, but I was a good patron at my daughter's beachside restaurant, dutifully receiving my red plastic pail of "spaghetti and meatballs." I used my blue plastic shovel to "taste" spoonfuls of sandy, snarled-up seaweed and was effusive in my praise. It was easy to love my daughter's spaghetti and meatballs because hers were the only ones I consumed that week.

Hannah Neeleman (@ballerinafarm) might have served her seven kids meatballs made from Ballerina Farm's own pasture-raised cows, but I didn't know. Julie D. O'Rourke (@rudyjude) might have eaten spaghetti cranked through a pasta maker by her extremely capable three-year-old, but I didn't know. Amanda

Watters (@mamawatters) might have posted a perfectly lit photo of spaghetti curled into a vintage stoneware bowl I could potentially buy at her online shop Homesong Market, but I didn't know. The counter upon which the vintage stoneware bowl of spaghetti rested might have been clean. But I didn't know. I didn't know if Naomi Davis (@taza) had returned to Instagram to share photos of a riotous spaghetti party. Maybe there was a cute photo of one of the twins slurping up a saucy noodle. I didn't know.

And the not knowing was bliss.

ACKNOWLEDGMENTS

Thank you to my agent, Amy Elizabeth Bishop, for seeing something in a completely unsellable essay collection three-ish years ago and sticking with me ever since. I'll never forget our first phone call, when we talked about *Anne of Green Gables* as I leaked breast milk and prayed my two-week-old wouldn't wake up from his nap. Thank you to my brilliant editor, Maya Fernandez, for locating missed opportunities for deeper reflection in early drafts and generally making this book infinitely stronger than it otherwise would've been without your thoughtful eye. Thank you Susan Lumenello and Emily Jane Shelton for your razor-sharp copyedits, and thank you to the rest of the Beacon team—Caitlin Meyer, Priyanka Ray, Alyssa Hassan, and Sanj Kharbanda—for bringing this book to as many readers as possible. Thank you Hillary Brenhouse for helping me shape the book proposal that became *Momfluenced*. Our "yes girl yes" calls energized and inspired me.

To the many, many, many people I interviewed for *Momfluenced*. Even if your interview didn't end up in the book, I learned something from each and every one of you, and I'm so grateful for you sharing your stories, your experiences, and your perspectives with me, particularly about such vulnerable subject material. Thank you so much.

Emily J. Smith, thank you for always *getting* me (and my writing) and for reading more trash first drafts of my shit than anyone. Your feedback is always just like you: smart, funny, and loving.

■ ■ ■

I didn't pursue writing as a career until relatively late in life (motherhood was the inciting incident), and I would probably still be cluelessly googling my way into and around the publishing industry were it not for the many generous writers I've met along the way.

Thank you Jo Piazza, Kate Baer, Amanda Montell, Carla Ciccone, Leslie Jamison, Erin Langner, Sarah Kasbeer, Chloe Caldwell, Julia Fine, Katie Gutierrez, Rachel Vorona Cote, Angela Garbes, Eve Rodsky, Kathryn Jezer-Morton, Emily Adrian, Kimberly Harrington, Rainesford Stauffer, Frankie de la Cretaz, Nina Boutsikaris, Sarah Chavez, Katie Simon, Garrard Conley, Dan Blank, Erin Khar, Anne Helen Petersen, and Lyz Lenz for sharing your stories, your pitches, your newsletter strategies, your book proposals, your insights, and for responding to a panoply of frantic texts and emails with validation, empathy, humor, and care.

Thank you Virginia Sole-Smith for everything.

I could not have written *Momfluenced* without the many wonderful babysitters who gave our kids a break from their cranky, burnt-out parents during the pandemic, particularly Ella Gianino and Li Ping Titterington. Thank you!

To the mom friends who have transcended mom-friendship: Holly Cerny, Molly Heaney, Rory Vogel, Kaitlin Stanton, Whitney Swaffield, Cate Smith, Kelly Millar, and Andrea Birkel. It is such a joy and an honor to mother alongside you.

To Kelly Murphy, my first book friend. Our adolescent Slattery's dates encouraged me to take myself seriously as a thinker.

To my sisters—some in blood and all in life: Megan Petersen, Kate Hart, Andrea Petersen, Phoebe Hart, Hannah Rindlaub, Lauren Richards, Renee Theodorou, Stephanie Pearl, Lisa Trask. I love you so much. Let's build our compound sooner rather than later.

To my aunts and grandmothers: you all showed me different ways to embody motherhood, and you all did (do) so with tenderness, individuality, and creativity. I'm grateful for you all.

I would never have had the courage to dream about books without the support, unfaltering love, and belief of my parents. I love you.

To Brett, who hauled our three kids to countless playgrounds, McDonald's drive-throughs, and weekend pool visits so I could type and think in total silence like the writing monk I am. Thank you for believing I was destined to be a guest on *Fresh Air* way before such a thought was remotely reasonable. You are my rock.

To my three children: becoming your mother radicalized me in the best way possible, and you make my world so much bigger. To my daughter: if you ever choose to become a mother, I hope you do so on your own terms, unburdened by anyone else's idea of an ideal anything. Fly free.

FOR FURTHER READING

A not-exhaustive reading list of books that informed or inspired *Momfluenced*

Andrews-Dyer, Helena. *The Mamas: What I Learned About Kids, Race, and Class from Moms Not Like Me.* New York: Crown, 2022.

Austin, Nefertiti. *Motherhood So White: A Memoir of Race, Gender, and Parenting in America.* Naperville, IL: Sourcebooks, 2019.

Beck, Koa. *White Feminism: From the Suffragettes to Influencers and Who They Leave Behind.* New York: Atria Books, 2021.

Berg, Allison. *Mothering the Race: Women's Narratives of Reproduction, 1890–1930.* Urbana: University of Illinois Press, 2002.

Berlant, Lauren. *Cruel Optimism.* Durham, NC: Duke University Press, 2011.

———. *The Female Complaint: The Unfinished Business of Sentimentality in American Culture.* Durham, NC: Duke University Press, 2008.

Brooks, Kim. *Small Animals: Parenthood in the Age of Fear.* New York: Flatiron Books, 2018.

Chan, Jessamine. *The School for Good Mothers: A Novel.* New York: Simon & Schuster, 2022.

Chayka, Kyle. *The Longing for Less: Living with Minimalism.* New York: Bloomsbury, 2020.

Coontz, Stephanie. *The Way We Never Were: American Families and the Nostalgia Trap.* New York: Basic Books, 2016.

Cooper, Brittney C. *Beyond Respectability: The Intellectual Thought of Race Women.* Urbana: University of Illinois Press, 2017.

Cottom, Tressie McMillan. *Thick: And Other Essays.* New York: New Press, 2019.

Cusk, Rachel. *A Life's Work: On Becoming a Mother.* New York: Picador USA, 2002.

Darby, Seyward. *Sisters in Hate: American Women on the Front Lines of White Nationalism.* New York: Little, Brown, 2020.

Douglas, Susan J., and Meredith W. Michaels. *The Mommy Myth: The Idealization of Motherhood and How It Has Undermined All Women.* New York: Free Press, 2005.

Duffy, Brooke Erin. *(Not) Getting Paid to Do What You Love: Gender, Social Media, and Aspirational Work.* New Haven, CT: Yale University Press, 2017.

Dungy, Camille T. *Guidebook to Relative Strangers: Journeys into Race, Motherhood, and History.* New York: W. W. Norton & Co., 2017.

Ehrenreich, Barbara, and Deirdre English. *For Her Own Good: Two Centuries of the Experts' Advice to Women.* New York: Anchor Books, 2005.

Frier, Sarah. *No Filter: The Inside Story of Instagram.* New York: Simon & Schuster, 2021.

Garbes, Angela. *Essential Labor: Mothering as Social Change.* New York: Harper Wave, 2022.

———. *Like a Mother: A Feminist Journey through the Science and Culture of Pregnancy.* New York: Harper Wave, 2018.

Gumbs, Alexis Pauline, China Martens, and Mai'a Williams, eds. *Revolutionary Mothering: Love on the Front Lines.* Oakland, CA: PM Press, 2016.

Hamad, Ruby. *White Tears/Brown Scars: How White Feminism Betrays Women of Color.* New York: Catapult, 2020.

Harper, Kimberly C. *The Ethos of Black Motherhood in America: Only White Women Get Pregnant.* Lanham, MD: Lexington Books, 2021.

Harrington, Kimberly. *Amateur Hour: Motherhood in Essays and Swear Words.* New York: Harper Perennial, 2018.

Harris, Taylor. *This Boy We Made: A Memoir of Motherhood, Genetics, and Facing the Unknown.* New York: Catapult, 2022.

Heti, Sheila. *Motherhood.* New York: Picador USA, 2019.

hooks, bell. *Feminist Theory: From Margin to Center.* Cambridge, MA: South End Press, 2000.

Johnson, Bethany L., and Margaret M. Quinlan. *You're Doing It Wrong! Mothering, Media, and Medical Expertise.* New Brunswick, NJ: Rutgers University Press, 2019.

Jones, Feminista. *Reclaiming Our Space: How Black Feminists Are Changing the World from the Tweets to the Streets.* Boston: Beacon Press, 2019.

Leaver, Tama, Tim Highfield, and Crystal Abidin. *Instagram: Visual Social Media Cultures.* Cambridge, UK: Polity, 2020.

Lenz, Lyz. *Belabored: A Vindication of the Rights of Pregnant Women.* New York: Bold Type Books, 2020.

Lloyd, Ellery. *People Like Her: A Novel.* New York: Harper, 2022.

Manguso, Sarah. *Ongoingness: The End of a Diary.* Minneapolis, MN: Graywolf Press, 2015.

Matchar, Emily. *Homeward Bound: Why Women Are Embracing the New Domesticity.* New York: Simon & Schuster, 2013.

McClain, Dani. *We Live for the We: The Political Power of Black Motherhood.* New York: Bold Type Books, 2019.

McCulloch, Gretchen. *Because Internet: Understanding the New Rules of Language.* New York: Riverhead Books, 2019.

Menkedick, Sarah. *Ordinary Insanity: Fear and the Silent Crisis of Motherhood in America.* New York: Pantheon Books, 2020.

Mitchell, Koritha. *From Slave Cabins to the White House: Homemade Citizenship in African American Culture.* Urbana: University of Illinois Press, 2020.

Montell, Amanda. *Cultish: The Language of Fanaticism.* New York: Harper Wave, 2021.

Morris, Amelia. *Wildcat: A Novel.* New York: Flatiron Books, 2022.

Noble, Safiya Umoja. *Algorithms of Oppression: How Search Engines Reinforce Racism.* New York: New York University Press, 2018.

O'Connell, Meaghan. *And Now We Have Everything: On Motherhood Before I Was Ready.* New York: Back Bay Books, 2019.

Platt, Christine A. *The Afrominimalist's Guide to Living with Less.* New York: Simon Element, 2022.

Rich, Adrienne. *Of Woman Born: Motherhood as Experience and Institution.* New York: W. W. Norton & Co., 1986.

Róisín, Fariha. *Who Is Wellness For? An Examination of Wellness Culture and Who It Leaves Behind.* New York: Harper Wave, 2022.

Rose, Jacqueline. *Mothers: An Essay on Love and Cruelty.* New York: Farrar, Straus and Giroux, 2018.

Schuller, Kyla. *The Trouble with White Women: A Counterhistory of Feminism.* New York: Bold Type Books, 2021.

Tolentino, Jia. *Trick Mirror: Reflections on Self-Delusion.* New York: Random House, 2019.

Vandenberg-Daves, Jodi. *Modern Motherhood: An American History.* New Brunswick, NJ: Rutgers University Press, 2014.

Wayland-Smith, Ellen. *The Angel in the Marketplace: Adwoman Jean Wade Rindlaub and the Selling of America.* Chicago: University of Chicago Press, 2020.

Yoder, Rachel. *Nightbitch: A Novel.* New York: Doubleday, 2021.

Zakaria, Rafia. *Against White Feminism: Notes on Disruption.* New York: W. W. Norton & Co., 2021.

NOTES

CHAPTER 1: "PERFORMING MOTHERHOOD WITH A HASHTAG"

1. Naomi Davis, comment on Instagram, https://ww.instagram.com/taza/?hl=en, accessed November 29, 2021.
2. Nona Willis Aronowitz, "Sister Bloggers: Why So Many Lifestyle Bloggers Happen to Be Mormon," *Good Magazine*, December 1, 2011, https://www.good.is/articles/sister-bloggers.
3. Nona Willis Aronowitz, "The Education of Natalie Jean," *Elle*, November 5, 2019, https://www.elle.com/life-love/a29438763/natalie-lovin-mommy-blog-influencer.
4. Paris Martineau, "The Wired Guide to Influencers," *Wired*, December 6, 2019, https://www.wired.com/story/what-is-an-influencer.
5. Lyz Lenz, "The Mommy Blog Is Dead. Long Live the Mommy Blog," *Topic*, May 2019, https://www.topic.com/the-mommy-blog-is-dead-long-live-the-mommy-blog, accessed June 22, 2022.
6. Shanicia Boswell, email interview, December 4, 2020.
7. Meghan Holohan, "Meet the Mom Who Hosts a Period Party to Make Periods 'Positive,'" *Today*, February 18, 2021, https://www.today.com/parents/period-party-makes-periods-positive-helps-period-poverty-t209430.
8. Alice Greczyn, Twitter post, February 11, 2021, https://twitter.com/alicefood/status/1359898142104190977.
9. Maya Kosoff, "Help! I'm Obsessed with Trad Wife Influencers!" *Medium*, January 22, 2021, https://kosoff.medium.com/help-im-obsessed-with-trad-wife-influencers-75286510ac31.
10. Kelly Havens Stickle, Instagram post, posted January 17, 2021, https://www.instagram.com/p/CKKDs01nvPS.
11. Maya Kosoff, email interview, February 12, 2021.
12. I could find only limited information about Hannah Neeleman's husband: Ian Mount, "JetBlue Founder's Revenge: A New Airline," *CNN Money*, March 20, 2009, https://money.cnn.com/2009/03/19/smallbusiness/jetblue_founder_flies_again.fsb/index.htm.

13. Sharon Haddock, "Modesty, Frugality, Is Important to Miss New York City," *Deseret News*, August 12, 2011, https://www.deseret.com/2011 /8/12/20386368/modesty-frugality-is-important-to-miss-new-york -city#hannah-wright-and-her-new-husband-daniel-neeleman; Ballerina Farm, Instagram post, December 28, 2015, https://www.instagram .com/p/_2-9LXK6Dj/?hl=en.

14. Haddock, "Modesty, Frugality, Is Important to Miss New York City."

15. Alexandra Tanner, "My Mommies and Me," *Jewish Currents*, December 18, 2020, https://jewishcurrents.org/my-mommies-and-me.

16. Alexandra Tanner, email interview, February 12, 2021.

17. Colleen McKeegan, "What's It *Really* Like to Be a Mom Influencer?," *Glamour*, February 10, 2021, https://www.glamour.com/story/whats-it -really-like-to-be-a-mom-influencer.

18. Jo Piazza, phone interview, December 4, 2020.

19. Piazza, phone interview.

20. Stephanie McNeal, "This HBO Documentary About Influencers Is So Condescending," *BuzzFeed*, February 5, 2021, https://www.buzzfeed news.com/article/stephaniemcneal/fake-famous-hbo-influencers.

21. Lissette Calveiro, Instagram post, February 12, 2021, https://www .instagram.com/p/CLNEJuWn0GB.

22. Tanya Chen, "An Influencer Is Defending Her Decision to Post a Photo Shoot of Her Motorcycle Accident on Instagram," *BuzzFeed*, August 19, 2019, https://www.buzzfeednews.com/article/tanyachen/nashville -influencer-claims-smartwater-featured-motorcycle.

23. "Tiffany Mitchell: When Buzzfeed Attacks," *The Creative Influencer*, November 20, 2019, https://podcasts.apple.com/us/podcast/tiffany -mitchell-when-buzzfeed-attacks/id1413350305?i=1000457378578.

24. "Tiffany Mitchell: When Buzzfeed Attacks."

25. Tiffany Mitchell, email interview, December 3, 2020.

26. Mitchell, email interview.

27. Erin Boyle, phone interview, February 11, 2021.

28. Boyle, phone interview.

29. Bekah Martinez, Instagram post, December 1, 2021, https://www .instagram.com/p/CW9Y0PcPvgR/.

30. Bekah Martinez, phone interview, July 26, 2021.

31. Martinez, phone interview.

32. Myleik Teele, Zoom interview, July 28, 2021.

33. Teele, Zoom interview.

34. Teele, Zoom interview.

35. Teele, Zoom interview.

36. Teele, Zoom interview.

37. Teele, Zoom interview.

38. Teele, Zoom interview.

39. Teele, Zoom interview.

40. Teele, Zoom interview.
41. Hitha Palepu, phone interview, March 18, 2022.
42. Palepu, phone interview.
43. Palepu, phone interview.
44. Palepu, phone interview.
45. Palepu, phone interview.
46. Shanicia Boswell, Zoom interview, February 15, 2021.
47. Boswell, Zoom interview.
48. Matt Klein, email interview, February 10, 2021.
49. Klein, email interview.
50. Klein, email interview.

CHAPTER 2: IN PURSUIT OF CLEAN COUNTERTOPS
AND A SHOPPABLE LIFE

1. Ellen Wayland-Smith, "The Angel in the Market," *Aeon*, September 17, 2020, https://aeon.co/essays/from-home-to-market-a-history-of-white-womens-power-in-the-us.
2. Emily Hund and Lee McGuigan, "A Shoppable Life: Performance, Selfhood, and Influence in the Social Media Storefront," *Communication, Culture, and Critique* 12, no. 1 (2019): 18–35.
3. Sadhbh O'Sullivan, "The Internet Is Obsessed with Parasocial Relationships," *Refinery29*, October 4, 2021, https://www.refinery29.com/en-gb/parasocial-relationships-online-cancelling-bon-appetit.
4. Coventry Patmore, "The Angel in the House," Project Gutenberg, https://www.gutenberg.org/files/4099/4099-h/4099-h.htm, accessed June 23, 2022.
5. Susan J. Douglas and Meredith W. Michaels, *The Mommy Myth: The Idealization of Motherhood and How It Has Undermined All Women* (New York: Free Press, 2004), 4.
6. Douglas and Michaels, *The Mommy Myth*.
7. Alexa, Instagram post, May 9, 2021, https://www.instagram.com/p/COqhJviDzH4.
8. Laura Turner, "The Good Wife: How the Cult of Domesticity Still Reigns in the 21st Century," *Pacific Standard*, September 10, 2015, https://psmag.com/social-justice/the-21st-century-cult-of-domesticity.
9. Koritha Mitchell, *From Slave Cabins to the White House: Homemade Citizenship in African American Culture* (Urbana: University of Illinois Press, 2020), 237.
10. Mitchell, *From Slave Cabins to the White House*, 95.
11. Mitchell, *From Slave Cabins to the White House*, 96.
12. Mitchell, *From Slave Cabins to the White House*, 189.
13. Mitchell, *From Slave Cabins to the White House*, 189.
14. Mitchell, *From Slave Cabins to the White House*, 190.
15. Mitchell, *From Slave Cabins to the White House*, 191.

16. Mitchell, *From Slave Cabins to the White House*, 192.

17. Mitchell, *From Slave Cabins to the White House*, 193–94.

18. Ellen Wayland-Smith, *The Angel in the Marketplace: Adwoman Jean Wade Rindlaub and the Selling of America* (Chicago: University of Chicago Press, 2020), 29.

19. Wayland-Smith, *The Angel in the Marketplace*.

20. Hannah Neeleman, Instagram post, July 12, 2020, https://www.instagram.com/p/CCh7N40gsi2.

21. Wayland-Smith, *The Angel in the Marketplace*, 33.

22. Wayland-Smith, *The Angel in the Marketplace*, 33.

23. Wayland-Smith, *The Angel in the Marketplace*, 34.

24. Wayland-Smith, *The Angel in the Marketplace*, 120.

25. Wayland-Smith, *The Angel in the Marketplace*, 152.

26. Anne Helen Petersen, "Unpacking the Nap Dress," *Culture Study Substack Newsletter*, June 24, 2021, https://annehelen.substack.com/p/unpacking-the-nap-dress.

27. Wayland-Smith, *The Angel in the Marketplace*, 189.

28. Cheridan Christnacht and Briana Sullivan, "The Choices Working Mothers Make," US Census Bureau, May 8, 2020, https://www.census.gov/library/stories/2020/05/the-choices-working-mothers-make.html.

29. Wayland-Smith, *The Angel in the Marketplace*, 137.

30. Wayland-Smith, *The Angel in the Marketplace*, 137.

31. Emily Gould, phone interview, June 21, 2021.

32. Wayland-Smith, *The Angel in the Marketplace*, 141.

33. Gould, phone interview.

34. Chavie Lieber, "She Was the 'Queen of the Mommy Bloggers.' Then Her Life Fell Apart," *Vox*, May 2, 2019, https://www.vox.com/the-highlight/2019/4/25/18512620/dooce-heather-armstrong-depression-valedictorian-of-being-dead.

35. Jo Piazza, phone interview, June 22, 2021.

36. Piazza, phone interview.

37. Grant McCracken, "Who Is the Celebrity Endorser? Cultural Foundations of the Endorsement Process," *Journal of Consumer Research* 16, no. 3 (1989): 310–21.

38. Hund and McGuigan, "A Shoppable Life."

39. Faith Hitchon, email interview, June 24, 2021.

40. Hitchon, email interview.

41. Hitchon, email interview.

42. Hitchon, email interview.

43. Brooke Erin Duffy, phone interview, June 24, 2021.

44. Atlas Obscura Contributor, "The Liberating Corsets of the Warner Brothers Corset Factory," *Slate*, January 10, 2017, https://slate.com/human-interest/2017/01/the-warner-brothers-corset-factory-made-health-corsets-that-were-a-step-toward-liberating-women-s-bodies.html;

Jonteel advertisement, *Good Housekeeping* 68 (1919), found via Google-Books, tinyurl.com/dddjyjph.

45. Duffy, phone interview.
46. Brooke Erin Duffy, *(Not) Getting Paid to Do What You Love: Gender and Aspirational Labor in the Social Media Economy* (New Haven, CT: Yale University Press, 2017), 16.
47. Hund and McGuigan, "A Shoppable Life."
48. Hund and McGuigan, "A Shoppable Life."
49. Joe Pinsker, "How Marketers Talk About Motherhood Behind Closed Doors," *The Atlantic*, October 10, 2018, https://www.theatlantic.com/family/archive/2018/10/marketing-conference-moms/572515.
50. Pinsker, "How Marketers Talk About Motherhood Behind Closed Doors."
51. Pinsker, "How Marketers Talk About Motherhood Behind Closed Doors."
52. Hund and McGuigan, "A Shoppable Life."
53. Shanicia Boswell, email interview, December 4, 2020.
54. Bekah Martinez, phone interview, July 26, 2021.
55. Tiffany Mitchell, email interview, December 3, 2020.
56. Hund and McGuigan, "A Shoppable Life."

CHAPTER 3: MIRROR NEURONS AND CRINGE FOLLOWS

1. Kelly Havens Stickle, Instagram post, June 28, 2021, https://www.instagram.com/p/CQrN-39H0SO.
2. Kate Lindsay, "Screw It. I'm Going Full Trad Wife," nofilter, October 15, 2020, https://nofilterpub.com/tradwife-homestead-influencers.
3. Lindsay, "Screw It. I'm Going Full Trad Wife."
4. Kate Lindsay, Zoom interview, July 15, 2021.
5. Kelly Havens Stickle, Instagram post, May 24, 2017, https://www.instagram.com/p/BUfBhOcgkXI.
6. Kelly Havens Stickle, Instagram post, May 15, 2017, https://www.instagram.com/p/BUHn7pRAfFy.
7. Kelly Havens Stickle, Instagram post, January 26, 2017, https://www.instagram.com/p/BPwBZD1As2k.
8. Kelly Havens Stickle, Instagram post, August 6, 2020, https://www.instagram.com/p/CDjwX66pPS-.
9. Lindsay, Zoom interview.
10. Lindsay, Zoom interview.
11. Lindsay, Zoom interview.
12. Lindsay, Zoom interview.
13. Lindsay, Zoom interview.
14. Lindsay, Zoom interview.
15. Elizabeth Nathanson, email interview, December 4, 2020.
16. Tomi Akitunde, Zoom interview, August 26, 2021.

17. Ashley Simpo, "Single Moms Are Not Synonymous with Struggle," *mater mea*, https://matermea.com/single-moms-not-synonymous-with -struggle-ashley-simpo, accessed November 30, 2021.
18. Akitunde, Zoom interview.
19. Akitunde, Zoom interview.
20. Akitunde, Zoom interview.
21. Tomi Akitunde, "Black Mothers Are the Worst?," *Huffington Post*, February 24, 2014, https://www.huffpost.com/entry/black-mothers-are-the -wor_b_4820530.
22. Akitunde, Zoom interview.
23. Akitunde, Zoom interview.
24. Katherine, email interview, September 21, 2021.
25. Sabia Wade, email interview, July 28, 2021.
26. Laura, email interview, July 9, 2021.
27. Amanda Montell, phone interview, July 27, 2021.
28. Montell, phone interview.
29. Montell, phone interview.
30. Montell, phone interview.
31. Susan J. Douglas and Meredith W. Michaels, *The Mommy Myth: The Idealization of Motherhood and How It Has Undermined All Women* (New York: Free Press, 2004), 25.
32. Kendra Cherry, "Social Comparison Theory in Psychology," Very Well Mind, September 19, 2020, https://www.verywellmind.com/what-is -the-social-comparison-process-2795872.
33. Mara Moujaes and Diarmuid Verrier, "Instagram Use, Instamums, and Anxiety in Mothers of Young Children," *Journal of Media Psychology: Theories, Methods, and Applications* 33, no. 2 (October 2020): 72–81, doi .org/10.1027/1864-1105/a000282.
34. Moujaes and Verrier, "Instagram Use, Instamums, and Anxiety in Mothers of Young Children."
35. Moujaes and Verrier, "Instagram Use, Instamums, and Anxiety in Mothers of Young Children."
36. Mara Moujaes, email interview, September 16, 2021.
37. Moujaes, email interview.
38. Dara Mathis, phone interview, July 19, 2021.
39. Mathis, phone interview.
40. Rachel Hollis, Instagram post, March 21, 2015, https://www.instagram .com/p/0fwr9Dl-VK/?utm_source=ig_embed&ig_rid=3ca51ab5-7288 -441b-b1e3-c6a8fe9db845.
41. Nora Krug, "Rachel Hollis Has Wooed Millions of Women with Her Book. What's Her Message?," *Washington Post*, November 12, 2018, https:// www.washingtonpost.com/entertainment/books/how-rachel-hollis--a -texas-mom-of-four--ended-up-writing-one-of-the-years-biggest-books /2018/11/10/59d3e89e-d9e1-11e8-a10f-b51546b10756_story.html.

42. Fourth Trimester Bodies Project, Instagram bio, https://www.instagram
.com/4thtribodies/?hl=en, accessed November 30, 2021.

43. Pooja Lakshmin, professional website, https://www.poojalakshmin.com,
accessed June 27, 2022.

44. Pooja Lakshmin, Zoom interview, September 30, 2021.

45. Lakshmin, Zoom interview.

46. Nicole Beurgen, phone interview, August 22, 2021.

47. Beurgen, phone interview.

48. Stephanie Hegarty, "What Phantom Limbs and Mirrors Teach Us
About the Brain," *BBC News*, December 5, 2011, https://www.bbc.com
/news/magazine-15938103.

49. Beurgen, phone interview.

50. Hannah Rindlaub, text interview, October 21, 2021.

CHAPTER 4: PRETTY/UGLY

1. Amanda Watters, Instagram post, March 25, 2020, https://www
.instagram.com/p/B-LCehpAAFs.

2. Amanda Watters, Instagram post, April 17, 2019, https://www
.instagram.com/p/BwW0wxhAK7M.

3. William Sears, "Holistic Ways to Manage Postpartum Depression," Ask
Dr. Sears, https://www.askdrsears.com/topics/pregnancy-childbirth
/manage-postpartum-depression, accessed November 30, 2021.

4. Amanda Watters, Instagram post, March 21, 2020, https://www
.instagram.com/p/B-ABNl2gcZU.

5. Homesong Market, accessed August 24, 2022, https://homesong
market.com/products/large-woven-laundry-basket?_pos=4&_sid
=58240d6cc&_ss=r.

CHAPTER 5: MINIMALIST MOMS, COOL MOMS,
AND UNFILTERED MOMS

1. Sarah Frier, *No Filter: The Inside Story of Instagram* (New York: Simon &
Schuster, 2020), 24.

2. Frier, *No Filter*, 4.

3. Frier, *No Filter*, 23.

4. Frier, *No Filter*, 25.

5. Frier, *No Filter*, 29.

6. Frier, *No Filter*, 31.

7. Frier, *No Filter*, 118.

8. Kyle Chayka, *The Longing for Less: Living with Minimalism* (New York:
Bloomsbury, 2020), 4.

9. Chayka, *The Longing for Less*, 5.

10. Chayka, *The Longing for Less*, 13.

11. Lisa Abend, "How *Kinfolk* Magazine Defined the Millennial Aesthetic . . .
and Unraveled Behind the Scenes," *Vanity Fair*, March 19, 2020,

https://www.vanityfair.com/style/2020/03/how-kinfolk-magazine
-defined-the-millennial-aesthetic-and-unraveled-behind-the-scenes.

12. Abend, "How *Kinfolk* Magazine Defined the Millennial Aesthetic."

13. Leslie Jamison, "*Kinfolk* Began as a Labor of Love, But Didn't Turn Out as Planned," *Elle*, March 30, 2020, https://www.elle.com/culture/art
-design/a27560262/kinfolk-magazine-katie-searle.

14. Abend, "How *Kinfolk* Magazine Defined the Millennial Aesthetic."

15. Chayka, *The Longing for Less*, 8.

16. Chayka, *The Longing for Less*, 9.

17. Chayka, *The Longing for Less*, 14.

18. Chayka, *The Longing for Less*, 21.

19. Christine Platt, phone interview, September 14, 2021.

20. Christine Platt, *The Afrominimalist's Guide to Living with Less* (New York: Tiller Press, 2021), 80.

21. Platt, *The Afrominimalist's Guide to Living with Less*, 80.

22. Platt, *The Afrominimalist's Guide to Living with Less*, 80.

23. Platt, *The Afrominimalist's Guide to Living with Less*, 55.

24. Platt, phone interview.

25. Platt, phone interview.

26. Platt, phone interview.

27. Platt, phone interview.

28. Platt, phone interview.

29. Platt, phone interview.

30. Valerie Metz, phone interview, September 10, 2021.

31. Metz, phone interview.

32. Stacey-Ann Blake, phone interview, December 10, 2021.

33. Bethanie Garcia, Zoom interview, September 15, 2021.

34. Garcia, Zoom interview.

35. Stephanie McNeal, "Instagram Is Investigating These Influencers Who Are Hosting a Car Giveaway," *BuzzFeed*, May 19, 2020, https://www
.buzzfeednews.com/article/stephaniemcneal/instagram-car-giveaway
-influencers-spam.

36. Garcia, Zoom interview.

37. Garcia, Zoom interview.

38. Mel (@unconventional_acres), Instagram post, November 29, 2021, https://www.instagram.com/p/CW3WKyFrhjK.

39. TheGarciaDiaries, https://www.instagram.com/thegarciadiaries/, accessed September 1, 2022.

40. Garcia, Zoom interview.

41. Garcia, Zoom interview.

42. Garcia, Zoom interview.

43. Stephanie Land, "The Class Politics of Decluttering," *New York Times*, July 18, 2016, https://www.nytimes.com/2016/07/18/opinion/the
-class-politics-of-decluttering.html.

44. Kathryn Jezer-Morton, Zoom interview, November 15, 2021.
45. Jezer-Morton, Zoom interview.
46. Jezer-Morton, Zoom interview.
47. Jezer-Morton, Zoom interview.
48. Laura Norkin, phone interview, November 3, 2021.
49. Norkin, phone interview.
50. Norkin, phone interview.
51. Norkin, phone interview.
52. Norkin, phone interview.
53. Norkin, phone interview.
54. Eva Chen, Instagram post, August 20, 2014, https://www.instagram
    .com/p/r65E-ZPPe1/?utm_source=ig_embed&ig_rid=8398eef3-21f9
    -4b0e-ad1d-04a13f7551fe.
55. Gina Marinelli, "Eva Chen Announces Her Pregnancy in the Most
    Eva Chen Way Possible," *Refinery29*, August 20, 2014, https://www
    .refinery29.com/en-us/2014/08/73147/eva-chen-pregnancy
    -announcement.
56. Eva Chen, Instagram post, July 17, 2015, https://www.instagram.com
    /p/5PWWf2vPfk/?utm_source=ig_embed&utm_campaign=loading.
57. Norkin, phone interview.
58. Anna Wallack, phone interview, July 9, 2021.
59. Wallack, phone interview.
60. Wallack, phone interview.
61. Norkin, phone interview.
62. Norkin, phone interview.
63. Karni Arieli, Zoom interview, November 4, 2021.
64. Arieli, Zoom interview.
65. Claire Dam, Instagram post, December 8, 2021, https://www
    .instagram.com/p/CXOj_iFIG3-.
66. Mairéad Heffron, Instagram post, October 23, 2021, https://www
    .instagram.com/p/CVYO0MEIeX4.
67. Maisie Cousins, Instagram post, March 8, 2021, https://www.instagram
    .com/p/CMKiZHhnX2a.
68. Arieli, Zoom interview.
69. Arieli, Zoom interview.
70. Arieli, Zoom interview.

CHAPTER 6: GOOD (WHITE) MOMS

1. Rose Henges, @ roseuncharted, Instagram post, June 23, 2021, https://
   www.instagram.com/p/CQejf8YtMcW.
2. Rose, Instagram post, May 21, 2021, https://www.instagram.com/p
   /CPIx0QrN1_4.
3. "Racial and Ethnic Disparities Continue in Pregnancy-Related Deaths,"
   Centers for Disease Control and Prevention (CDC), September 5, 2019,

https://www.cdc.gov/media/releases/2019/p0905-racial-ethnic
-disparities-pregnancy-deaths.html.

4. Dovile Vilda, Maeve Wallace, Lauren Dyer, Emily Harville, and Katherine Theall, "Income Inequality and Racial Disparities in Pregnancy-Related Mortality in the US," National Library of Medicine, August 8, 2019, https://www.ncbi.nlm.nih.gov/pmc/articles/PMC6734101.

5. "Working Together to Reduce Black Maternal Mortality," CDC, April 6, 2022, https://www.cdc.gov/healthequity/features/maternal
-mortality/index.html; Katy B. Kozhimannil, Julia D. Interrante, Alena N. Tofte, and Lindsay K. Admon, "Severe Maternal Morbidity and Mortality Among Indigenous Women in the United States," *Obstetrics and Gynecology*, published online January 9, 2020, https://www.ncbi
.nlm.nih.gov/pmc/articles/PMC7012336.

6. Virginia Sole-Smith, "When You're Told You're Too Fat to Get Pregnant," *New York Times*, June 18, 2019, https://www.nytimes.com/2019
/06/18/magazine/fertility-weight-obesity-ivf.html.

7. Rose, Instagram post, October 15, 2020, https://www.instagram.com
/p/CGYW6PnndVS.

8. Julia Duin, "'This Is All About Jesus': A Christian Rocker's COVID Protest Movement," *Politico*, October 25, 2020, https://www.politico
.com/news/magazine/2020/10/25/sean-feucht-christian-rocker-covid
-protest-movement-431734.

9. Duin, "'This Is All About Jesus.'"

10. Alejandra Molina, "Hate Watch Groups Voice Alarm About Sean Feucht's Portland Security Volunteers," Religion News Service, August 13, 2021, https://religionnews.com/2021/08/13/hate-watch-groups
-look-into-worship-leader-sean-feuchts-security-team-for-extremist-ties.

11. Kevin Roose, "QAnon Followers Are Hijacking the #SaveTheChildren Movement," *New York Times*, August 12, 2020, https://www.nytimes.com
/2020/08/12/technology/qanon-save-the-children-trafficking.html.

12. Mia Bloom, "We Knew QAnon Was Anti-Semitic. Now We Know It's Racist Too," *The Bulletin*, July 5, 2021, https://thebulletin.org/2021/07
/we-knew-qanon-is-anti-semitic-now-we-know-its-racist-too.

13. Rose, Instagram post, July 3, 2020, https://www.instagram.com/p
/CCL247cno-Z.

14. Rose, Instagram post, December 10, 2019, https://www.instagram.com
/p/B55k-jSH_aH; Rose, Instagram post, March 26, 2020, https://
www.instagram.com/p/B-NRTv2nvF9.

15. Rose, Instagram post, July 28, 2020, https://www.instagram.com/p
/CDMYJIzn5_O.

16. Seyward Darby, *Sisters in Hate: American Women on the Front Lines of White Nationalism* (New York: Little, Brown, 2020), 127.

17. T-shirt text from Loves Sales, accessed May 25, 2022, tinyurl.com/2v7
wdkyd.

18. Kathryn Jezer-Morton, "Did Moms Exist Before Social Media?," *New York Times*, April 16, 2020, https://www.nytimes.com/2020/04/16/parenting/mommy-influencers.html.

19. Amanda Montell, Instagram post, August 13, 2021, https://www.instagram.com/p/CTPhh_OCUhw.

20. Jo Piazza text, January 5, 2022.

21. Bec, Instagram post, December 3, 2021, https://www.instagram.com/p/CXC54G_tmza.

22. Bec, Instagram post, November 30, 2021, https://www.instagram.com/p/CW7MujXt_Vl.

23. Anne Helen Petersen, "The Real Housewives of QAnon," *Elle*, October 29, 2020, https://www.elle.com/culture/a34485099/qanon-conspiracy-suburban-women.

24. Petersen, "The Real Housewives of QAnon."

25. Petersen, "The Real Housewives of QAnon."

26. Annie Kelly, "Mothers for QAnon," *New York Times*, September 10, 2020, https://www.nytimes.com/2020/09/10/opinion/qanon-women-conspiracy.html.

27. Kelly, "Mothers for QAnon."

28. Kelly, "Mothers for QAnon."

29. Kelly, "Mothers for QAnon."

30. Bec, Instagram post, September 19, 2021, https://www.instagram.com/p/CUbc8wiN0qe; Rose, Instagram post, December 17, 2021, https://www.instagram.com/p/CXmHnOHu99X.

31. Constance Grady, "How Beyoncé Infused Her Social Media Pregnancy Announcement with High Art," *Vox*, February 3, 2017, https://www.vox.com/culture/2017/2/3/14484610/beyonce-social-media-pregnancy-art-venus-virgin-mary-mami-wata-awol-erizku; Darby, *Sisters in Hate*, 93.

32. Darby, *Sisters in Hate*, 94.

33. Annie Kelly, "The Housewives of White Supremacy," *New York Times*, June 1, 2018, https://www.nytimes.com/2018/06/01/opinion/sunday/tradwives-women-alt-right.html.

34. Danielle Kwateng-Clark, "The Beyoncé Pregnancy Backlash Is Unwarranted," *Essence*, October 26, 2020, https://www.essence.com/culture/beyonce-pregnancy-backlash.

35. Ayla, Instagram post, May 13, 2019, https://www.instagram.com/p/BxbAOKSAXtZ.

36. Darby, *Sisters in Hate*, 98–99.

37. Darby, *Sisters in Hate*, 176.

38. Darby, *Sisters in Hate*, 105.

39. Darby, *Sisters in Hate*, 107.

40. Darby, *Sisters in Hate*, 112.

41. Darby, *Sisters in Hate*, 121.

42. Darby, *Sisters in Hate*, 109.
43. Darby, *Sisters in Hate*, 157.
44. Darby, *Sisters in Hate*, 123.
45. Darby, *Sisters in Hate*, 140–41.
46. Darby, *Sisters in Hate*, 142.
47. Darby, *Sisters in Hate*, 145.
48. Darby, *Sisters in Hate*, 115.
49. Darby, *Sisters in Hate*, 116.
50. Darby, *Sisters in Hate*, 119.
51. Darby, *Sisters in Hate*, 121.
52. Kaylyn Mead, Instagram post, December 13, 2021, https://www.instagram.com/p/CXb38hgOVIP.
53. Darby, *Sisters in Hate*, 121.
54. Darby, *Sisters in Hate*, 152–53.
55. Darby, *Sisters in Hate*, 153.
56. Bernadine, Instagram post, December 12, 2021, https://www.instagram.com/p/CXY8Il1OzhL; Bernadine, Instagram post, November 29, 2021, https://www.instagram.com/p/CW3QiWZlNBo.
57. Bernadine, Instagram post, November 29, 2021.
58. Patricia Hill Collins, "It's All in the Family: Intersections of Gender, Race, and Nation," *Hypatia* 13, no. 3, Border Crossings: Multicultural and Postcolonial Feminist Challenges to Philosophy (Part 2) (Summer 1998): 65.
59. Collins, "It's All in the Family," 69.
60. Michelle Clare, Instagram post, December 24, 2021, https://www.instagram.com/p/CX3iBbQKeGK.
61. Koritha Mitchell, email interview, March 6, 2021.
62. Mitchell, email interview.
63. Mitchell, email interview.
64. @roseuncharted Instagram story, accessed September 1, 2022.
65. Yolande Norris Clarke, Instagram post, December 17, 2021, https://www.instagram.com/p/CXk2sDfuAr9.
66. Kendra, Instagram post, May 4, 2021.
67. Hayla Wong, Instagram post, November 9, 2021, https://www.instagram.com/p/CWEYD4SgHuE/?hl=en
68. Hayla Wong, Instagram post, November 9, 2021, https://www.instagram.com/p/CWEYD4SgHuE.
69. Eva Wiseman, "The Dark Side of Wellness: The Overlap Between Spiritual Thinking and Far-Right Conspiracies," *Guardian*, October 17, 2021, https://www.theguardian.com/lifeandstyle/2021/oct/17/eva-wiseman-conspirituality-the-dark-side-of-wellness-how-it-all-got-so-toxic.
70. Hayla Wong, text interview, November 23, 2021.
71. Wong, text interview.
72. Wong, text interview.

73. "5 Reasons 'Rise with Rachel Hollis' Is Worth the Money," *Eat, Drink, and Save Money Blog*, https://eatdrinkandsavemoney.com/5-reasons -rise-with-rachel-hollis-is-worth-the-money, accessed January 14, 2022.

74. Stephanie McNeal, "Rachel Hollis Has Apologized After Posting a Maya Angelou Quote Without Attribution," *BuzzFeed*, April 27, 2020, https://www.buzzfeednews.com/article/stephaniemcneal/rachel-hollis -apology-maya-angelou-quote; Constance Grady, "Why the Author of *Girl, Stop Apologizing* Had to Apologize Twice in a Week," *Vox*, April 9, 2021, https://www.vox.com/culture/22373865/rachel-hollis -controversy-harriet-tubman-girl-wash-your-face-stop-apologizing -unrelatable.

75. Grady, "Why the Author of *Girl, Stop Apologizing* Had to Apologize Twice in a Week."

76. Rachel Hollis, Instagram post, February 24, 2020, https://www .instagram.com/p/B888S4lHbHA.

77. Joseph Ax and Lisa Shumaker, "U.S. Reports Nearly 1 Mln COVID-19 Cases in a Day, Setting Global Record," Reuters, January 5, 2020, https://www.reuters.com/world/us/us-reports-nearly-1-mln-covid -19-cases-day-setting-global-record-2022-01-04.

78. Rachel Hollis, Instagram post, January 7, 2020, https://www.instagram .com/p/B7BKkAGHwKE.

79. Rachel Hollis, Instagram post, December 29, 2019, https://www .instagram.com/p/B6qaTcvFhwh.

80. Kimberlé Crenshaw, "Demarginalizing the Intersection of Race and Sex: A Black Feminist Critique of Antidiscrimination Doctrine, Feminist Theory, and Antiracist Politics," *University of Chicago Legal Forum*, no. 1, article 8 (1989), https://chicagounbound.uchicago.edu/cgi/view content.cgi?article=1052&context=uclf, accessed June 30, 2022.

81. Matilda Boseley, "'My Feminism Will Be Intersectional or It Will Be Bullshit': What's Next for the March 4 Justice," *Guardian*, March 17, 2021, https://www.theguardian.com/australia-news/2021/mar/17 /my-feminism-will-be-intersectional-or-it-will-be-bullshit-whats-next -for-the-march-4-justice.

82. Koa Beck, *White Feminism: From the Suffragettes to Influencers and Who They Leave Behind* (New York: Atria Books, 2021), xvii.

83. Beck, *White Feminism*, xviii.

84. Beck, *White Feminism*, 39.

85. Beck, *White Feminism*, 11.

86. Sam Miller, "'The Future Is Female' Is Not A Progressive Slogan," *Left Voice*, February 21, 2017, https://www.leftvoice.org/the-future-is-female -is-not-a-progressive-slogan-1492.

87. Beck, *White Feminism*, 104.

88. Beck, *White Feminism*, 104.

89. Beck, *White Feminism*, 105.

90. Katherine Rosman, "Girl, Wash Your Timeline," *New York Times*, April 29, 2021, https://www.nytimes.com/2021/04/29/style/rachel-hollis -tiktok-video.html.

91. Louiza Doran, Instagram Live video, April 2, 2021, https://www .instagram.com/tv/CNLzy9qHgmF.

92. Louiza Doran, Zoom interview, January 13, 2022.

93. Doran, Zoom interview.

CHAPTER 7: DISRUPTING THE FEED

1. Erica Nolan, Zoom interview, January 7, 2022.

2. Nolan, Zoom interview.

3. Nolan, Zoom interview.

4. Nolan, Zoom interview.

5. Nolan, Zoom interview.

6. Doran, Zoom interview.

7. Doran, Zoom interview.

8. Doran, Zoom interview.

9. Mia O'Malley, Zoom interview, January 7, 2022.

10. O'Malley, Zoom interview.

11. O'Malley, Zoom interview.

12. Mia O'Malley, "My Invisible Plus-Size Pregnancy," Plus Size Birth, https://plussizebirth.com/my-invisible-plus-size-pregnancy, accessed February 9, 2022.

13. O'Malley, Zoom interview.

14. O'Malley, Zoom interview.

15. O'Malley, Zoom interview.

16. O'Malley, Zoom interview.

17. O'Malley, Zoom interview.

18. O'Malley, Zoom interview.

19. O'Malley, Zoom interview.

20. O'Malley, Zoom interview.

21. Aaronica Cole, phone interview, February 1, 2022.

22. Cole, phone interview.

23. Cole, phone interview.

24. O'Malley, Zoom interview.

25. O'Malley, Zoom interview.

26. Koa Beck, *White Feminism: From the Suffragettes to Influencers and Who They Leave Behind* (New York: Simon & Schuster, 2021), 42.

27. Beck, *White Feminism*, 44.

28. Feminista Jones, *Reclaiming Our Space: How Black Feminists Are Changing the World from the Tweets to the Streets* (Boston: Beacon Press, 2019), 5–6.

29. Jones, *Reclaiming Our Space*, 29.

30. Beck, *White Feminism*, 180.

31. Lyz Lenz, "How America Weaponizes Motherhood," *Washington Post*, June 30, 2020, https://www.washingtonpost.com/lifestyle/2020/07/29/how-america-weaponizes-motherhood.

32. Beck, *White Feminism*, 181–82.

33. Beck, *White Feminism*, 182.

34. Andrea Landry, phone interview, January 6, 2022.

35. Landry, phone interview.

36. Landry, phone interview.

37. Landry, phone interview.

38. Landry, phone interview.

39. Fakiha Baig, "Indigenous Women Still Forced, Coerced Into Sterilization: Senate Report," Canadian Press, June 3, 2021, https://globalnews.ca/news/7920118/indigenous-women-sterilization-senate-report.

40. Landry, phone interview.

41. Landry, phone interview.

42. Rebekah Taussig, Zoom interview, September 8, 2021.

43. Taussig, Zoom interview.

44. Taussig, Zoom interview.

45. Rebekah Taussig, Instagram post, January 13, 2022, https://www.instagram.com/p/CYsBV9QFiH7.

46. Taussig, Zoom interview.

47. Taussig, Zoom interview.

48. Taussig, Zoom interview.

49. Taussig, Zoom interview.

50. Taussig, Zoom interview.

51. Ashley Simpo, Instagram post, December 6, 2021, https://www.instagram.com/p/CXJgUR0lV-W.

52. Ashley Simpo, Instagram post, December 22, 2021, https://www.instagram.com/p/CXytUj8lUEE.

53. Ashley Simpo, Zoom interview, November 17, 2021.

54. Simpo, Zoom interview.

55. Simpo, Zoom interview.

56. Simpo, Zoom interview.

57. Jones, *Reclaiming Our Space*, 121.

58. Jones, *Reclaiming Our Space*, 122.

59. Rochaun Meadows-Fernandez, "Med School Student's Illustration Shows a Black Fetus in Utero—Here's Why It Went Viral," *Parents*, December 8, 2021, https://www.parents.com/kindred/med-school-students-illustration-shows-black-fetus-in-utero-heres-why-it-went-viral.

60. Jones, *Reclaiming Our Space*, 120.

61. Jones, *Reclaiming Our Space*, 122.

62. Jones, *Reclaiming Our Space*, 129.

63. Patricia Hill Collins, "A Comparison of Two Works on Black Family Life," *Signs* 14, no. 4, Common Grounds and Crossroads: Race,

Ethnicity, and Class in Women's Lives (Summer 1989): 875–84, https://www.jstor.org/stable/3174688.

64. Simpo, Zoom interview.
65. Jones, *Reclaiming Our Space*, 142.
66. Jones, *Reclaiming Our Space*, 146.
67. Jones, *Reclaiming Our Space*, 150.
68. Jones, *Reclaiming Our Space*, 159.
69. Simpo, Zoom interview.
70. Simpo, Zoom interview.
71. Jones, *Reclaiming Our Space*, 120.
72. Simpo, Zoom interview.
73. Simpo, Zoom interview.
74. Simpo, Zoom interview.
75. Simpo, Zoom interview.
76. Imani Payne, Zoom interview, September 13, 2021.
77. Payne, Zoom interview.
78. Payne, Zoom interview.
79. Payne, Zoom interview.
80. Jones, *Reclaiming Our Space*, 22.
81. Imani Payne, Instagram post, June 30, 2021, https://www.instagram.com/p/CQwoexLLDBr/.
82. Payne, Instagram post.
83. Payne, Instagram post.
84. Payne, Zoom interview.
85. Laura Danger, Zoom interview, February 3, 2022.
86. Danger, Zoom interview.
87. Danger, Zoom interview.
88. Danger, Zoom interview.
89. Danger, Zoom interview.
90. "About MomsRising," MomsRising Together, https://www.momsrising.org/about, accessed August 1, 2022.
91. Kristin Rowe-Finkbeiner, phone interview, February 2, 2022.
92. Rowe-Finkbeiner, phone interview.
93. Rowe-Finkbeiner, phone interview.
94. Julia Wolfe, Jori Kandra, Lora Engdahl, and Heidi Shierholz, *Domestic Workers Chartbook*, Economic Policy Institute, May 14, 2020, tinyurl.com/ye29suh2.
95. Rowe-Finkbeiner, phone interview.
96. Rowe-Finkbeiner, phone interview.
97. Rowe-Finkbeiner, phone interview.
98. Rowe-Finkbeiner, phone interview.
99. Rowe-Finkbeiner, phone interview.
100. Rowe-Finkbeiner, phone interview.
101. Lauren Smith Brody, phone interview, February 7, 2022.

102. Smith Brody, phone interview.
103. Smith Brody, phone interview.
104. Smith Brody, phone interview.
105. Smith Brody, phone interview.

CHAPTER 8: CRUEL OPTIMISM AND DREAMS OF MOTHERHOOD "DESTINED TO BE DASHED"

1. Naomi Davis, Instagram post, October 1, 2021, https://www.instagram.com/p/CUgnIzrFwTV.
2. Sara Petersen, @slouisepetersen, Twitter thread, March 1, 2022, https://mobile.twitter.com/slouisepetersen/status/14987101426821201 92.
3. Jordan Reid, phone interview, October 28, 2021.
4. Lydia Kisling, "The Evolution of a Mormon Mommy Blogger," *The Cut*, June 7, 2018, https://www.thecut.com/2018/06/what-happened-to-natalie-jean-nat-the-fat-rat.html.
5. *GOMI* post, March 28, 2021, https://gomiblog.com/forums/mommy-bloggers/love-taza-naomi-davis/page-1823.
6. *GOMI* post, July 6, 2017, https://gomiblog.com/forums/lifestyle-bloggers/ramshackle-glam-jordan-reid/page-542.
7. Reid, phone interview.
8. @milkgiver, Instagram post, April 6, 2022, https://www.instagram.com/p/CcBudWXldOy.
9. Reid, phone interview.
10. Reid, phone interview.
11. Amanda McMaster and Yi-Jin Yu, "Mom Influencer Opens Up About Why She Erased Her Kids' Faces from Social Media," *Good Morning America*, February 17, 2022, https://www.goodmorningamerica.com/family/story/mom-influencer-opens-erased-kids-faces-social-media-82928115.
12. Katy Rose Prichard, Zoom interview, March 1, 2022.
13. Prichard, Zoom interview.
14. Prichard, Zoom interview.
15. Prichard, Zoom interview.
16. Palepu, phone interview.
17. Stephanie McNeal, email interview, March 21, 2022.
18. Virginia Duan, "How My Parenting Style of Benign Neglect Has Raised Useful (Happy) Humans," *ScaryMommy*, November 13, 2020, https://www.scarymommy.com/parenting-style-benign-neglect.
19. Virginia Duan, phone interview, November 6, 2021.
20. Duan, phone interview.
21. Lynzy Coughlin, "Why I Am Leaving Instagram," *Lynzy and Co.*, November 30, 2021, https://lynzyandco.com/why-i-am-leaving-instagram.

22. Emily Hund and Lee McGuigan, "A Shoppable Life: Performance, Selfhood, and Influence in the Social Media Storefront," *Communication, Culture & Critique* 12, no. 1 (March 2019): 13.

23. Prichard, Zoom interview.

24. Amil Niazi, email interview, January 11, 2022.

25. Sarah Frier, *No Filter: The Inside Story of Instagram* (New York: Simon & Schuster, 2020), 278.

26. Barrett Prendergast, phone interview, June 16, 2021.

27. Coughlin, "Why I Am Leaving Instagram."

28. Hannah Schwär, "How Instagram and Facebook Are Intentionally Designed to Mimic Addictive Painkillers," *Insider*, August 11, 2021, https://www.businessinsider.com/facebook-has-been-deliberately-designed-to-mimic-addictive-painkillers-2018-12.

29. Courtney Klein and Grace Kapin, "You Should Definitely Breastfeed, But I Would Rather Not Have to See It," *Medium*, December 12, 2019, https://medium.com/storq/you-should-definitely-breastfeed-but-i-would-rather-not-have-to-see-it-1aa0474a6d2e.

30. Klein and Kapin, "You Should Definitely Breastfeed."

31. Grace Kapin, email interview, February 1, 2021.

32. Kapin, email interview.

33. Karni Arieli, Zoom interview, November 4, 2021.

34. Arieli, Zoom interview.

35. Arieli, Zoom interview.

36. Bethanie Garcia and Tami Nealy, Zoom interview, September 15, 2021.

37. "Taza Talks: A Chat About Motherhood, with Hannah Neeleman of @BallerinaFarm," Instagram, May 5, 2021, https://www.instagram.com/tv/COgThV6Dtgp/?igshid=Y2ZmNzg0YzQ%3D.

38. Hund and McGuigan, "A Shoppable Life," 5.

39. Jorie Lagerwey, email interview, November 30, 2020.

40. Lauren Berlant, *The Female Complaint: The Unfinished Business of Sentimentality in American Culture* (Durham, NC: Duke University Press, 2008), 1.

41. Berlant, *The Female Complaint*, 5.

42. Lydialyle Gibson, "Sentimental Education," *University of Chicago Magazine*, July 2008, http://magazine.uchicago.edu/0878/investigations/sentimental_ed.shtml, accessed July 14, 2022.

43. Berlant, *The Female Complaint*, 5.

44. Aimée Morrison, Zoom interview, July 21, 2021.

45. Morrison, Zoom interview.

46. Morrison, Zoom interview.

47. Morrison, Zoom interview.

48. Hua Hsu, "Affect Theory and the New Age of Anxiety," *New Yorker*, March 18, 2019, https://www.newyorker.com/magazine/2019/03/25/affect-theory-and-the-new-age-of-anxiety.

49. Morrison, Zoom interview.

50. Morrison, Zoom interview

51. Morrison, Zoom interview.

52. Hsu, "Affect Theory and the New Age of Anxiety."

53. Hsu, "Affect Theory and the New Age of Anxiety."

54. Angela Garbes, *Essential Labor: Mothering as Social Change* (New York: Harper Wave, 2022), 24.

55. Garbes, *Essential Labor*, 68.

56. Garbes, *Essential Labor*, 25.

57. Garbes, *Essential Labor*, 60.